The Research Process
in Educational Settings

The Research Process
in Educational Settings:
TEN CASE STUDIES

Edited by
Robert G. Burgess

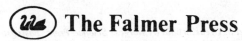 **The Falmer Press**

A member of the Taylor & Francis Group
London and New York

UK   The Falmer Press, Falmer House, Barcombe, Lewes, East Sussex, BN8 5DL

USA   The Falmer Press, Taylor & Francis Inc., 242 Cherry Street, Philadelphia, PA 19106-1906

First published in 1984. Reprinted in 1993

Library of Congress Cataloging in Publication Data

Main entry under title:

The research process in educational settings.

   Includes bibliographies and index.
   Contents: The old girl network/Sara Delemont —
The researcher exposed/Martin Hammersley — Beachside
reconsidered/Stephen J. Ball — [etc.]
   1. Education—Research—Great Britain—Case studies.
I. Burgess, Robert G.
LB1028.R376 1984   370′.7′8041 83-20796
ISBN 0-905273-92-3
ISBN 0-905273-91-5 (pbk.)

Typeset in 11/13 Garamond
by Imago Publishing Ltd., Thame, Oxon.

*Printed in Great Britain by Burgess Science Press, Basingstoke
on paper which has a specific pH value on final paper
manufacture of not less than 7.5 and is therefore 'acid free'.*

Contents

Preface

The shape, substance and style of educational research and evaluation have undergone considerable change in the last ten years. No longer are researchers who work within this field preoccupied with quantitative methods based upon statistical sampling, measurement and experiment for much research now uses qualitative as well as quantitative methods. Among the qualitative methods most commonly used are observation, participant observation and informal or unstructured interviews alongside documentary data. Depending on the initial training and disciplinary allegiance of the researcher in anthropology, sociology or educational studies this style of qualitative research is known by such terms as ethnography, fieldwork, field research and case study; all of which are characterized by intensive investigation by the researcher.

While there is now a range of textbooks and papers on this style of research, much of the material is American and is based upon anthropological or sociological problems. However, there is very little literature that addresses the specific problems that arise when studying education and educational settings. Nevertheless, much can be learned from those accounts that do not merely focus upon qualitative methods as a set of techniques but also examine the relationship between theories, methods and substantive issues taking into account the social, ethical and political problems that surround the research process. Indeed, first person accounts that combine together discussions of the research process with research technique can help us to advance our knowledge of research practice.

Accordingly, this set of essays is designed to address major issues in the process of utilizing qualitative methods in the study of educational settings. The contributors are drawn from different disciplines: social anthropology, sociology, history and educational studies and use different combinations of qualitative methods in educational research and evaluation in Britain. In these first person accounts the authors demonstrate how they handled problems associated with ethnographic or case study research in a variety of educational settings. The focus is, therefore, upon the researcher and the research process in the study of education.

All the essays were specially commissioned to demonstrate the range of research experience that has been gained in the study of educational settings. The result is not a 'how to do it' manual for students and researchers in education but a collection of essays that demonstrate how different researchers have encountered and handled major issues and problems whilst doing educational research. Accordingly, it is hoped that the material presented in these essays will provide undergraduates, postgraduates and researchers with some insights on the research process in the study of educational settings.

Each of the contributions to this book was originally presented to a two day workshop on 'the ethnography of educational settings' that was held at Whitelands College, London in March 1982. As all the papers for the workshop were pre-circulated the emphasis was upon discussion and debate. In revising this material for wider dissemination the authors have drawn on the discussions that were all tape recorded. In addition to the contributors to this volume the following individuals also took part in the discussion: Clem Adelman, Ann Borthwick, Brian Davies, Tony Edwards, Maurice Galton, Tony Green, Christine Griffin, Andy Hargreaves, Colin Lacey, Jon Nixon, Andrew Pollard, Sue Scott, Helen Simons, Marten Shipman, John Wakeford, Rob Walker and Peter Woods; all of whom helped to focus attention on the key issues involved in conducting research in educational settings.

The workshop was made possible by a grant that I received from the University of Warwick Research and Innovations Fund. I am, therefore, most grateful to the members of the Research and Innovations Sub-Committee who supported my proposal for work in this area of study. I would also like to thank all those who contributed to our discussions and who gave encouragement to our work. In the course of editing this material I have received much help from the contributors and I am particularly grateful to David Jenkins, Marten Shipman and Helen Simons who were kind enough to provide detailed comments on early drafts of my material. As always Hilary Burgess provided help, encouragement, support and advice in equal measure. Finally, but by no means least I have had a range of expert secretarial assistance from Sarah Fulton, Eunice Hodgekinson, Pam

Smitham, Frances Jones, Christine Cluley and Hilary Pearce. Any errors or omissions, of course, remain my own.

Robert Burgess
University of Warwick

Introduction

Robert G. Burgess

Researchers who study educational settings encounter 'education' in a number of different ways. First, there are the educational activities of the individuals and groups who are the 'subjects' of their studies. Secondly, there is the research process itself that involves a learning experience and finally, the product of the research that is often examined for a higher degree and frequently contributes to the knowledge base of our disciplines. While 'education' and educational activities are frequently questioned by researchers, the familiar world of the social researcher with its own educational experiences is often taken as given and remains unquestioned. For social scientists have been relatively slow to provide public accounts of their own educational experiences whilst doing research. Yet as anyone who hangs around the fringe of conference bars and research seminars knows, there is a wealth of academic gossip about the false starts and *faux pas* that are part of the everyday world of the social researcher.

It is only in the last decade that social researchers in Britain have begun to raise questions about what constitutes 'doing research', for social and educational research has been surrounded by a conspiracy of silence (at least in public and in printed form). Here, researchers and research methodologists have both been guilty parties to the conspiracy. Among researchers we have had few details in the final research report about how the research was actually done. Indeed, when this has been provided it has taken the form of a summary of the aims, methods and findings of the investigation. According to such accounts researchers start their work with a problem, go out to the field of investigation and collect their data before returning to the university or research unit to analyze this data and write the research report. As Medawar (1963), writing on natural science indicates, such accounts are fraudulent as they perpetuate the myth that research procedure involves a series of steps or stages which the researcher follows.[1] Yet these accounts link neatly with the discussions in methodology textbooks about the mechanics of doing research (Goode and Hatt, 1952; Madge, 1953; Moser and Kalton, 1971; Bailey, 1978; Cohen and Manion, 1980). In these terms, social and educational research appears to be little more than the use of samples, questionnaires, interview schedules, participant observation and documentary materials as this approach overlooks the fact that research is infused with assumptions about the social world and is influenced by the researcher. Indeed, as Gouldner (1971) argues, every method of social research makes assumptions about how research may be conducted:

> Viewed from one standpoint 'methodology' seems a purely technical concern devoid of ideology; presumably it deals only with methods of extracting reliable information from the world, collecting data, constructing questionnaires, sampling and analyzing returns. (Gouldner, 1971, p. 50)

However, he continues:

> it is always a good deal more than that, for it is commonly infused with ideologically resonant assumptions about what the social world is, and what the nature of the relation between them is. (Gouldner, 1971, pp. 50-1)

Accordingly, researchers and research methodologists need to get closer to research processes as well as research procedures if we are to understand what constitutes 'methodology' and the conduct of social research.

Recent developments in research methodology indicate that 'methodology' involves a consideration of research design, data collection, data analysis, and theorizing together with the social, ethical and political concerns of the social researcher. In short, research is no longer viewed as a linear model but as a social process (Bechhofer, 1974; Stacey and Burgess, 1979; Burgess, 1982a). Accordingly, questions now need to be raised about the *actual* problems that confront researchers in the course of their investigations and some consideration needs to be given to the ways in which techniques, theories and processes are developed by the researcher in relation to the experience of collecting, analyzing and reporting data. One way in which this approach has been developed is through the publication of first person accounts of social research; that is, reports that focus upon the relationships between research and biography and between personal, political and procedural issues in social research.

Developing First Person Accounts

First person accounts have been developed particularly by sociologists and social anthropologists working in the USA. The most celebrated sociological account is Whyte's appendix to *Street Corner Society* (Whyte, 1955) which outlines how the research was done 'warts and all'. However, it is important to recall that the study had originally been published in 1943 without any discussion of the research experience. Indeed, the difficulties of publishing such accounts in the 1940s are detailed by Wax (1971) in the preface to her book, *Doing Fieldwork*, where she writes:

> When, in 1946, I wrote a detailed account of my fieldwork in the centers where the Japanese Americans were confined during World War II, Robert Redfield and Alfonso Villa Rojas suggested that I try to get it published. After several publishers had rejected the manuscript as 'fascinating but unpublishable', I set it aside. In 1963 I wrote a similar but shorter account of fieldwork on the Thrashing Buffalo reservation. Once again I approached a publisher with the suggestion that I prepare a book on fieldwork and once again I was discouraged. (Wax, 1971, p. ix)

This account standing alone might suggest that it was conservatism among publishers that prevented the publication of research experiences. However, turning to the 1950s we find that the anthropologist Laura Bohannon produced an account of her field experiences in the form of a novel entitled *Return to Laughter* which was published under the pseudonym Elenore Smith-Bowen (1954). A note at the beginning of the book states her position clearly:

> All the characters in this book, except myself, are fictitious in the fullest meaning of that word. I knew people of the type I have described here; the incidents of the book are of the genre I myself experienced in Africa. Nevertheless, so much is fiction. I am an anthropologist. The tribe I have described here does exist. This book is the story of the way I did fieldwork among them. The ethnographic background given

here is accurate, but it is neither complete nor technical. When I write as a social anthropologist and within the canons of that discipline, I write under another name. Here I have written simply as a human being, and the truth I have tried to tell concerns the sea change in one's self that comes from immersion in another and alien world. (Smith-Bowen, 1954, p. 5)

This statement indicates that the dearth of accounts on doing research could not be attributed merely to problems surrounding the economics of publishing but also to the state of the disciplines, the subject matter involved and the style of academic reports. Certainly, the accounts that have been provided do represent a different perspective on doing research as they focus upon what *actually* happened rather than what *should* have happened.

The potential usefulness of such accounts was identified by individuals working in different sociological traditions at the end of the 1950s. The celebrated methodologist, Paul Lazarsfeld, writing a 'state of the art' essay on methodology (Lazarsfeld, 1959) remarked that the teaching of methodology was severely handicapped as it lacked appropriate materials such as analytic documents in which the merits and shortcomings of published work could be evaluated alongside a discussion of the decisions that lay behind the final product. For as far as Lazarsfeld was concerned sociologists tended to shy away from the kind of autobiographical account provided by Whyte (1955) with the result that there were few opportunities to learn about the intricacies of social research which were much broader than a knowledge of technical skills. Writing from a different perspective Wright Mills (1959) remarked: 'It is much better to have one account by a working student of how he is going about his work than a dozen "codifications of procedure" by specialists who often as not have never done much work of consequence' (Mills, 1959, p. 195). For Mills considered that the sense of theory and method could only be effectively communicated by experienced researchers reporting in some detail about the ways in which they went about their work. Mills attempted to promote this style of work by drawing on his own research experience in the essay, 'On intellectual craftsmanship'. Here, he began to demonstrate the relationships between life experience and intellectual work and the way in which social research involves a degree of untidiness as researchers direct and redirect their studies in response to the questions which they pose.

This approach was further developed in the USA by sociologists and social anthropologists writing in the 1960s and 1970s.[2] Among the most powerful collections of essays within this genre were those published by Hammond (1964) and by Vidich, Bensman and Stein (1964). Both sets of accounts emphasized the importance of the circumstantial and irrational alongside the logical and systematic, and portrayed the disorderly relationship between theory and method in the social sciences (cf. Shils, 1957). Theory and method were therefore discussed in relation to research experience so that the formal and informal processes of doing research could be examined in the context of social investigations. For both volumes the authors were asked to draw on their own experiences in order that methodological self-consciousness could be developed.

While the aim of the Hammond collection was to focus on the context of discovery in social research, the essays in Vidich, Bensman and Stein's collection, attempted to contribute to methodology by: 'continuing to keep the issue of methodology an open issue which never has a solution independent of particular substantive problems and investigators' (Vidich, Bensman and Stein, 1964, p. xiv). Accordingly, they asked their contributors to write specifically about research themes in relation to specific problems in the conduct of community studies (Vidich, Bensman and Stein, 1964, p. xiii). This approach was also used by Habenstein (1970) who got researchers who had worked in a variety of organizational settings to address a set of questions about field problems, with the result that the papers in his collection focus on the practical problems involved in doing research in a variety of organizations: a college, a hospital, a business, the military and a union, among many others.

Meanwhile in Britain, this approach has been slow to develop. The first set of essays to be produced was that by Shipman (1976) who invited authors of eight of the most quoted books in the behavioural sciences related to education to 'describe their research in full, including its origins, organization and implementation.' Furthermore, they were asked to 'include not only the research design, but the personal and professional problems that had to be overcome, the thinking that lay behind their work and the way it was finally produced for publication' (Shipman, 1976, p. ix). In all Shipman persuaded six authors to write about longitudinal studies (Douglas, 1976; Newson and Newson, 1976), school studies (Ford, 1976; Lacey, 1976) and policy studies (Barker-Lunn, 1976; Dale, 1976).

Beyond educational studies, Bell and Newby (1977) produced a set of essays on the practical, philosophical and political aspects of sociological research. In the introduction to their collection they draw a distinction between the normative accounts of research method in contrast to the experience of 'doing research' with which researchers are familiar. Accordingly, the focus of their materials was upon the social processes of doing research as they invited contributors to write descriptive accounts about the conduct of their investigations. In writing to their contributors they indicated the kind of account they were aiming at by stating:

> we feel that you should if possible write yourself into your account — the best essays we know on this topic are quasi-autobiographical, e.g. Whyte's account of doing *Street Corner Society*. Some account of the 'institutional' setting of your research — be it university, research unit, or the whole complex of problems associated with being a research student or assistant (power and authority in research) — would be helpful. Why did you do this or that piece of research, when you did it in the way you did? How did you actually go about your research — what were the false starts, brilliant ideas and so on? What were the reactions, if any to publication? What have been the personal consequences for you for the research? These are the kinds of things, by no means an inclusive nor an imperative list, we would like to encourage you to write about. (Bell and Newby, 1977, p. 12)

It was, therefore, their hope that this style of work would contribute not only to the practicalities of doing research but also to the epistemological and theoretical problems.[3] Subsequently, Helen Roberts has developed this approach to focus on similar issues in relation to sexual divisions. Accordingly, the contributors to her volume take up theoretical, methodological, practical and ethical issues in relation to feminist research (Roberts, 1981).[4]

While these accounts have been widely used in both undergraduate and postgraduate teaching (see the syllabuses in Wakeford, 1979 and Burgess, 1979 respectively) they have nevertheless come in for considerable criticism (cf. Burgess and Bulmer, 1981; Payne, Dingwall, Payne and Carter, 1981; and Kent, 1981). A common thread that runs through all the criticisms is that these accounts are descriptive narratives of events in the conduct of inquiry rather than discussions of what was actually done in terms of research design, research procedure and theorizing. Nevertheless, such accounts do begin to demystify the ways in which research is conceived, funded, managed, conducted, written and published.

Developing First Person Accounts on the Study of Educational Settings

While in recent years there has been a range of research activities in the field of education all of which utilize qualitative methods, there is a dearth of relevant literature on *how* research is conducted in educational settings. For although there is much in common between educational settings and other social milieux and between schools and other organizations, there are particular circumstances which shape the pattern of social relationships and the associated strategies of social investigation. There are specific problems associated with observing in classrooms, interviewing teachers and pupils, and examining and evaluating the curriculum. Indeed, there are also further problems about what constitutes 'education' in settings that occur beyond the world of schools and classrooms.

Yet there appears to be relatively little that has been produced in Britain about the content of educational research. In terms of methodological discussions involving sociological studies of schools and classrooms there are few accounts beyond appendices to studies (Hargreaves, 1967; Sharp and Green, 1975; Woods, 1979; Turner, 1983) and autobiographical accounts by Lacey (1976) Hamilton (1981) and Walker (1981). The result is that researchers who wish to use a qualitative approach in the study of education are forced to turn to anthropological accounts (Jongmans and Gutkind, 1967; Henry and Saberwal, 1969; Spindler, 1970; Freilich, 1977) and to sociological accounts (Hammond, 1964; Vidich, Bensman and Stein, 1964; Habenstein, 1970; Bell and Newby, 1977; Bell and Encel, 1978; Roberts, 1981) in doing research in a variety of social settings in different societies. While this may sensitize the researcher to general issues and approaches involved in this style of research it still does not provide specific guidance on methodological problems and the methodology that is appropriate for the study of educational settings (Burgess, 1980; 1982b). Indeed, Eggleston (1980) has argued that we need further first-hand accounts of research projects in the field of education similar to those that were collected by Shipman (1976).

Accordingly, this set of essays attempts to address key questions on methodology: on the relationships between theory and method and between data collection and data analysis in the context of the substantive study of educational settings in Britain. When issues such as these are raised it becomes more evident that we lack first-hand autobiographical accounts on qualitative research in educational settings which highlight the principles and processes involved in the actual conduct of social research. It is this gap that these essays attempt to address. Here the focus is upon the gap in the literature rather than upon the principles of 'how to do' research. It is often the case that such accounts are high on description and low on analysis; that is, they lack detail on the relationships between the formal and informal procedures in social research. In an attempt to overcome this problem all the contributors were invited to write accounts that examined research experiences and research strategies in educational settings including the methodological principles that were actually used. The following guide was, therefore, provided to help contributors direct their discussion towards some of the major issues:

1   What was the origin of the project?
2   What were the research aims and objectives? What key questions were addressed? How were they developed? When were they developed? Why were they developed?
3   What form did research design take? What are the technical procedures? How were the procedures modified by research practice?
4   How was access obtained? Who were the sponsors? What were your relationships with sponsors and gatekeepers? How did these relationships influence data collection and analysis?
5   What sampling procedures were adopted? How were they used? Why were they used? How were sampling procedures modified?
6   What major groups and events were studied? Who were the main informants? How were they selected? What was their role in the project?
7   What methods of social investigation were used? Methods of observation, participant observation, conversations, informal interviews, group interviews, documentary methods, unobtrusive measures. What relationships existed between the methods? How were the methods modified in relation to the project?
8   What form did field relations take? What roles were taken in the project? What were your relationships with the informants? What was the influence of sex and gender on field relations? In the case of research teams, what were the relationships among team members? What were the power relations on the project?
9   What language skills were required in data collection and

data analysis? What linguistic skills were developed in the field and how important was this for field relations?

10 What data recording procedures were used? What methods were used for recording, organizing and filing field notes and keeping field diaries?

11 What was the relationship between data collection and data analysis? What were the informal processes involved in data analysis? What technical procedures were used for analyzing field data? What form did the writing up take?

12 What was the role of theory in the project? What was the relationship between theory, data collection and data analysis? What form did theorizing take?

13 What ethical problems were confronted in the project? How were these problems handled?

14 What form did data dissemination take? What was the impact of the project on sociology, educational studies, policy and practice?

15 In what ways would you develop further projects in this area? What methodological advice would you offer?

In short, the contributors were invited to write autobiographical accounts that dealt with the formal and informal processes of doing research alongside technical procedures — what *actually* happens in terms of success, failure and discovery during a research project. However, it was indicated that not all questions were to be covered as I wrote: 'you may wish to follow up particular questions that are relevant in your research project. I do not intend all these questions to be addressed in each account nor do I consider that this is an exclusive list.'

The contributions that are included in this collection, therefore, focus on broadly similar issues involving techniques, strategies, processes and procedures associated with the collection and analysis of qualitative data in the course of conducting research in a variety of educational settings. The essays have not been grouped into sections according to the topics covered as many involve a complex set of issues that are interwoven in different ways no matter whether the research concerns schools or other educational institutions, the curriculum or curriculum evaluation. In turn, the essays focus on the different ways in which similar problems confront the research novice writing a PhD thesis or an experienced researcher developing research expertise or extending his or her research repertoire. The contributors indicate how they handled research problems in the context of their own studies and their own research careers. Together they demonstrate that there is no universal set of procedures involved in the conduct of qualitative research nor even in qualitative research in educational settings. Yet they do highlight the principles, processes and problems to which researchers need to be sensitized in the study of education.

Acknowledgements

I would like to thank all the workshop participants who provided helpful comments on an earlier draft of this material at 'The Ethnography of Educational Settings' Workshop held at Whitelands College in March 1982. In particular, I would like to thank Marten Shipman and Helen Simons who were kind enough to provide me with detailed written comments. All weaknesses are, of course, my own.

Notes

1 For a first person account of doing research from a natural scientist see, for example, Watson (1968).
2 See, for example, in sociology: Hammond (1964), Vidich, Bensman and Stein (1964), Horowitz (1967), Sjoberg (1967), Habenstein (1970) and in social anthropology Spindler (1970), Freilich (1977). More recently further American collections have been published and include Shaffir, Stebbins and Turowetz (1980) and some accounts on educational settings in Popkewitz and Tabachnick (1981) and in Spindler (1982) (see especially part one).
3 A further set of accounts in relation to Australian experiences of doing research was edited jointly by Bell and Encel (1978).
4 A subsequent volume is to appear that is jointly edited by Colin Bell and Helen Roberts that is the successor to their previous collections. See Bell and Roberts (1984).

References

BAILEY, K.D (1978) *Methods of Social Research*, New York, Free Press.
BARKER-LUNN, J. (1976) 'Streaming in the primary school: Methods and problems', in SHIPMAN, M. (Ed.) *The Organisation and Impact of Social Research*, London, Routledge and Kegan Paul.
BECHHOFER, F. (1974) 'Current approaches to empirical research: Some central ideas', in REX, J. (Ed.) *Approaches to Sociology: An Introduc-*

tion to Major Trends in British Sociology, London, Routledge and Kegan Paul.

BELL, C. and ENCEL, S. (Eds) (1978) *Inside the Whale*, Oxford, Pergamon.

BELL, C. and NEWBY, H. (Eds) (1977) *Doing Sociological Research*, London, Allen and Unwin.

BELL, C. and ROBERTS, H. (Eds) (1984) *Social Researching: Policies, Problems and Practice*, London, Routledge and Kegan Paul.

BURGESS, R.G. (Ed.) (1979) *Teaching Research Methodology to Postgraduates: A Survey of Courses in the U.K.*, Coventry, University of Warwick.

BURGESS, R.G. (1980) 'Some fieldwork problems in teacher-based research', *British Educational Research Journal*, 6, 2, pp. 165–73.

BURGESS, R.G. (Ed.) (1982a) *Field Research: A Sourcebook and Field Manual*, London, Allen and Unwin.

BURGESS, R.G. (1982b) 'The practice of sociological research: Some issues in school ethnography', in BURGESS, R.G. (Ed.) *Exploring Society*, London, British Sociological Association.

BURGESS, R.G. and BULMER, M. (1981) 'Research methodology teaching: Trends and developments' *Sociology*, 15, 4, pp. 477–89.

COHEN, L. and MANION, L. (1980) *Research Methods in Education*, London, Croom Helm.

DALE, R.R. (1976) 'Mixed or single sex school?: A comment on a research study', in SHIPMAN, M. (Ed.) *The Organisation and Impact of Social Research*, London, Routledge and Kegan Paul.

DOUGLAS, J.W.B. (1976) 'The use and abuse of national cohorts', in SHIPMAN, M. (Ed.) *The Organisation and Impact of Social Research*, London, Routledge and Kegan Paul.

EGGLESTON, J. (1980) 'The perspectives of the educational research project', *British Educational Research Journal*, 6, 1, pp. 85–9.

FORD, J. (1976) 'Facts, evidence and rumour: A rational reconstruction of "social class and the comprehensive school"', in SHIPMAN, M. (Ed.) *The Organisation and Impact of Social Research*, London, Routledge and Kegan Paul.

FREILICH, M. (Ed.) (1977) *Marginal Natives at Work*, New York, Wiley.

GOODE, W.J. and HART, P.K. (1952) *Methods in Social Research*, New York, McGraw Hill.

GOULDNER, A.W. (1971) *The Coming Crisis of Western Sociology*, London, Heinemann.

HABENSTEIN, R.W. (Ed.) (1970) *Pathways to Data*, Chicago, Aldine.

HAMILTON, D. (1981) 'In search of structure: An afterword', in *Reader C of the Study Guide to Curriculum Research*, Open Campus Program, Deakin University, Australia.

HAMMOND, P. (Ed.) (1964) *Sociologists at Work*, New York, Basic Books.

HARGREAVES, D.H. (1967) *Social Relations in a Secondary School*, London, Routledge and Kegan Paul.

HENRY, F. and SABERWAL, S. (Eds) (1969) *Stress and Response in Fieldwork*, New York, Holt, Rinehart and Winston.

HOROWITZ, I.L. (1967) *The Rise and Fall of Project Camelot*, Cambridge, Mass., MIT Press.

JONGMANS, D.G. and GUTKIND, P.C.W. (Eds) (1967) *Anthropologists in the Field*, Assen, Mouton.

KENT, R.A. (1981) *A History of British Empirical Sociology*, Aldershot, Gower.

LACEY, C. (1976) 'Problems of sociological fieldwork: A review of the methodology of "Hightown Grammar"', in SHIPMAN, M. (Ed.) *The Organisation and Impact of Social Research*, London, Routledge and Kegan Paul.

LAZARSFELD, P.F. (1959) 'Problems in methodology', in MERTON, R.K., BROWN, L. and COTTRELL, L.S. (Eds) *Sociology To-day: Problems and Prospects Volume I*, New York, Harper and Row.

MADGE, J. (1953) *The Tools of Social Science*, London, Longmans.

MEDAWAR, P. (1963) 'Is the scientific paper a fraud?', *The Listener* (12 September).

MILLS, C.W. (1959) *The Sociological Imagination*, Oxford, Oxford University Press.

MOSER, C.A. and KALTON, G.K. (1971) *Survey Methods in Social Investigation*, 2nd ed., London, Heinemann.

NEWSON, J. and NEWSON, E. (1976) 'Parental roles and social contexts', in SHIPMAN, M. (Ed.) *The Organisation and Impact of Social Research*, London, Routledge and Kegan Paul.

PAYNE, G., DINGWALL, R., PAYNE, J. and CARTER, M. (1981) *Sociology and Social Research*, London, Routledge and Kegan Paul.

POPKEWITZ, T.S. and TABACHNICK, B.R. (Eds) (1981) *The Study of Schooling: Field Based Methodologies in Educational Research and Evaluation*, New York, Praeger.

ROBERTS, H. (Ed.) (1981) *Doing Feminist Research*, London, Routledge and Kegan Paul.

SHAFFIR, W.B., STEBBINS, R.A. and TUROWETZ, A. (Eds) (1980) *Fieldwork Experience: Qualitative Approaches to Social Research*, New York, St. Martin's Press.

SHARP, R. and GREEN, A. (1975) *Education and Social Control*, London, Routledge and Kegan Paul.

SHILS, E. (1957) 'Primordial, personal, sacred and civil ties: Some particular observations on the relationships of sociological theory and research', *British Journal of Sociology*, 8, pp. 130–45.

SHIPMAN, M. (Ed.) (1976) *The Organization and Impact of Social Research*, London, Routledge and Kegan Paul.

SJOBERG, G. (Ed.) (1976) *Ethics, Politics and Social Research*, London, Routledge and Kegan Paul.

SMITH-BOWEN, E. (Bohannon, Laura) (1954) *Return to Laughter*, London, Gollancz.

SPINDLER, G. (Ed.) (1970) *Being an Anthropologist: Fieldwork in Eleven Cultures*, New York, Holt, Rinehart and Winston.

SPINDLER, G. (Ed.) (1982) *Doing the Ethnography of Schooling: Educational Anthropology in Action*, New York, Holt, Rinehart and Winston.

STACEY, M. and BURGESS, R.G. (1979) The research process, Oxford, Sussex Publications (taped discussion).

TURNER, G. (1983) *The Social World of the Comprehensive School*, London, Croom Helm.

VIDICH, A.J., BENSMAN, J. and STEIN, M.R. (Eds) (1964) *Reflections on Community Studies*, New York, Harper and Row.

WAKEFORD, J. (Ed.) (1979) *Research Methods Syllabuses in Sociology Departments in the U.K.*, Lancaster, University of Lancaster.

WALKER, R. (1981) 'Getting involved in curriculum research', in LAWN, M. and BARTON, L. (Eds) *Rethinking Curriculum Studies*, London, Croom Helm.

WATSON, J.D. (1968) *The Double Helix*, Harmondsworth, Penguin.

WAX, R. (1971) *Doing Fieldwork*, Chicago, University of Chicago Press.

WHYTE, W.F. (1955) *Street Corner Society*, 2nd ed., Chicago, University of Chicago Press.

WOODS, P. (1979) *The Divided School*, London, Routledge and Kegan Paul.

1 The Old Girl Network: Recollections on the Fieldwork at St Luke's

Sara Delamont

Editor's Commentary. Although there are now many accounts of the social processes involved in 'doing sociological research', there are still relatively few systematic analyses of being a PhD candidate. Accordingly, many postgraduates could gain the impression that established researchers did not experience the trials and traumas associated with writing a PhD thesis. Sara Delamont's chapter, therefore, helps to rectify this glaring gap in our knowledge of a crucial period in which postgraduate students become researchers.

Drawing on her own experience in the University of Edinburgh, Delamont provides a commentary on her research apprenticeship. Her account is made all the more interesting as she provides extracts on the research process that were written for her PhD thesis in 1973 together with a commentary that has been written ten years later. Sara Delamont's account of her research at St Luke's (a girl's public school in Edinburgh) that has been discussed in her book *Interaction in the Classroom* and in several papers, is contextualized in relation to the key issues in the study of school classrooms when she began her work in 1968 and in relation to the work of her peers in Edinburgh.

In common with many other contributors to this collection she looks at gaining access, sampling, data collection, data analysis and the ethics of doing research. Delamont indicates that these aspects of the research process were taken for granted and seen as relatively unproblematic when she produced her thesis in 1973, while today she rigorously questions the processes and procedures in which she was involved. Among the questions that her chapter addresses are: how does the researcher attempt to integrate different kinds of data? In what ways can protection be given to informants? These and other key issues that confront the PhD candidate in the course of becoming a researcher are discussed in this chapter.

In England we possess, in the great boys' schools, what is (in spite of all defects) probably the finest system for the training of men in manly qualities that the world knows; it is all the

more pity that we have so signally failed to evolve a corres-
ponding organization for the rearing of womanly women.

Meyrick Booth wrote that condemnation of the education provided
in the girls' public schools in 1927. In 1971 Mallory Wober described
the *English Girls' Boarding Schools* and came to an effectively similar
conclusion when he criticized them for failing to teach cookery and
childcare. In 1969 and 1970 I was engaged in research in several of the
fee-paying, elite girls' schools in Edinburgh, imbued with the opposite conviction. I had, as I still have, a belief that such schools were an
embodiment of the best kind of education for girls. Single-sex,
academic, achievement-oriented institutions dedicated to producing
scholars rather than womanly women seemed to me highly desirable.
This paper is an autobiographical account of my PhD fieldwork at St
Luke's: the pseudonym I gave the expensive girls' public school
where I did observation in 1970.[1] The full ethnography is written up
in Delamont (1973) and remains substantially unpublished.

There are four main sections to the paper. The first is essentially
a *caveat*, because I have certain reservations about discussing the
material so long after the events. The central core is made up of
extracts from the relevant chapters of the PhD thesis with an
intercalated commentary written in the 1980s. This is followed by a
discussion of some further issues on data collection and analysis
which have relevance to the current state of educational research and
to this volume. The fourth section is a postscript, in which some 'if
only' comments are made.

Caveats

At the outset I would like to stress how long ago this work was done.
I graduated in 1968, spent 1968–69 working on paper and pencil tests
about study habits, and did the observational work in 1969–70. At
that time the 'new' sociology of education was not 'public'. I had
completed my data collection by the 1970 BSA conference at which
the paradigm change was announced (Brown, 1973). Also work on
females was very unfashionable, and 'women's studies' had barely
begun even in the USA. This means that there are at least two major
research topics — gender and the content of the curriculum — which
would have been treated as problematic if I had done the fieldwork in
the mid-1970s. However, they were not seen then as central or even
significant topics for research, and I cannot say much about them. I

believe that bad ethnographic writing comes from taking data collected with one frame of reference and writing it up using a different one, because the researcher has usually focused on issues and personnel relevant to the first perspective, and lacks insight on different questions. The work of Sharp and Green (1975) seems to me a particularly vivid warning to other ethnographers in this regard. It does not appear either possible or desirable to write about the St Luke's work as if I had read classification and framing (Bernstein, 1971) or Millman and Kanter (1974) while I was doing the research. The study is, therefore, notable for failing to make either the curriculum, or the issues of gender, problematic.

A second caveat concerns the status of the research, and its historical context. Since the St Luke's fieldwork I have never had the luxury of spending longer than a month engaged in research full-time, so in some ways the three years of full-time study (and two years of part-time work) spent on the project should make it a model ethnography. However, it was a higher degree project, and therefore a learning exercise; an apprenticeship. I would not want any other researcher, novice or experienced, to do exactly what I did, and I would not now tackle the project in precisely the same way myself.

The whole context of classroom research has changed so markedly since 1969 that many aspects of the St Luke's study seem quaint; sepia-tinted; 'long ago and far away'. As the extracts from the thesis, used in the next section, show the combination of a novel research topic and method with being a candidate for a higher degree gives the thesis a defensive tone. My recollection of writing up the thesis is that, as well as being extremely hard work, the process was frightening. The criteria for success were largely indeterminate, my supervisor had no experience in submitting ethnographic work for higher degree examination, and the professor (who controlled the selection of an external and an internal examiner) capricious. I now know from a survey of higher degree students (Eggleston and Delamont, 1983) that most feel worried by the indeterminacy of thesis examination, and that inexperienced supervisors are common. Today I warn graduates that research is a lonely, unsettling experience, and doing a thesis is rather like an initiation ceremony where young warriors have to live all alone in the wilderness for long periods before rejoining the tribe as adults. At the time, the intellectual isolation and responsibility I felt scared me.

It can be argued that such isolation is necessary, as well as common, among postgraduates (Eggleston and Delamont, 1983). I can see that, as one of a group of research students Liam Hudson had gathered in Edinburgh, I was lucky to share my stumbling discovery of school and classroom ethnography with a group of others. Hudson (1977) has written an article about the student ethnographers he fostered in Edinburgh, in which he describes us as an intellectual and social clique with considerable hostility to other schools of methodology. His detailed analysis of the internal structure of the student group is highly inaccurate, but his general characterization of us as mutually supportive both intellectually and personally is reasonable. The central links formed then can still be seen in the publications of the core members of the clique.[2] The Edinburgh group was not only mutually supportive in developing ethnographic methods in education, it has also come to be seen as a pioneering group for developing educational ethnography. Professor E.C. Wragg's (1982) evidence to the Rothschild Enquiry, for example, cites us as a shining example of the role of SSRC studentships in fostering scholarly work of major national importance. Certainly if I had not had the friendship of Paul Atkinson, David Hamilton, Michael Stubbs, Margaret Reid, Brian Torode and Margo Galloway I would never have written the thesis and submitted it. As it was, I planned carefully to submit while Liam Hudson was on sabbatical, and was awarded the degree by Don Swift and Boris Semeonoff.

The final caveat is that, because the bulk of the research is unpublished, much of what follows may be obscure. Ball and Atkinson, among others in this volume, are writing accounts of how well-known ethnographies were done. Readers of this book will have read *Beachside Comprehensive*, and can relate the account to the finished project. The data on St Luke's lie, relatively unknown, in the Edinburgh University Library. This is not because I was ashamed of my work, but the result of a series of accidents. I submitted the thesis in August 1973, and started work at Leicester in September. I had asked Routledge (who had published Roy Nash's PhD (1973)) if they wanted to see mine, and despatched it as I left for Leicester. Some six to nine months later, having heard nothing, I wrote to ask for my manuscript back. Routledge replied that they had lost it, would pay for a Xerox, and wished to have a photocopy so that they could consider it for publication. The second submission reached an academic referee (Brian Davies) who recommended that a revised manuscript be published. Routledge rejected this advice, pleading the economic climate, and so I was back at Square One. However, by this time John Eggleston had asked me to write *Interaction in the Classroom* (1976a), so the thesis was put aside. Thus, apart from four papers (Delamont, 1976b, 1976c, 1984b; Atkinson and Delamont,

1977), the research described below is only known from *Interaction in the Classroom*. The material which follows, therefore, describes the collection, analysis and presentation of a PhD thesis, not a book or a research report to a sponsor like most of the other contributors to this volume.

The next section presents material from the PhD thesis, *Academic Conformity Observed: Studies in the Classroom*, set in italics, with a commentary written in 1982–83.

Doing the Research at St Luke's

The introduction to the thesis describes the central features of my research at St Luke's, in the context of 1972–73.

The Scope and the Methods

This thesis discusses the intellectual perspectives and work-habits of adolescents at a variety of Scottish schools; with particular emphasis on one sample of girls who are analyzed in the context of the teaching they experienced and their institutional and social setting. Three traditionally separate methods of data collection have been used, together with aspects of their related theories.

The first of these three normally distinct methodologies uses inventories, questionnaires, or mental tests; and has traditionally formed the cornerstone of most educational psychology and educational sociology. Both the other two methods are based on observation, but used in rather different ways. In one tradition, which I have called systematic *observation the observer uses a schedule of some description, which has been devised in advance, and allows the observer to code behaviour as he observes it, usually so that it can later be quantified, (Medley and Mitzel, 1963). The other tradition of observation I have called* unstructured, *because the observer is concerned to* discover *the interrelationship of variables in the social situation by observing social action.*

These three particular methods of data collection have not, to my knowledge, been used in conjunction before. As a result there is no obvious precedent in the literature either for combining the results gathered in the separate traditions or for presenting it in a coherent monograph with the related theory. This lack of precedent has affected the form which this thesis takes and the style in which it is written. The authors who have conducted research in the three traditions relevant to this thesis have done so largely in mutual isolation. In consequence I have dispensed with the standard 'review of the literature' chapter, in favour of discussing the relevant literature at the appropriate point in the thesis. Stylistically, the lack of precedent has led me to expose the 'bare bones' of the research design rather more than usual — to explain and justify my use of the various data collection techniques at each stage of the discussion.

My comments today on this extract are, firstly: it is odd I use 'he' for 'the researcher', and secondly, I am surprised by the defensiveness. The thesis had ten chapters in three sections — one on the pupils and the teachers based on questionnaires, interviews, and documents; the next on the systematic observation; and then one on the unstructured observation which built to a theorized crescendo. After the description of what was in the ten chapters, I reviewed some basic literature on the 'Three Traditions', in the following ways:

THE THREE TRADITIONS: *Paper and Pencil Measures, Systematic and Unstructured Observation*

My work on teacher and pupil's styles has only a tangential connection with the mainstream of work in either the mental testing field or that of questionnaire and survey based educational psychology. However, it does have close ties with some of the less orthodox work which has developed from that tradition, in particular that of Hudson, (1966, 1968a, 1968b) on differences in intellectual styles, which grew out of intelligence testing, and Parlett (1967 and 1970) on individual work-styles. The study described below used a variety of questionnaires and inventories, in particular a version of the syllabus-bound inventory developed by Parlett for use among students at MIT (Parlett, 1967) and also Hudson on English schoolboys (Hudson, 1968a). The questionnaire and inventories used in this study have provided much of the quantifiable data, and the means of comparing samples of pupils at different schools. The main emphasis of this study was, however, placed on observation within schools rather than on inventories, questionnaires or tests.

Here I rehearsed the growth of systematic observation in the USA via Medley and Mitzel (1963) and Rosenshine (1970). I said that:

Some of these systems are mentioned briefly later in this chapter. A more thorough review of the relevant literature occurs in Chapter 6.

At this point it is enough to say that this part of the research is well documented and has clear precedents.

This was to draw a contrast with:

unstructured observation techniques [which] have remained largely neglected. Handbooks of research methods in the social sciences, particularly anthropology, discuss unstructured observation, but handbooks on educational research do not. There have, however, been a few studies done in recent years using unstructured techniques, in particular the work of Becker and his associates in higher education and professional socialization (Becker et al., 1961, 1968).... Four studies of schools using unstructured techniques have been useful during my research; two studies of English secondary schools (Hargreaves, 1967; Lacey, 1970), and two of American elementary classes (Smith and Geoffrey, 1968; Jackson, 1968).

Writing today, it is very striking how little observational work was published on schools in 1970–3, and how unknown some of the available studies from the USA were in Britain. None of the ethnographies I traced was about girls, and the few books on girls' schools (e.g. Wober, 1971) were not recognizable to me as research. I corresponded with Audrey Lambart about her Manchester study, but at that time she had not written up her Master's thesis and so had nothing to send me. To date her work is less well-known than the classics (Hargreaves, 1967 and Lacey, 1970) by her colleagues, and only two articles (Lambart 1982) have been published. Since 1973 there have been a few papers on the schooling of girls published (Fuller, 1980; Llewellyn, 1980) but a contemporary research student studying St Luke's would not find a full-length published ethnography of girls to use as a model. I based the structure of my thesis on *Making the Grade* (Becker *et al.*, 1968), and it would have been easier to have a British ethnography of a school to use as a blueprint. At the time, I did not labour those points, but emphasized to the reader of the thesis that I had used Flanders Interaction Analysis Categories (FIAC) (1970) *with* a loosely symbolic interactionist-observational approach. I explained this at the time as follows:

The decision to integrate data gathered from different traditions into one coherent monograph was initially the product of disappointment. During 1968–9 I conducted a study of syllabus-bound and syllabus-free pupils in some secondary schools based solely on questionnaires and inventories. This research raised more questions than it resolved. I found that differences between samples from the various schools visited were great, even when the pupils were of the same age, sex and social class. Nothing in the questionnaire data explained the wide range of scores, and the answers appeared to lie in the internal structures of the schools. A research project which was based on observation within one or more schools, designed to illuminate the subtle variations which had eluded the questionnaire-based study, was indicated.

When I came to the literature on observation in schools I was intrigued by the existence of two disparate traditions of observation — the systematic and the unstructured apparently in mutual isolation. I felt that the two types of observation had been used for tackling different research problems, and so were not necessarily incompatible. The project at St Luke's was therefore planned to involve both methods, each in the area where it was most appropriate. While in the field I found that the two techniques were indeed compatible, and the problems which were raised by the combination of methods were relatively slight. However, the difficulties of producing a coherent report of the study utilising all the data are considerable. This is due, at least in part to the lack of any previous work attempting the same combination of techniques, and the resulting lack of any established conventions for presenting such data.

This is still true in 1983, in that no published work has attempted to do what I did! However the ORACLE book on transfer to middle and secondary schools (Galton and Willcocks, 1983) does draw on data collected with Deanne Boydell's two observational schedules and ethnographic fieldnotes (see Galton and Delamont, 1984). At the time I stressed the uneasy relationship(s) between quantitative and qualitative data.

The relationship between the unstructured methods of observation and either the data produced by 'paper and pencil' measures or that from systematic observation is an uneasy one. It is, of course, merely a part of the wider problem which faces anyone using unstructured techniques: how to handle and present the data and whether or not to attempt to quantify them. A comparison of those authors whose work with unstructured observation has influenced this research shows vividly that there is no consensus about the extent to which other types of data should be incorporated.

At one extreme the two books produced by the Manchester 'anthropologists' Hargreaves (1967) and Lacey (1970) contain far more data derived from written questionnaires than actual accounts of the observation. Lacey includes a long historical section derived from published records, and quotes at length from diaries kept by the boys, apparently at his request. Hargreaves uses questionnaire responses extensively in his book, although his subjects would probably have been more articulate in interviews than on paper. Both men relied very heavily on sociometric data to establish social relations among the boys, and apparently paid little attention to recording actual patterns of interaction among the boys while they were in the schools. This reliance on written material means that their books tell us more about social relations expressed in writing than they do about what the fieldworker actually saw. Neither book contains detailed accounts of the lessons observed: neither their intellectual content, nor the teachers' actions, nor the pupils' reactions and classroom behaviour.

This passage shows how dominant Hargreaves (1967) and Lacey (1970) were at the time, and how I saw my work as an attempt to do better. I wanted to see how far Hargreaves and Lacey were producing findings about boys which would not be applicable in girls' schools; *or* about streamed schools which would not turn up in institutions with subject sets and mixed ability groups; *or* about schools with an intake from different social classes or home circumstances. That is, if one looked at girls, and at a non-streamed school, and at a 'one-class' school, would one find polarized peer groups? So I wanted expensive, single-sex schools where there were subject sets but not fixed streams, where I could study peer-group formation. When I came to write up the thesis I dignified the choice of school type as 'theoretical sampling' (Glaser and Strauss, 1967) but only when writing up. In 1969 I just thought Lacey and Hargreaves had three variables confused, and it was necessary to separate them.

The thesis chapter goes on to compare the role of the observer doing FIAC with that of the ethnographer. I contrasted the non-involved FIAC-user with Becker talking to medical students as they sat around in Kansas, emphasizing that 'full' participation is not possible in the type of school studied. The thesis chapter continues:

In my study I attempted to play both types of observational role within the school, depending on the situations which arose. Within the ordinary, largely silent classroom I acted as an entirely non-participant, 'fly-on-the-wall' observer, and concentrated on using two systematic schedules, augmented by notes of other events. In those lessons where the girls were sometimes free to move around and to talk amongst themselves (such as Needlework, Art, the three sciences, and games), I circulated among the pupils during the appropriate periods, talking to them and to the teacher. In the episodes where attention was focused on the teacher I reverted to the non-participant role, and used my systematic techniques if they were applicable. Throughout the rest of the school day I concentrated on participating in the life of the staff-room and the playground, engaging in conversations with teachers and pupils, during breaks, lunch-hours, free lessons, the intervals between lessons and the extra-curricular activities.

With this combination of techniques I tried to make the best possible use of my time in the school, to provide coherent accounts of both the highly regulated, and the relatively free, episodes in the school day of my sample. It appeared to be perfectly possible to play both roles while observing in the same school, because each role is used in the context where it is closest to the behaviour of the people being observed. Within a secondary school, at least, the two methods of observing are not incompatible.

As part of the contrast, I did stress that Jackson (1968), Smith and Geoffrey (1968) and Blanche Geer (1964) had tried to make the familiar strange, and that was what I, too, had tried to achieve. There is more detail about the FIAC observation in a later chapter, but no more discussion about the ethnography. For this paper I have written something on access, data collection and recording, analysis, and ethics, none of which is discussed in the thesis. In retrospect it appears that I took 'participant observation' as a relatively unproblematic, taken-for-granted, activity, which did not need further discussion.

Some Previously Unconsidered Trifles

In this part of the paper I comment upon several aspects of the research which were not discussed in Delamont (1973) and are previously unpublished. Access, data collection and recording, analysis, writing up, and ethics are recollected in this section.

Gaining Access

The general strategy for gaining access to a school to observe, interview or give out questionnaires, was a polite, but vague letter asking to see the Head. Once inside her room, I would specify what I hoped to be allowed to do. All the schools studied in Edinburgh were independent, fee-paying girls' schools, so the local authority and the Scottish Education Department (SED) did not have to be approached. As far as I know all the heads made their own decision, and did not consult the Governors. When I saw heads I always wore a conservative outfit and real leather gloves. I had a special grey dress and coat, for days when I expected to see the head and some pupils. The coat was knee-length and very conservative-looking, while the dress was mini-length to show the pupils I knew what the fashion was. I would keep the coat on in the head's office, and take it off before I first met pupils. When observing I tried to dress like the student teachers who were common in all the schools: no trousers, unladdered tights, and no make up.

No head ever asked me to explain my project to her staff, but rather did any explaining herself. I do not think any head let me into her school without warning her teachers, an experience reported by Atkinson (q.v.) and Llewellyn (1980). I never approached teachers myself, and the pupils were never asked, by anyone, if they minded completing questionnaires or being observed.

None of the 'posh' girls' schools in Edinburgh refused access. I visited six elite girls' schools (including the one used for the Jean Brodie story) for questionnaire sessions, or observation, or both. Paper and pencil 'tests' were done in several girls' schools during 1968–69, and I had negotiated observation of a few lessons. When I decided to concentrate on observational methods I did a short period (2–3 weeks) in December 1969 on one school, 'The Laurels', as a 'pilot' for a half-term at St Luke's.[3] Some observation was done in four different schools, but the thesis was concentrated on the half-term at St Luke's. Accordingly I have focused on that work in this paper. However, I can honestly say I did not have any access problems, and all the heads — gatekeepers — were very cooperative. I used to be nervous before I saw them, but no-one ever objected to the research taking place.

The phrase 'old-girl network' is used as the title because I think the fact that the headmistress of St Luke's was an old Girtonian and warmed to me when told I had been at Girton, led to allowing me to stay in the school for half a term and to leaving me unharassed. She asked the staff if they would let me into their classes, but in my absence. Only one teacher refused to have me in her lessons, her public reason being that she had just had a student teacher for eight weeks and wanted some privacy. The girls told me that she frequently lost her temper and 'explained' her refusal in that way. This refusal meant I only saw one French teacher in action, although I was able to see German and Spanish taught. Mrs Michaels, the head, also wrote to parents asking them to allow me to interview her pupils. Only one set of parents among the forty-four girls in the year I was studying refused me permission to interview their daughter, Deborah. With the inevitability of sod's law, Deborah was the isolate of the year, chosen as a friend by no-one, and was a highly significant, negative reference point for all the other girls. They thought her parents were overprotective and that she was babyish and yielded too much to her family! I regret to this day that I did not get a talk with her, because her classroom behaviour was unusual: she volunteered a lot in class, but the teachers ignored her raised hand to a noticeable degree. (Her school career was reasonably successful, however, in that she eventually left with nine SCE O-grades and six 'Highers').[4] The other girls either gained their parents' permission for the interview, or were given the freedom to make their own decision. (They were 14 and 15 during the study). All in all, Mrs Michaels was extremely supportive towards the research, as were the staff of St Luke's, who largely treated me with benign neglect.

Sampling

I worked with a whole year group, of 14/15-year-olds who were third years in Scottish terms[5] (fourth years in English terms) — that is, one year away from SCE O-grades. There were forty-four girls in the year in two parallel forms, taught as ability sets for some subjects and in option groups for others. I had a sampling problem over which lesson to watch when three or four were sometimes happening at once. For example, Physics, Biology, Greek, and Dress and Design were timetabled simultaneously, so that I could not observe the girls taking Greek *and* those doing needlework. I chose to concentrate on large classes (Physics with twenty girls rather than Greek with three) and avoided the languages I did not speak myself (German and Spanish). However, I made sure that every teacher had me at least once, so they all shared the burden, except the 'refuser'. I kept a careful record of where I had been, and watched an equal number of lessons taught by the 'majority' teachers: that is, I systematically went to one English teacher and then the other to make sure I had an equal sample of 'A' and 'B' English lessons. The whole year group was my 'sample', or rather population, and all the teachers who taught them, except the visiting music teachers of violin, trumpet, etc.

(Among these peripatetic staff were the only males in the building apart from the caretaker.)

Data Collection and Recording

During the first two weeks I did FIAC in all lessons, before I knew any of the participants. Then I watched the lessons, concentrating on the pupils, coding their contributions with a schedule of my own devising (see Appendix) and made 'fieldnotes' of 'interesting' pieces of dialogue. It was not possible to do anything but sit silently in most lessons, because that is what the girls did. The classes at St Luke's were silent, or had one person talking at a time. Pupil conversations were rare, because the girls worked nearly all the time, or switched off. In lessons where talk was allowed, I mixed with the pupils: for example, Physics, Chemistry and Biology group work, and PE. However, I tried to be passive — I did not play hockey or lacrosse as Mandy Llewellyn (1980) did — but did tie the girls' team numbers on for them if they asked. At break and lunch I went to the staffroom and chatted to the teachers.

My main focus was pupils' study habits, especially their verbal contributions to classroom discourse. I wanted to see if there were polarized peer groups, and whether there were cliques with similar participatory styles or not. I expected to find individual differences in classroom participation — both between the girls, and when the same pupil was taught by different teachers. Accordingly that was my main focus, and I did not look for many other things which were undoubtedly going on. To collect material on the girls' perception of, and strategies for dealing with, each other and their teachers, I interviewed all the fourth year except Deborah. I interviewed the boarders one evening in the boarding house, and the day-girls at Paul Atkinson's flat during the holidays. They came in groups (if they wished) and sat reading magazines while I interviewed them one at a time in a separate room. The groups they formed to come for interview gave me an unobtrusive measure of their sociometric structure.

Overall I do not think what I did can usefully be called *participant* observation, because I did not participate in any meaningful way. Instead I 'lurked' and watched. I think I fell into the category in the school occupied by student teachers, who also lurked about the school, often without any clear function.

There were four kinds of data: questionnaires completed by the girls; tape-recorded interviews with pupils; the FIAC data; and my fieldnotes. Specimens of all the questionnaires, and the interview schedule, are reproduced in an Appendix to the thesis, and are not discussed further here. I taped pupil interviews, *and* took notes on them, in case of the recorder failing, which it did on one occasion. The interview covered peer group membership, perceptions of teachers elicited with their names on cards presented in threes following Kelly's procedure (Bannister and Fransella, 1971), career ambitions, leisure activities and general views of St Luke's. I also asked what sort of pupil teachers liked and disliked, eliciting a description of a 'Good Pupil' Ideal Type. These data have subsequently confused several commentators, notably Rosemary Deem (1978).[6] The interviews also went into some detail about subject choice, and the role of parents and teachers in the process.

The two kinds of observational data were recorded in different ways. Coding classroom talk with FIAC involves writing a number every three seconds (800 in a forty-minute lesson) with the sequence preserved. I sat at a desk with a stopwatch, and wrote the coding numbers on A-4 lined paper turned sideways to give me columns; each minute of interaction took one column. (I prepared pages with horizontal lines at fifteen, thirty and forty-five seconds to keep the coding neatly arranged and to enable me to check that I was recording at three-second intervals). My other observational records were kept in spiral-bound shorthand pads. The 'notes' in the shorthand books included: a seating plan for each lesson and the mixture of notes and my pupil talk schedule. Things that happened in the staffroom, at hockey or on the bus home were noted down in the same books. I did not keep a separate field diary, nor did I rewrite my notes afterwards in any proper way. Looking back I realize how badly I did the recording: *but* I do have an excellent memory. I take better, fuller and more kinds of notes today because I know better, from reading books on ethnographic methods, and other people's 'methods' appendices! I would not let any graduate student I supervise escape with so little in writing, or such undigested records.

Data Analysis

Other students at Edinburgh, notably Brian Torode, constructed elaborate indexes of their material. I did not do any indexing of fieldnotes, because I usually remembered which lessons included examples of whatever behaviour or person I was interested in, and was able to turn to it. If I wanted any incident I knew where to find it, by running the fieldwork through my head and picturing the relevant pages in my notebooks. I still do this — running the 'film' of a lesson in my head, and then running over the 'film' of my notes till I can 'see' where the incident is.

Analyzing the FIAC data took a long time. I followed his instruction manual (now superseded by Flanders (1970)), transferring each code number onto a 10 × 10 matrix and then totalling the codings. I worked out all the ratios — I/D, TTR, etc. by hand. As this was done according to an explicit, published manual I will only say here that it was a chore — if I ever do that again I'll use a computer!

All the paper and pencil tests and questionnaires were coded or scored, and the numbers were punched (by me) and handled with SPSS, mainly to do cross-tabs. Liam Hudson was very hostile to factor analysis, and we were none of us urged to use multivariate analysis. Charles Jones taught me how to prepare punch cards, and get simple SPSS runs done by the Edinburgh Regional Computing Centre, and sorted out my botched jobs. In return I spent time collating, stapling and distributing the questionnaires on which his PhD was based. Brian Torode had invented a cluster analysis programme, for his seating plans, and he used it on mine, too, though I did not report any detail of it in the thesis. The results did not seem to make sense, and neither Brian nor I could see why a programme that produced beautiful sociometric clusters in his school did not on the St Luke's data. The idea was to put the seating plans drawn in every lesson into the cluster analysis, and see which pupils habitually sat together, weighting the tie between a pair who sat side by side more heavily than the links between those sitting one behind the other, or separated by gangways. In his school this produced magnificent sociograms, at St Luke's it seemed to reflect only the setting arrangements: girls who said they were not friends, but were in the same set for maths, English or French, came out as highly associated. I went to a series of seminars on cluster analysis and multi-dimensional scaling run by Peter Buneman and Tony Coxon, heard several experts in maths and computing science show cluster analysis to be very problematic, and quietly abandoned the data from the Torode programme.

The 'fieldnotes' were not analyzed. I read through them over and over again, and picked out bits to illustrate the argument I was developing. When I wrote up I was still analyzing data, and I tried to say things for which I had evidence of two different kinds (for example, a questionnaire and a classroom extract). I was unselfconscious and non-reflexive at the time and it is hard now to reconstruct what I did. I can describe how I arrived at the sociometric structure of the year group I presented in the thesis and elsewhere (Delamont, 1976c). I had two sources of data, apart from the seating charts. In each girl's interview I asked who she went around with in school, who her friends were. When the girls arranged the appointments for their interviews I suggested that they could come in groups, and so I was able to see a pattern of voluntary, holiday time, association which gave me an unobtrusive measure. Thus, when Tessa told me her closest friend was Zoe, and when she arrived for her interview with Zoe (and Zoe's sister) I felt I had tapped something solid. Some girls said they did not see school friends outside, and they all came alone, or with a friend who was not from St Luke's. The confidence I had in this as an unobtrusive measure was strengthened when the clique who prided themselves on being 'mature' and 'grown up', because they had boyfriends, wore make-up, drank coffee, smoked, dressed fashionably, and went out dancing, arrived with a group of boys, having been thrown out of a coffee bar for noisy behaviour. The party sat in the flat playing strip poker (though none of the girls took off anything more than shoes, hair-ribbons, watches and jackets) while I interviewed members of my sample.

It was important that, as we wrote our theses, we all read bits of each other's work, and commented on the analyses. David Hamilton, for example, read my chapter on FIAC very thoroughly, while I read Margo Galloway's work, and so on. This gave us, I imagine, some similarity of style, and of literature cited, and meant that we tried out our arguments for plausibility in a sympathetic atmosphere.

Finally in this section, the issue of ethics in the St Luke's research has to be mentioned.

Ethics

Too many researchers, especially the illuminative evaluators, discuss 'ethics' instead of focusing on methodological reflexivity or theorizing. This argument is made elsewhere (Atkinson and Delamont, 1984) and I do not wish to elaborate it here. There were some problems which arose during the fieldwork, because every ethnographer in a school learns things about pupils which could cause them trouble with staff, and possesses 'guilty knowledge' about teachers pupils would relish. The St Luke's girls were not engaged in criminal acts, but because it was a school used by university families (a Dean of Social Sciences had a child in the school), I knew the parents of two of my sample. The two girls concerned took the double relationship in their stride, but it could have caused problems. The main ethical issue on which I felt, and feel, strongly, is the importance of protective pseudonyms. Until this paper I have always used the coy phrase 'a Scottish city' instead of Edinburgh. In talks great stress was laid on the research being conducted in *all* the fee-paying girls' schools in Edinburgh, to confuse those who knew the city. When challenged by anyone who had guessed the real identity of St Luke's, I have always refused to make any comment, and pointed out that it could have been X, Y, Z or W school instead. The official history of the school was mentioned in the thesis, but no reference is given in the bibliography. All the teachers and pupils have pseudonyms which have been used so often it is hard to remember their 'real' equivalents. I am a believer in pseudonyms rather than real names because the individuals should be protected whether they like it or not. Any school prepared to have a researcher in deserves that protection, because researchers know what harm can be done to teachers and pupils better than schools can. The determination and care exercised in protecting the participants at St Luke's was rewarded for me when a colleague announced that his/her research assistant was one of my sample. The young woman had been given *Interaction in the Classroom* to read, and returned having recognized her schooldays in the examples. Finding that one of my sample is now an active educational researcher seems a good enough reason to maintain all the pseudonyms twelve years on.

Maintaining pseudonyms is aided by spending considerable time inventing them with a logical relationship to the real names, attaching them early on, and always writing and talking about the research from the earliest drafts and most informal chats with the pseudonyms. It soon becomes easier to remember that Tessa and Zoe are friends than that A and B are. Indeed it is harder today to recall the real names of my sample than the pseudonyms.

Retrospect and Prospect

In retrospect, greater attention should have been paid to the content of the curriculum, especially the reasons for the large number of girls doing science, and to the importance of the school as an all-female institution. The school had a feminist tradition, founded in the nineteenth century as part of the pioneering educational campaigns. For seventy-five years it had sent many girls to university, especially Oxbridge, and the large numbers doing physics in 1970 symbolized the high academic standards. Gender was, therefore, important but not a matter thought about at the time. I was glad that the school was of that kind and not the 'finishing-school' type, but I only thought through the implications of the gender issue much later when writing 'The Girls Most Likely to' (Delamont, 1976c) which tried to look at St Luke's as a school reproducing Scottish elite strata. The historical tradition is recounted in the thesis, and the concept of 'double conformity' (Delamont, 1978) was evolved (in discussion with Paul Atkinson) for the thesis. It would have been nice, I now realize, to enquire systematically about the impact of that pioneer tradition on the school in 1970.

The lack of a published monograph on the material is a cause for regret. In addition to a 500-page thesis, there is enough unused draft to produce a further 250 pages. Data lying unpublished sadden me. It is probably *hubris* to imagine that a full-length monograph would have had the impact of Lacey (1970) or Willis (1977), because sociologists of education are uninterested in research on elite groups. It would be nice if the data from St Luke's were to make a dent in the inverted snobbery of sociologists, which makes it OK to research the bad and the poor, but not to study elite groups. However, the St Luke's work is always rejected as 'irrelevant' because of the class, ability, and elite status of the school (for example, Deem, 1978) as if the way the upper class is educated were unimportant.[7] For five or six years the study was also 'written off' because its focus was girls, and that at least has changed. I still believe there is a desperate need for ethnographies in prep, public and other elite schools, so we know how the top people are educated. We are also very short of published work on girls in all social classes.

There is one further paper on these girls awaiting publication (Delamont, 1984b), including data on their O-grade, H-grade and A-level results and school careers until the upper sixth. These data allowed me to 'follow up' the pupils, and even test my hunches about who would 'succeed' in the school. The characterization of St Luke's as a highly academic school can be seen in the exam results obtained in 1973 (when my sample left the sixth).[8] In 1970 there were three large cliques, two small ones and a few marginal girls. The three large cliques were the boarders, the 'debs and dollies', and the 'intellectuals'. One small group consisted of the keen horsewomen, and the other of the weakest pupils academically who spent their leisure time with their parents. At 14 the boarders and the 'intellectuals' were the most academically successful, and the keenest sportswomen came from the boarding house and a subset within the 'teenage' group. These patterns of abilities and interests at 14 were sustained until the girls left at the end of their school careers.

The group who described themselves as 'academic' were the most successful in obtaining exam passes, university places, school offices in the intellectual activities and provided the Head Girl (Jill). Three members (Jill, Penny and Evelyn) got three A-levels at Grade A. Michelle went to Oxford, Henrietta to medical school, Evelyn won a bursary to St Andrews, and Charmian a prize as an outstanding scientist. None of this group was involved in sport, but they were the presidents of the school societies (historical, musical and literary).

The boarders had been the most enthusiastic sportswomen at 14, and in the sixth form they were the dominant presence in the school teams. Mary was captain of hockey, squash and badminton as well as playing tennis and lacrosse for the school. Alexandra was captain of tennis, and in the first team for hockey and lacrosse. The boarders also provided the mainstay of the choir, and most got enough H-grades and A-levels to enter higher education. The sporting members of the 'debs and dollies' clique had survived into the sixth, also getting entry qualifications for university. Tessa became captain of lacrosse and vice-captain of hockey, and Monica not only captained the school fencing team but represented Scotland. The prefects, house captains and winners of merit badges came from all three groups.

This pattern came as a relief, because the thesis argued that the involvement in youth culture shown by the 'debs and dollies' was *not* a signal that they were to be school dropouts or academic failures. However, data on their occupations and marriage patterns in 1990 will be needed to test the hypotheses about elite reproduction made in Delamont (1976c).

Conclusion

The study, as conducted, has many flaws of omission and commission. However the basic topics, the choice of school, and the structure of the thesis still appear to me to be soundly chosen.

Notes

1 During the fieldwork I was supported by a three-year SSRC award. The thesis was written in the evenings while I worked for Dr J.A.M. Howe, supported by a grant from the Scottish Council for Research in Education. I am grateful to both these funding bodies. Paul Atkinson and Bob Burgess have given me substantial criticisms of this paper, and I am very grateful to them. Mrs Myrtle Robins typed this manuscript into an acceptable form, and I am deeply indebted to her.
2 Most obviously in the contributions to Chanan and Delamont (1975), the volume edited by Stubbs and Delamont (1976), *Explorations in Classroom Observation*; papers in Delamont (1984a); Atkinson, Reid and Sheldrake (1977); Dingwall, Heath, Reid and Stacey (1977), and Adelman (1981).
3 Throughout this paper all schools, teachers and pupils have their pseudonyms firmly attached.
4 Readers unfamiliar with Scottish education may need to know that the Scottish Certificate of Education (SCE) exam system has O-grades at 16, Higher H-grades at 17 and then a certificate of sixth form studies for 18-year-olds. Fee-paying schools like St Luke's often put pupils heading for university in for English A-levels at 18, so they take major public exams three summers running. At St Luke's the brightest girls did this, so Charmian got ten O-grades, six H-grades and three A-levels.
5 Transfer to secondary education is at 12 in Scotland, so O-grades are taken at the end of the fourth year.
6 Rosemary Deem (1978, pp. 40–1), drawing only on *Interaction in the Classroom* rather than the thesis or published articles, says that the girls of St Luke's: 'seem to have almost an obsessive concern with being quiet, good at school work, and getting teachers to like them.... Boys seldom perceive their role in this way and there can be few boy pupils of whom it could be said, as it was of one girl in Delamont's study ... that "she only answers when she's sure she's right".' While I fail to understand how anyone could misread the relevant section of *Interaction in the Classroom* (pp. 68–71) completely, I have amended the section in the second edition (Delamont, 1983). I asked the girls: 'If you had a sister coming to St Luke's who wanted to be popular with teachers, and asked you how, what would you tell her to do?' The characteristics of the ideal pupil elicited in this way were in no sense a description of behaviors any of my sample wished to engage in. Every girl said that only 'goody-goodies', 'wets', 'swots' and 'babies' wanted to be popular with teachers and no sister of theirs would be so feeble. However, they did produce descriptions of a 'teacher's pet' for me, which is revealing about *their* views of what *teachers* like. But, in justice to Alexandra, Zoe, Wendy and the rest, I must record that they did not *want* to be swots and weeds.

There is, to my knowledge, no evidence that boys' perceptions of what teachers like are different. Boys also think teachers like well behaved, quiet, clever, hardworking pupils, and there are plenty of quiet, conscientious boys who only answer when they are sure they have the correct reply in the classrooms of Britain. Beynon and Atkinson (1984) show a thoroughly rebellious boy describing 'teachers' pets' in language almost identical to that used by the St Luke's girls, twelve years later and in a South Wales comprehensive.

7 Deem (1978, p. 40) dismisses the whole ethnography (without having read the thesis) by saying that 'in any case the girls studied are a quite atypical group in class terms', as if that made them unworthy of research attention.

8 In the fourth year forty-seven girls took 381 O-grades and only ten results were graded below 'C'. Girls in their fifth and sixth years added twenty-eight further O-grades in sixteen subjects to their fourth year totals. 'Highers', taken in fifth and sixth years, produced 234 passes in seventeen subjects among eighty pupils. Thirteen different A-level subjects were available, and eight pupils took three subjects, eight took two, and seven took one. There were forty passes, and three of my sample (Jill, Penny and Evelyn) got three A-levels at Grade A.

Appendix: Table of Pupil Talk Categories

CODE	EXPLANATION
VR	A correct, or at least, acceptable answer, produced by a volunteer.
VW	An incorrect, or unacceptable answer, produced by a volunteer.
VT	A volunteered translation.
AR	A correct answer, produced on demand.
AW	An incorrect answer, produced on demand.
AT	A translation, produced on demand.
HUNA	A pupil raises her hand, but is not asked by the teacher.
QDSP	A dependence-seeking question, concerning procedure.
QDSF	A dependence-seeking question, concerning facts.
RNA	A question revealing that a pupil has not been paying attention.
REP	A reprimand.
QEI	A question asking for extra information.
QUIB	A quibble with the teachers' explanations, etc.
VPO	A volunteered personal experience or opinion.
APO	A personal experience or opinion produced on demand.
ST	A pupil doing seat work indicates that she is stuck.
HELP	A teacher gives a pupil doing seat work some individual help.
T	Pupil talk, taking place, illegally, during lessons.

References

ADELMAN, C. (Ed.) (1981) *Uttering, Muttering*, London, Grant McIntyre.

ATKINSON, P. (1984) *q.v.*

ATKINSON, P. and DELAMONT, S. (1977) 'Mock-ups and cock ups', in HAMMERSLEY, M. and WOODS, P. (Eds), *The Process of Schooling*, London, Routledge and Kegan Paul.

ATKINSON, P. and DELAMONT, S. (1984) paper to appear in SHIPMAN, M. (Ed.) *Contemporary Analysis in Education* Lewes, Falmer Press.

ATKINSON, P. *et al.* (1977) 'Medical mystique', *Sociology of Work and Occupations*, 4, 3, pp. 243–80.

BALL, S. (1981) *Beachside Comprehensive*, Cambridge, Cambridge University Press.

BANNISTER, D. and FRANSELLA, F. (1971) *Inquiring Man*, Harmondsworth, Penguin.

BECKER, H.S. *et al.* (1961) *Boys in White*, Chicago, University of Chicago Press.

BECKER, H.S. *et al.* (1968) *Making the Grade*, New York, Wiley.

BERNSTEIN, B. (1971) 'Classification and framing', in YOUNG, M.F.D. (Ed.), *Knowledge and Control*, London, Collier-Macmillan.

BERNSTEIN, B. (1974) 'Class and pedagogy', in *Class, Codes and Control Vol. 1*, London, Routledge and Kegan Paul.

BEYNON, J. and ATKINSON, P. (1984) paper to appear in DELAMONT, S. (Ed.) *Reader in Classroom Interaction*, London, Methuen.

BOOTH, M. (1927) 'The present day education of girls: An indictment', *The Nineteenth Century and After*, 102, August, pp. 259–69.

BROWN, R. (Ed.) (1973) *Knowledge, Education and Cultural Change*, London, Tavistock.

CHANAN, G. and DELAMONT, S. (Eds) (1975) *Frontiers of Classroom Research*, Slough, NFER.

DEEM, R. (1978) *Women and Schooling*, London, Routledge and Kegan Paul.

DELAMONT, S. (1973) *Academic Conformity Observed: Studies in the Classroom*, unpublished PhD thesis, University of Edinburgh.

DELAMONT, S. (1976a) *Interaction in the Classroom*, London, Methuen.

DELAMONT, S. (1976b) 'Beyond Flanders Fields', in STUBBS, M. and DELAMONT, S. (Eds), *Explorations in Classroom Observation*, Chichester, Wiley.

DELAMONT, S. (1976c) 'The girls most likely to', *Scottish Journal of Sociology*, 1, 1, pp. 29–43; reprinted in PARSLER, R. (Ed.) (1980) *Capitalism, Class and Politics in Scotland*, Farnborough, Gower.

DELAMONT, S. (1978) 'The contradictions in ladies' education', in DELAMONT, S. and DUFFIN, L. (Eds), *The Nineteenth Century Woman*, London, Croom Helm.

DELAMONT, S. (1983) *Interaction in the Classroom*, 2nd ed., London, Methuen.

DELAMONT, S. (Ed.) (1984a) *Reader in Classroom Interaction*, London, Methuen.

DELAMONT, S. (1984b) 'Debs, dollies, swots and weeds', in WALFORD, G. (Ed.), *Sociological Perspectives on the Public Schools*, Lewes, Falmer Press.

DINGWALL, R. *et al.* (Eds) (1977) *Health Care and Health Knowledge*, London, Croom Helm.

EGGLESTON, J.F. and DELAMONT, S. (1983) 'A necessary isolation?', in EGGLESTON, J.F. and DELAMONT, S. (Eds), *The Admission, Supervision and Examination of Higher Degrees in Education*, Birmingham, BERA.

FLANDERS, N.A. (1970) *Analysing Teaching Behaviour*, New York, Addison-Wesley.

FULLER, M. (1980) 'Black girls in a London comprehensive school', in DEEM, R. (Ed.), *Schooling for Women's Work*, London, Routledge and Kegan Paul.

GALTON, M. and DELAMONT, S. (1984) 'Speaking with forked tongue', in BURGESS, R.G. (Ed.) *Field Methods in the Study of Education*, Lewes, Falmer Press.

GALTON, M. and WILLCOCKS, J. (1983) *Moving from the Primary Classroom*, London, Routledge and Kegan Paul.

GEER, B. (1964) 'First days in the field', in HAMMOND, P. (Ed.), *Sociologists at Work*, New York, Basic Books.

GLASER, B. and STRAUSS, A. (1967) *The Discovery of Grounded Theory*, Chicago, Aldine.

HARGREAVES, D.H. (1967) *Social Relations in a Secondary School*, London, Routledge and Kegan Paul.

HUDSON, L. (1966) *Contrary Imaginations*, London, Methuen.

HUDSON, L. (1968a) *Frames of Mind*, London, Methuen.

HUDSON, L. (1968b) 'Student style and teacher style', *British Journal of Medical Education*, 2, pp. 28–32.

HUDSON, L. (1977) 'Picking winners: A case study of the recruitment of research students', *New Universities Quarterly*, 32, 1, pp. 88–106.

JACKSON, P.W. (1968) *Life in Classrooms*, New York, Holt, Rinehart and Winston.

LACEY, C. (1970) *Hightown Grammar*, Manchester, Manchester University Press.

LAMBART, A. (1976) 'The Sisterhood', in HAMMERSLEY, M. and WOODS, P. (Eds), *The Process of Schooling*, London, Routledge and Kegan Paul.

LAMBART, A. (1982) 'Expulsion in context; a school as a system in action', in FRAN KENBERG, R. (Ed.) *Custom and Conflict in British Society*, Manchester, Manchester University Press.

LLEWELLYN, M. (1980) 'Studying girls at school', in DEEM, R. (Ed.), *Schooling for Women's Work*, London, Routledge and Kegan Paul.

MEDLEY, D.M. and MITZEL, H.E. (1963) 'Measuring classroom behaviour by systematic observation', in GAGE, N.L. (Ed.), *Handbook of Research on Teaching*, Chicago, Rand McNally.

MILLMAN, M. and KANTER, R.M. (Eds) (1974) *Another Voice*, New York, Anchor Books.

NASH, R. (1973) *Classrooms Observed*, London, Routledge and Kegan Paul.

PARLETT, M. (1967) *Classroom and Beyond*, Boston, Mass., Education Research Center, MIT.

PARLETT, M. (1970) 'The syllabus-bound student', in HUDSON, L. (Ed.), *The Ecology of Human Intelligence*, Harmondsworth, Penguin.

ROSENSHINE, B. (1970) 'Some criteria for evaluating category systems', in GALLAGHER, J.J. *et al.* (Eds), *Classroom Observation*, Chicago, Rand McNally.

SHARP, R. and GREEN, A.G. (1975) *Education and Social Control*, London, Routledge and Kegan Paul.

SMITH, L.M. and GEOFFREY, W. (1968) *Complexities of an Urban Class-*

room, New York, Holt, Rinehart and Winston.

STUBBS, M. and DELAMONT, S. (Eds) (1976) *Explorations in Classroom Observation*, Chichester, Wiley.

WILLIS, P. (1977) *Learning to Labour*, Farnborough, Saxon House.

WOBER, M. (1971) *English Girls' Boarding Schools*, London, Allen Lane.

WRAGG, E.C. (1982) Evidence submitted to the Rothschild Enquiry into the SSRC.

2 The Researcher Exposed: A Natural History

Martyn Hammersley

Editor's Commentary. Many sociologists give the impression that they became interested in conducting a particular research project after reading the work of other researchers. While there is some truth in this statement it does oversimplify the situation. In this chapter Martyn Hammersley shows how the origins of his research were based on his personal, political and sociological interests. Indeed, he shows that shifts in emphasis in a research programme are not merely the result of new developments in the area of study but also a consequence of the changing personal circumstances of the social researcher. Hammersley's account charts his interest in classroom interaction from his early days as an MA student through his period as a PhD candidate to his time as a lecturer at the Open University. He indicates how his work has been the product of a complex interaction between his fieldwork, his writing for teaching and research and his personal, political and sociological interests in the field of study.

Martyn Hammersley provides a candid portrait of the sociologist at work. His chapter charts the unsteady start of the research novice who gradually develops expertise. He addresses such questions as: how can access be achieved? How is data collection conducted? At this point Hammersley not only considers such practical matters as writing letters, keeping field notes and making tape recordings but also some key issues associated with sampling. Indeed, his chapter shows how doing research is not merely a mechanical operation based on the management of research tools but a social process that involves theoretical as well as practical decisions where there are few rules and few guides. Finally, Hammersley highlights the way in which he learned several sociological lessons while contributing to our knowledge of classroom life.

Descartes would have us believe that he had read scarcely anything. That was a bit too much. Yet it is good to study the discoveries of others in a way that discloses to us the source of the discoveries and renders them in a sort our own. And I

wish that authors would give us the history of their discoveries and the steps by which they have arrived at them.
(Leibniz, 1887, Vol. III, p. 568; quoted in Merton, 1967, p. 5)

In recent years there have increasingly been calls for sociology to
become more reflexive, though we can see from the above quotation
that the idea is perhaps not quite as new as we are sometimes inclined
to believe. It has been suggested that sociological analysis, which
often delights in revealing ulterior motives, guilty knowledge and
secret deviance, should be trained on sociologists themselves (Gouldner, 1970). Indeed, the gap between the idealized versions of research
appearing in methodology texts on the one hand and available
accounts of actual research practices on the other, suggests that this is
a promising line of investigation (Bell and Newby, 1977).

Sometimes the motive underlying these calls for reflexivity seems
to be some notion of just desserts, that it is only fair that sociologists
themselves be exposed to public view in the same way as those they
study. But there are other, more substantial, motives. These arise
from the abandonment of naive positivistic views about the nature of
research in which validity can be ensured by following the rules of
'scientific method'. It has come to be recognized that scientific
research is a complex activity involving metaphysical presuppositions
and tacit knowledge not directly open to test (Polanyi, 1958; Kuhn,
1962). Furthermore, scientists are people with all the normal range of
interests, emotions and frailties; not clinically neutral cognitive
supermen or wonderwomen: they are more like Captain Kirk than
Mr Spock (Watson, 1968). More emphasis is now placed on the role
of the scientist, and of the scientific community, in generating and
testing knowledge (Barnes, 1974; Bloor, 1976).

Within sociology this view has sometimes converged with
opposition to correspondence theories of knowledge, on occasion
reaching the point where the existence of any world independent of
the researcher is denied (McHugh *et al*, 1974; for a 'translation' see
Heritage, 1975). In the same way there has been increasing opposition
to the doctrine of value-freedom, on the grounds that interests and
values inevitably shape all aspects of the research process. Once again
this has sometimes been taken to the point where it is suggested that
all research is necessarily 'political' (for a discussion see MacKinnon,
1977), and that any attempt to discount the effects of values and
interests is futile.

It has often been argued that research biographies can play a key
role in enhancing the reflexivity of sociology. Some commentators

demand that the whole research process be explicated and laid out before the reader as a warrant for the validity of the findings. At its most extreme, what is required here is not simply a natural history describing the process of research, but that the research take as its focus the interpretive methods by which it is itself accomplished. Any failure fully to explicate a particular interpretation is regarded as automatically undercutting the validity of the findings, on the grounds that it introduces a reliance on common sense rather than established scientific knowledge (Sacks, 1963; Hitchcock, 1983). However, the arguments against the very possibility of finding some fundamental and indubitable base from which to start, whether this be sense data or interpretive methods, are overwhelming (Harris, 1970; Bauman, 1978). Not only can no ultimate foundation be discovered, at each point in the research process more explication can always be demanded (as is clear from Garfinkel, 1967).

The alternative argument for the importance of reflexive accounts in the evaluation of data and findings is more modest and limited. It begins from a recognition that the researcher always has some impact on the setting he or she is studying, that the selectivity necessarily involved in research activity will shape the data and findings, and that researchers are by no means immune to the effects of interests and values. These three features open up research to a wide range of potential threats to validity, from reactivity of one kind· or another to bias on the part of the researcher in interpreting the data. In this light the function of a reflexive account is to indicate the nature and likelihood of such threats, as well as outlining what has been and could be done to deal with them. It is in this spirit that the present account is written.

Initial Orientations

The origins of my research probably lie in an early interest in existentialism and the debate between moral absolutism and relativism. Later, I studied sociology at LSE in those eventful years 1967–70, the peak of 'the student revolt'. While I was only on the margins of that movement, undoubtedly this experience, and especially the occupation of the premises in October 1968 (Hoch and Schoenbach, 1969), had an important 'radicalizing' effect on my political views. The events of those years provided evidence of the 'repressive' character of educational institutions and of the joys of 'solidarity'. It fuelled previous ideas about 'authoritarian absolutism'

seemed to me to be the most significant area in which the 'cultural imperialism' of schooling would show itself.

I was never at ease with the teachers or the pupils. Indeed, I spent most break times alone, hanging around the hall or yard, and I went home for lunch to ease the strain. I feared that going into the staffroom would be regarded as threatening by the teachers, and would endanger my continued presence in the school! It is worth examining the probable sources of this anxiety. First, I had difficulty in feeling adult in relation to the teachers. I was closer in age to the pupils than to most of them, and I was, of course, still only a student. The fact that they were teachers added to this. As an ex A-stream pupil in a secondary modern school myself, I tended to feel deferential towards teachers, despite my political views; perhaps this derived from the fact that I had, as it were, been sponsored after initial failure (Turner, 1960). Indeed, it might even be that my political views at this time owed something to this aspect of my biography.

Secondly, there was the conflict between my political opinions and the views and practices of the teachers. This had two consequences. For one thing, despite choosing the school as an example of authoritarianism, and despite my own experience as a pupil in a similar school, I was shocked by the way in which the pupils were treated: in particular the extent of control over their behaviour the teachers claimed and the insults that were constantly hurled at them. Then again, I thought it clearly necessary to conceal my purposes and views from the teachers; I implied to them that I was primarily interested in the pupils. This deception was a source of strain and guilt. I also felt guilty because I was doing nothing to help the pupils. In part through the influence of Gamson, a deviant, mildly progressive teacher at the school, I came to feel that if I really wanted to do anything about the situation I ought to be teaching myself.

Finally, perhaps as a result of inadequate preparation before entering the field, I found it difficult to see what analytic payoff I was going to be able to derive from the data I was collecting. There were few mentions of intelligence in my fieldnotes and they did not seem substantial enough to shore up the kind of analysis I wanted to make. With a rapidly mounting sense of my own incompetence and increasing doubts about the value of my work, I abandoned the fieldwork after only five days. If that seems a very short period, I can only say that at the time it seemed very much longer!

His Master's Thesis

After the abortive first few days in the field I decided to aim at completing my Master's thesis in the remainder of the year, leaving open the question of whether I would later return to the field, or turn to teaching or something else. In the thesis I set out to apply to what I already knew about schools the range of ideas I had discovered in the literature. I came to feel that my failure to make much of the fieldwork was in large part the product of the limited analytic resources that had been available to me: I had not thought through how interpretive sociology, the theoretical approach I favoured, might be applied to schools.

Around that time I began to realize that I was not alone in my views about the current state of the sociology of education, and that others too were exploring the implications of interpretive sociology in the field of education. This was symbolized by the appearance of *Knowledge and Control* (Young, 1971) and the Open University reader, *School and Society* (Cosin *et al.*, 1971). The discovery that others were on the same trail was both a relief, and at the same time a threat. It quelled some doubts about my project, but also took the edge off my sense of originality. This was to be a recurring experience as my work took longer and longer to complete, while more and more articles and books appeared in a similar vein.

However, this was not the only kind of threat to emerge at this time. What had been a substantially interactionist department at Manchester was changing its character, with a number of its most vociferous members being drawn into ethnomethodology. The effect of this was to challenge my self-identity as theoretically 'radical', since in several key respects ethnomethodology represented an extreme version of interactionism: notably in its even more exclusive focus on meaning and process, the social construction of the world and the rationality of actors (Pollner, 1974). On the other hand, I felt unable to follow this trend, partly because ethnomethodology seemed to proscribe my concern with practical political payoff, and also because I felt it reduced the research focus of sociology to trivia, for example, to the details of casual conversations.[3] Nevertheless, I had to come to terms with ethnomethodology and this involved trying to penetrate the opaque language of its literature and to overcome the understandable unwillingness of some of its representatives at Manchester to talk about what they called 'programmatics'.

My contact with ethnomethodology influenced me in a number of ways. First, my efforts to understand and counter it took an enormous amount of time, especially since they forced me deeper into linguistics, linguistic philosophy and phenomenology. Secondly, in the light of ethnomethodology, the work of documenting 'what happens in school' became much more problematic: painstaking and very detailed analysis of the process of schooling appeared to be necessary. At the same time, ethnomethodology reinforced my view that we knew very little about what went on in schools and added to it the feeling that finding out would take a long time. From this followed the conclusion that little immediate political payoff could be expected from research in this area. Finally, it seemed imperative that if I were to do further fieldwork, tape recordings of lessons should be my primary data source. Mistakenly, I came to the conclusion that transcripts of natural talk were the only really adequate form of data. Finally, ethnomethodology, and in particular Sacks' work on turn-taking, offered a way of grounding my concern with the cultural imperialism of schools. It facilitated analysis of the unequal distribution of interactional rights to be found in classrooms.

At precisely the same time as my 'theoretical radicalness' was under attack from ethnomethodology, my commitment to radical education was challenged by the deschooling movement. The demand that schools be liberated, with authoritarian relationships among teachers and pupils being replaced by more egalitarian and democratic forms, suddenly came to be presented as mere reformism. What was really necessary, the deschoolers argued, was that schools should be abolished. Once again what had happened, it seemed to me, was that the central tenets of my position had been taken to their logical, and absurd, conclusion. Even more damaging to my naive conception of politics at that time, a blend of anarchism and socialism, was the fact that deschooling, while apparently more radical than my position, had 'right wing' overtones to it.

So, in a matter of months, I discovered that my project was not as original as I had thought and I found myself out-radicalized (Cohen, 1974) on both theoretical and political fronts. The world was no longer a simple place.

Fieldwork Again

Despite this turmoil I resolved to begin fieldwork again. Indeed, perhaps the prospect of getting to grips with some 'real data' provided a kind of anchor in a now rather uncertain world. I decided to be more careful in the selection of a school than I had been previously. Though I didn't believe there was much sense in looking for typicality I did think I ought to avoid an obviously untypical school like the first one I had studied, with its small classes and small number of staff; and in any event I did not relish the idea of returning there.

Gaining Access

I wrote to the local education authority asking permission to approach schools with a view to carrying out research. The Chief Education Officer responded asking for fuller information and I replied in the following manner:

> Dear Sir,
> Thank you for your letter. I am employed as a research assistant in the Sociology Department of the University of Manchester. My assignment is to continue the research on social interaction in schools which I began last year in pursuing a course for the degree of MA (Econ) and which was partly based on five days exploratory fieldwork at Down-town County Secondary School (with your permission).
> The micro-sociological study of classroom interaction is one of the most underdeveloped and yet basic areas of the sociology of education; it is overdue for more research. The intention is to use methods of conversational and linguistic analysis in investigating behaviour in classrooms to produce data regarding the recurrent problems of the teacher in class and knowledge management.
> The fieldwork would involve observation and tape-recording of perhaps three teacher/class combinations through all their meetings over a period of up to six weeks and informal interviews with the head, the teachers concerned and possibly some of the pupils under study. Obviously I would endeavour to cause the least possible disturbance; technical problems permitting I shall be using a small battery-operated tape-recorder.
>
> Yours faithfully,
> Martyn Hammersley

A couple of weeks later I received this reply:

> Dear Mr Hammersley,
> I am writing in answer to your request to continue

fieldwork on social interaction in schools. I have consulted Mr Johnson the Headmaster of Downtown County Secondary Boys' School where you carried out your initial research. He and members of the staff of the school would be willing to welcome you and to co-operate in your work.

I should be grateful if you would now approach Mr Johnson to arrange with him a suitable programme for the work. I apologise for some delay in replying to your letter but it has taken a little time to consult the appropriate members of staff.

I hope that this arrangement will prove satisfactory.

Yours sincerely,
Chief Education Officer

Whether this unfortunate outcome was the result of misunderstanding or subtle strategy I cannot tell. However, I was faced with the choice of accepting what was offered or seeking to renegotiate permission to approach other schools. For a variety of reasons, not least because it was already well into the spring term, I decided to accept the offer. I consoled myself with the thought that typicality was a vain quest, and that my prior contact with the school would be an advantage.

As the letter from the Chief Education Officer had suggested I was welcomed by the headmaster (a new one) at Downtown. He delegated Walker, the English teacher of my acquaintance, to arrange my access to lessons. However, I learned from Walker that the teachers were rather reluctant to have me in the school. He explained this reluctance in terms of 'the *poor* quality of the work, the pupils are so *poor*'. Still, he reported that he had 'persuaded two of them other than myself to let you record a couple of their lessons'. This didn't seem too promising a beginning. The teachers were reluctant and clearly wanted me out as soon as possible; though the exact nature of the threat I posed was not very clear to me. From the beginning I stressed to Walker and the other teachers that I was not there to make any kind of evaluation but simply to describe and explain what was happening in the school. They, for their part, made it clear to me that I *had* no basis for any evaluation of them. Thus, on the first day:

[Staffroom: Some masters are off sick. Walker talking to Larson the deputy head in my presence. Glancing at me he says:]
Walker: You'll have to get him to take over.
Larson: Now that's an idea, you'd learn something then.

I take this to be not simply a minor expression of resentment at someone watching them at work, but also an insider argument: you'd only really know what it's all about if you had to teach here (Merton, 1972).

My relative youth probably aided access. While in the first few abortive days it had been a problem for me, and to some degree still was, I suspect that for the teachers it considerably reduced the threat I posed; for them credibility seemed to go with age and 'experience'. The presence of students on teaching practice in the first term of fieldwork probably also helped. The teachers treated me rather like a student, as someone who did not really know 'what was what'. I sought to capitalize on this by asking questions, including some naive ones, suppressing many of my political and educational views, nodding agreement when required, and on occasion offering supportive comments. The last was possible without hypocrisy because, and this came as a surprise to me, there were issues on which our views were similar; in particular the iniquity of the raising of the school leaving age. As a result, curiously, in the teachers' eyes I probably compared favourably with the students currently teaching in the school. One of them, Cobden, nicknamed 'The Maharishi' by the other teachers, was a source of some derision in the staffroom, and even the others, Wright and Roach, employed what to Downtown staff were 'progressive' classroom techniques. I, on the other hand, was not forced to show my hand in this way.

The teachers had an ambivalent attitude towards research and researchers. They were very dismissive of all 'experts', and there were comments within my earshot about the irrelevance of theory and the importance of practice and experience. (This was in any case a minor theme in the staffroom probably owing to the presence of the students.) At the same time, the teachers occasionally suggested that research *ought* to be done on 'these pupils', implying that the latter were beyond normal comprehension.

Initially, Walker acted as my sponsor in dealings with the staff (I suspect rather reluctantly). As I later discovered, he was subject to some questioning by the other teachers as to my purposes. During the first day, in conversation with him, I mentioned my interest in pupils' interpretations of teachers' questions. This immediately struck a chord, he called it 'pupil response'. He seemed impressed by this, and introduced this information about my interests in the staffroom saying, '*now* we know what he wants.' This coincidence between my interests and one of the concerns of the teachers was probably a great help in facilitating access, though it also had less desirable consequences: it emerged later that, despite my concern not to influence what was going on in the school, Walker was putting on oral lessons especially for me so that I would get plenty of data on pupil language!

After a few days in the school I took over the negotiation of access to lessons myself. With the exception of Greaves, the head of maths, all the teachers I asked willingly agreed for me to come into and tape their lessons; though at first they were cagey about *which* lessons I could observe. I did not push to go into those lessons where they were reluctant to have me. For this reason I abandoned my original intention to follow a couple of teacher-class groupings through all their lessons or to follow a particular class through its meetings with different teachers.

Collecting the Data

I focused heavily on the second year and included some first year classes as these seemed relatively unproblematic from the point of view of access. Later I branched out to cover what I assumed to be some of the more difficult classes, those in the third and fourth years. Within the second year I focused particularly on one class, trying to attend as many of their lessons as possible. This enabled me to learn the names of the pupils and to begin to get some sense of the class as an interactional unit.

In the face of the difficulties in organizing access, and of both focusing on a particular class and yet at the same time getting some overall view of all the classes, my embryonic belief in the need for systematic sampling broke down. As with my concern over the typicality of the school, when it came down to it I really didn't think it mattered all that much, or at least that's what I persuaded myself.[4] Also, systematic sampling might have meant observing games, wood-work, metalwork and PE lessons and I didn't count these as part of the 'serious' business of the school. Given the focus of the study, and the fact that this prejudice reflects the hierarchy of subjects within schools, this may not be a serious distortion; but it certainly reveals an important misconception on my part. Apart from any other consideration, for pupils these lessons are often of central significance, either because they are the only ones of any interest, or because they are a source of considerable fear and humiliation (Woods, 1979).

In the classroom I sought to play a minimal role, sitting at the back or side of the room away from the pupils; this was possible because of the small number of pupils in each class given the size of the rooms. However, while for the most part the pupils ignored me, this was not always true of the teachers. I was in their direct line of sight for much of the time. Furthermore, sometimes, having set written work, they would come over to talk, occasionally for the remainder of the lesson. This was often a useful source of data, though it involved the danger that they might be able to read my fieldnotes. To counteract this I made my writing even more illegible than it normally is and used a false front page. Quite why I was so concerned about them reading my fieldnotes I am not now sure. Presumably it was because I was afraid they would discover what I was really studying, though in fact I was becoming increasingly unsure myself about exactly what the focus of the research was.

When tape recording a lesson I usually placed the recorder on the teacher's desk at the front of the room. For the most part it seemed to be ignored by both teachers and pupils; apart from one occasion when, having run out of tape, it emitted a high pitched whistle in the middle of a lesson! For the reasons mentioned earlier I placed great emphasis on tape recording. But I soon realized that I was not going to be able to record a large number of lessons, both because of the time it took to transcribe tapes and because of the cost of constantly buying new cassettes. Originally, I had intended to re-use the same cassettes over and over again; but I soon discovered that I was unable to transcribe them quickly enough to do that; and I also came to think it important to keep the tapes since my transcripts were never complete. This posed sampling problems: which lessons to record. Once again I resolved this in a largely ad hoc fashion, averaging out my recording of lessons across the whole period of the fieldwork, and selecting lessons which promised to be primarily oral. This latter selection principle, while quite rational in itself, when combined with my overvaluation of transcript data, resulted in my focusing primarily on oral work in the classroom; despite the fact that the teachers seemed to regard written work as, if anything, more important. This is just one aspect of the general problem of the representativeness of my data to which the lack of systematic sampling gave rise. Whilst the representativeness of the transcripts can be checked against the classroom fieldnotes, the fact that the lessons *observed* were not selected by systematic sampling makes the test of limited value.

I also made fieldnotes of my informal talk with teachers on the way to and from lessons, and of staffroom conversations. It seemed to me that this might provide an important source of evidence about what was happening in the classroom. I relied on this informal data rather than using interviews both because I had come to regard interview data as 'artificial' and therefore virtually useless, and because I was afraid that asking for interviews with teachers might threaten my continued presence in the school, given my avowed interest in pupil language. (I am now convinced I was wrong on both counts.) As a result of a similar fear about 'pushing my luck' with teachers I did not request permission to sit in on staff meetings. (Once again this was a mistake since it would have provided important data and on the basis of subsequent experience in other schools I am sure that such a request would not have endangered my presence in the school.)

My staffroom data[5] are even more open to bias than the classroom data. I spent most break times and lunch times in the staffroom on the days I was present in the school: two or three days a week for nearly two terms. When I had no lesson to observe I returned to the staffroom where, often, there would be teachers spending free periods (especially in the first term when there were students on teaching practice in the school). There is unintentional and unprincipled sampling involved here: questions can be raised about how representative the exchanges I recorded were of the whole body of staff talk, even during the two terms when I was in the school. Had I realized the importance of this at the time, it might have been possible to sample staff interaction randomly over time, at least for a short period, for example by going into the staffroom on randomly chosen days and at random times.[6]

Another form of sampling bias occurred in my collection of staffroom data. My interactions with the staff were not equally distributed or equivalent. At first I was closely tied to Walker, and even as I became less closely associated with him I tended to associate much more with some of the teachers than with others. For a short time I tried to widen my associations by moving round the staffroom: spending a break time in one group, a lunchtime in another and so on. However, this created problems. While there did not seem to be seats reserved for particular teachers, on one occasion because of my presence at one of the tables in the staffroom there was no seat available for a regular member of the group which usually congregated there. On another occasion, in seeking to infiltrate a different group, I found myself expected to join in a game of bridge, a game I could not play. I suspected that there would be little tolerance for me as a learner bridge player *and* researcher, and so I withdrew. As a result of these problems I abandoned this strategy, though it was probably successful to some degree in widening my contacts with the teachers.

While sitting permanently at one of the tables, I still tried to listen to conversations going on over the other side of the room, sometimes not joining in conversations where I was sitting, pretending to read the newspaper and straining my ears to hear what was being said. In free periods, and during that part of lunchtime when some of the teachers were having lunch in the hall, I got access to conversations among teachers other than the stalwarts of 'my' table; either because they drew me into conversations or I joined in myself, or because they carried on conversations without me and the room was quiet enough for me to hear what was being said. Despite this it still seems likely that those teachers with whom I was more closely associated are overrepresented in my data. Once again unintentional and unprincipled, though probably inevitable, sampling was occurring.

While in the staffroom I listened and tried to note down as soon and as accurately as possible anything the teachers said which was remotely relevant to teaching, the school or the pupils; including at the limit, for example, comments about news items relating to the treatment of young offenders. Once again we have a sampling process here; though this time it is intentional, systematic and theoretically guided. Still, I may well have not recognized things which were actually very relevant or very useful indicators, and my conception of what was relevant may have changed over the course of the fieldwork (there is no sound basis for checking whether this is the case).[7]

Some of these problems might have been overcome by the tape recording of staffroom talk. I assumed from the start that this was impossible. I thought, probably quite rightly, that the teachers would either never allow it, or that if they did tape recording would distort what was said. Secret tape recording seemed to me to be unethical and probably impracticable too. Even secret note-taking raised the important ethical issues of deception and privacy, though it seemed to me that no breach of contract was involved and no damage to participants would ensue.[8]

Noting down what was said on the spot was very difficult, being done in a surreptitious and hurried manner. On one occasion I was forced to jot down notes on the newspaper I was reading, hoping that no-one would ask to borrow it. There had been comments on one occasion about me reading a 'liberal' newspaper like *The Guardian* and on that basis I hoped I was safe! Often the jotted notes had to be made after I had left the staffroom. While I tried to note down literally what was said, I may have made mistakes. While I can claim that even where I did not get the words exactly right I probably got the sense of what was said, that unfortunately builds in a reliance on the interpretations of sense I made on the spot. Also important here is the relevance of context. I often wonder now in reading these data whether anything was said before or after the recorded exchange which would modify interpretation of it. Once again there is reliance here on my on-the-spot decisions. Even more important, it is possible that on some occasions, rather than simply not remembering the exact words used, I may have forgotten whole sentences or stretches of conversation which came between one utterance and the next in the recorded exchange.

Besides the operation of this selectivity in perception and data recording, and the biases that may have been involved, there is also the question of the effects of my presence on what occurred in the staffroom. While one of the reasons for collecting data on staffroom talk rather than relying on interviews with teachers was to minimize the effects of the researcher on the data, such effects may still have been present. These are presumably likely to have been greatest where I was talking to a teacher on his own. The effect was quite noticeable in the case of one of the teachers, Webster, where what he said to me contrasted sharply with what he said in the presence of his colleagues. This is not necessarily to imply that what he said to me was invalid, simply that it represents a different kind of data from that more typical of staffroom exchanges.

Reactivity is likely to have varied in exchanges with groups of teachers according to the degree to which I participated in the discussion. Sometimes I was an active party to the conversation, asking questions and volunteering comments. Much more often I was a passive participant and sometimes not even a party to the conversation at all, simply in the room eavesdropping.[9] However, even my presence in the room may have had an effect on what was said. While, as far as I know, the teachers were not aware that I was taking notes on what they said in the staffroom, it is clear that at the very least *some* of the teachers were *sometimes* aware of the possible relevance of my latent researcher identity:

[Discussion in staffroom about the punishment of a pupil — a teacher had decided to keep a whole class away from games. Phillipson is reporting this to the rest of the staff, in the absence of the teacher concerned.]
Phillipson: I know Fred Baldwin'll disagree with that,

you'll disagree with the principle of the thing.

Baldwin: It's unfair on the rest of the class.

Holton: No, it's *him* [the pupil] who's keeping the others away from games, by his attitude.

Baldwin: No, it's Arthur, in choosing his punishments that's keeping them away.

[Holton seemed to accept this, or perhaps he didn't want to argue. At this point Greaves passes by the group on his way to make coffee.]

Greaves: You've got my permission to kick the bastard in the guts.

Holton: George! 'Kick the bastard in the guts', 'Kick the bastard in the guts'! You've been watching too much television. [Turning to the researcher] It's a pity you didn't have your tape recorder going.

However, this example suggests that my presence was not having too much effect since this is precisely the kind of comment one would expect to be withheld. It is possible that this occasion is an exception, that Greaves was breaking the rules and that Holton's comment was a deviance imputation (Hargreaves, Hester and Mellor, 1975). However, the controversial, and often racist, nature of much that was said in my presence in the staffroom makes this implausible (Hammersley, 1982). Similarly, conversations about the personal use of school resources frequently took place in front of me without the least self-consciousness. One afternoon Greaves, the teacher with whom I had the most difficult relationship, even asked me to cover for him leaving early:

[3.25 in the afternoon. I am working alone in the staffroom. Greaves comes in, puts his coat on, collects his briefcase and says to me, smiling:]

Greaves: If anybody comes after me you haven't seen me!

I tried to monitor staffroom events for any signs that a double standard was operating, comments for my consumption and different ones when I was absent — for example, uneasy silences when I entered the room, broken off sentences when it was realized I was there, significant exchanges of glances and so on — but I detected none. Still, perhaps the teachers were better at information games than I was.

I stayed at Downtown until the end of the school year, in all spending sixty-two days in the school. Despite being invited to return the following September, I did not do so; even though this would have allowed me to follow through the process of comprehensive reorganization. There were several reasons for this. Firstly, at that time the reorganization held little interest for me. From the point of view of my political views and my theoretical interest in the details of classroom interaction, I viewed it as almost an irrelevance. This reflects not only an absence of anything beyond a rudimentary macro-perspective on the education system and its role in society, but also my failure to heed the advice of interactionism, to look to what was important to the participants. Secondly, I was mentally ex-hausted, and the thought of returning to the school filled me with horror. In addition, I had an enormous amount of data, only a small proportion of which had been processed and none of which had been filed. I had just about managed to write up the fieldnotes during the data collection, but I had hardly made any impression on the pile of tapes to be transcribed or on the task of sorting my data into categories. At the same time I had a lot of ideas about how to analyze classroom interaction and I wanted to get on with developing and testing them out. These at least are the reasons I used to persuade myself not to return the following September. In retrospect my failure to follow through the process of reorganization seems a grave error. However, such a judgement probably reflects not simply the benefit of hindsight, but also perhaps that amnesia about the actual priorities and pressures of research characteristic of much reflection on it.

An important feature of my data collection is the extent to which it deviated from the model proposed by Glaser and Strauss (1967). They recommend analysis of the data during the course of the fieldwork and a shaping of the data collection process to develop that analysis, notably through theoretical sampling. While I was develop-ing ideas about how the data might be analyzed during the fieldwork, these did not significantly affect my data collection. I continued to select and tape lessons and make notes on staff interaction much as before. My approach approximated the opposite pole to theoretical sampling, what might be called 'dredging': choosing a setting and collecting all the data available in it relevant to particular foresha-dowed problems. Two things pushed me in this direction, both resulting from the influence of ethnomethodology. Firstly, my heavy reliance on taping and my inability to keep up with the transcription of tapes during the fieldwork. Secondly, the naive view that ethno-graphic research should involve the tapping of 'natural' events, of 'what's going on' in the school. Still, I suspect that dredging may be more common, and grounded theorizing less common, than is usually admitted.

An issue which has been given little attention in the literature on ethnographic research is the effects of the research process on the researcher (but see Schwartz and Schwartz, 1969; Johnson, 1975). Doing ethnographic research on the Downtown teachers had a curious effect on me. As I have explained, in the beginning one of my primary aims was a well-documented expose. But I was also committed to doing an interpretive ethnography, and one of the first requirements of such work is that the researcher empathize with the people under study, that an attempt be made to understand the world from their point of view. I therefore found myself facing a severe dilemma, especially since empathy tends to lead to sympathy.[10] The very process of gaining and maintaining access also pushed me in the direction of sympathy for the teachers: one cannot constantly present an image of agreement, friendliness and understanding without strong pressures towards experiencing such feelings. As a result, over the course of the fieldwork I came to question many aspects of my views on political, educational and theoretical issues, sometimes without finding anything to replace them. In the areas of politics and education in many respects I simply became uncertain and confused; and more and more I concentrated my energies simply on sociology. In fact I came to see my research as having no direct political relevance: as theoretical not applied, a distinction I would have rejected earlier.

I think it would be a mistake to dismiss my changing views, and the resulting change in my analysis of the Downtown situation, simply as an irrational response to role conflict. There was an important element of discovery. The process of research forced me to recognize features of the setting I would previously have ignored or misinterpreted. However, it also made me reconsider the nature of sociology and I began to question much that I had taken for granted hitherto (Hammersley, 1981).

The Long and Winding Road

Having 'dredged up' a very large amount of data, my task now was to try to complete the transcription of the tapes, and to begin the process of analysis. I had some twenty-two hours of lesson tapes to transcribe and I found that transcription was an extremely time-consuming business, especially since the recordings were rather poor.

For this reason I started to analyze my data long before I had finished transcription, working on ideas that had emerged during the fieldwork (in fact the transcription of the tapes was not completed until 1979). Over the course of the vacation following the fieldwork I prepared a paper 'The Ideal Pupil: Classroom Control' which was subsequently delivered to seminars, and later developed into three articles (Hammersley, 1974; 1976; 1977b). I also set to work on the staffroom data and an initial analysis was produced in late 1974, but for reasons already mentioned I did not publish it until much later (Hammersley, 1980b; 1981; 1982).

In the first year after the fieldwork I took on part-time teaching in the department at Manchester, partly because I thought it would be an opportunity to attempt 'non-authoritarian' teaching myself. This further undermined my initial simplistic notions about teaching and also forced me to read much more widely in sociology than I had done since starting the research. These tendencies were reinforced by my experience of the deepening crisis in sociology. From my point of view the whole area of social theory had become a battlefield in which, vicariously anyway, I was in the middle no longer 'radical' and now on the receiving end from all sides. This was not conducive to the analysis of empirical data. Not only were all kinds of fundamental, and probably unanswerable, questions being raised, but it was difficult to come to any conclusion as to how the research ought to be written up. Should I simply concentrate on a small amount of the transcript data and do conversational or some other kind of discourse analysis on it (Payne, 1976; Torode, 1977)? Should I attempt a more conventional interactionist ethnography? Should I try to relate my analysis of classroom processes to the deepening crisis of British capitalism? Shouldn't I concentrate on explicating my own activity as a researcher? Increasingly I came to see my work from several conflicting perspectives.[11] This again forced me to pay more and more attention to the nature of the sociological enterprise, to reconsider my own views about the kind of business I was in. Much of this period was therefore spent in reading and trying to come to grips with diverse theoretical approaches and the philosophical positions which underpinned them.

At the same time I was becoming worried about the untypicality of Downtown, and also about its newsworthiness. The days had long gone when the 'exposure' of traditional teaching as 'authoritarian' was news. The game now was to show that even progressive teaching is 'authoritarian', indeed that it reproduces the status quo in a subtle and therefore more insidious and effective way (Sharp and Green,

1975). I feared that my research was going to be of little value or interest. As a result I decided to spend the last year of my research assistantship at Manchester collecting data in another school. I chose Windsor Street, a school in the same locality as Downtown but which was much larger and had a reputation for being 'progressive', not least among Downtown teachers. In the event it turned out to be not particularly 'progressive', rather more difficult to study than Downtown, and I collected yet more data to analyze. This was, in retrospect, the biggest mistake of all — it postponed the completion of the research by several years and as yet I have made little direct use of the Windsor Street data.

When my research assistantship expired, I managed to secure a temporary lectureship at Manchester. However, this left me little time for the research and, midway through that year, having gained a permanent post at the Open University for the following October, I began preliminary work on units for the Open University course E202, *Schooling and Society*. In moving to the Open University the balance of theoretical influences upon me changed. Whereas at Manchester ethnomethodology was the most immediate and dominant influence, at the Open University those who had been involved in 'the new sociology of education' were now moving in a quite different direction, towards Marxism.[12] It was from this rather different angle that I now had to defend my continuing, if rather battered, commitment to interactionism. Work on E202, while closely related to my research, left virtually no time for it. It also forced me to think harder about what shape the analysis ought to take. The effect was to strengthen an emerging belief that much of the so-called crisis in sociology was manufactured, and that the differences between approaches did not generally lie at the level of ontology or epistemology, but were either crudely political or quite superficial, sometimes being simply terminological. I no longer saw interpretive sociology as a 'new paradigm' or indeed as any kind of paradigm, but rather as a useful set of ideas which in many respects complemented the emphases of other approaches and, taken alone, had serious defects (Hammersley, 1979; 1980a).

Immediately after completing work on E202 I joined the course team of a research methods course (DE304) on which I was the only ethnographer among survey researchers, mathematical modellers, statisticians and experimentalists. I now had to read the literature on ethnographic methodology more seriously. It turned out to be considerable, yet rather unsatisfactory as a resource for countering the criticisms of other course team members. I began to see ethnography in a rather different light, no longer as a methodology replacing 'positivism' but as a method with particular advantages and disadvantages in relation to the problems which face all social research; though it carried along with it some important methodological arguments neglected by the 'positivist' tradition.

My work on DE304 resulted in me coming to a less 'radical', rather eclectic, position in methodology, not unlike that I had already reached in the area of theory. These changes in my theoretical and methodological views created further serious problems for my research. I now regarded the data I had available to me as seriously inadequate, even those collected at Windsor Street. I considered abandoning the whole project and starting again. I decided though that such an impulse stemmed from a misguided pursuit of perfection. On that basis no research would ever get done. My conclusion was that I must simply make the most of the data I had and be honest about its deficiencies.

The 'crisis' in sociology had simply worsened a problem which is intrinsic to 'unstructured' research, and to ethnography in particular with its emphasis on the importance of discovery and the development of 'understanding' in the field. This is the problem, that one lacks a clear idea of what form the product will, or should, take. One is forced to operate instead with implicit, largely intuitive, notions of what is 'good analysis'. Moreover, as we might expect, there are multiple criteria and competing views on this issue. Some stress the 'news value' of the research, either in terms of its presentation of an original theoretical line or in more substantive terms, for instance in providing information about a hitherto neglected situation. Others place value instead on the exploration and description of the *details* of mundane interaction in familiar settings. Again, there are differences in view over the degree to which the analysis must be explicitly grounded in and checked out against the data. Often for those who stress 'news value' a lower emphasis is placed on methodological rigour; while those who stress detailed analysis of the mundane place great emphasis on rigour, sometimes to the point where the area of legitimate analysis is reduced considerably (as, for example, in the case of ethnomethodology).[13]

One of the key problems in ethnographic analysis is finding an overall theme, model or argument which organizes the data in a coherent and forceful way. Only then does the line between the relevant and irrelevant become clear. How ethnographers acquire such models is shrouded in mystery. Often, they simply talk of an overarching model 'emerging'. I had no problem on this score when I began the research, since I had very definite ideas about my purposes and what I would find. My problem was rather how to relate my theme — the 'authoritarian' character of much teaching — to the data, a partial solution to which was provided by Sacks' work on conversation. However, as I explored this aspect of classroom interaction, and under the influence of changes in my theoretical orientation, it became clear that I could not restrict my analysis to the structure of classroom interaction. I had also to take into account the broader perspectives of the participants, and how these were produced and maintained. As a result, it became less and less clear where my analysis should stop.

Over the course of my research I came to realize the considerable role pragmatic considerations play in shaping the scope and perhaps the actual content of analysis. This message was rammed home in the closing stages of my analysis. In the face of rapidly approaching and unavoidable deadlines, I reluctantly took two major decisions for the purposes of writing up my PhD thesis. Firstly, that I would concentrate entirely on the Downtown data, and leave analysis of the Windsor Street material until a later date. Secondly, and perhaps even more significantly, I decided that I would abandon my project of completely reconstructing the arguments of my earlier articles in favour of a much more modest reorganization. The more ambitious project would not only have taken a great deal of time, but was also fraught with difficulties. Thus, for example, I foresaw major presentational problems in combining my concern with the preconditions for the display of 'intelligence' in classrooms by pupils with the other major theme which had emerged over the period of analysis, the complex structuring of teachers' classroom perspectives and practices. My problem, in short, was that more than one 'overarching' model had 'emerged' and the linear structure of any kind of account imposes severe limits on the intelligible presentation of more than one 'story' at once. I decided not to run the risk of obscuring my basic arguments in this way.

I thus redefined my PhD thesis as a way-station on the route to the final product of research, a book for which I already had a contract with a publisher. Later on it became clear that the problem was not merely presentational. While there were several theoretical themes I wanted to pursue, because the data collection had never become narrowly focused I did not have the data to press any of these very far. Moreover, because of the changes in my theoretical and methodological views I became increasingly unwilling simply to make the most of the data I had. Four years later, the proposed book has taken on a very different form to the thesis, and is still in the process of being written.

Conclusion

The most striking feature of my experience of research, as I think emerges clearly from this account, is that it was a voyage of discovery and much of the time was spent at sea. I was led to rethink my views on many aspects of methodology and theory. In particular the experience forced me to question the naturalistic philosophy often invoked by ethnographers. Insofar as this is taken to imply that by being in a setting one can understand what is going on there and why, it is clearly misconceived (Hammersley and Atkinson, 1983, Ch. 1). Research in 'natural' settings is extremely valuable and is able to overcome some of the problems involved in reliance on experiments and interviews. But to be effective it must be systematically designed, albeit in the course of data collection rather than before it begins. In this respect I have come to take the notion of grounded theorizing much more seriously than I did in the past. Indeed, I would now go beyond Glaser and Strauss since I think it is as important to *test* theories as rigorously as possible as it is to *develop* them systematically (Hammersley, Scarth and Webb, 1983).

Such a concern with testing points to what I regard as the most important lesson of all that I have learned from doing the research whose history has been recounted here. This is that the organization of sociology around paradigms which conflate theoretical assumptions and political values, rather than around research problems, is counterproductive in the extreme. Apart from the time and energy it wastes in fruitless polemic, the 'paradigmatic mentality' also obscures methodological and theoretical issues and works against their resolution (Hammersley, 1983).

Of course, I wouldn't want to suggest that on the basis of my experience I now know conclusively how ethnography ought to be done. Social research will always be a learning experience, and so it ought to be. These are simply the lessons I think I have learned from my research.

Notes

1 See Newby (1977) for an account of research in another area which began as a political exposé.
2 This is reflected in the oddly eclectic bibliography of my MA thesis: Hammersley (1971).
3 See M. Atkinson (1977) for an account of a similar experience in a different field, but leading to a very different response.
4 Contrast this with Ball's laudable commitment to systematic sampling: Ball (this volume).
5 I called all these data 'staffroom data' since, while some did not derive from the staffroom, all seemed to conform fairly closely to the context of colleague talk.
6 For the only attempt at random sampling of this kind in ethnographic research on education of which I am aware, see Berlak *et al.* (1975).
7 This is a common problem in ethnographic research. While one can examine the data collected for any obvious changes in nature, it is difficult to tell whether these were the product of changes in the setting or in the researcher.
8 For some writers, for example, Erikson (1967), secret research is always ethically unacceptable, if not also methodologically unsound. It involves an invasion of privacy and threatens, once its results have been published, to spoil the field for others. However, the consensus among researchers seems to be that under certain circumstances, where the research is important and no other means of access is possible, secret research can be legitimate. (It has, in any case, been pointed out by Roth (1961) that there is no clear line dividing 'open' from 'secret' research, and that the practices of researchers in secret research often differ little from the practices of collecting information employed by actors in their everyday activities.) I believed, and believe, the staffroom to be an important setting in which to collect data, and that had I explicitly informed the teachers that I was collecting data there this would either have resulted in me being barred from participation, or in serious distortion of staffroom interaction. On the other hand, the teachers were, of course, aware that I would hear what was said in the staffroom, and they could reasonably expect that I might remember it. Whether my attempt to record systematically what was said there breaks the morality of the setting I cannot tell, but I still believe my actions to be justified. For me the most important consideration is the consequences of my recording and publishing staffroom talk. Here the key issue is the preservation of the anonymity of the school. I have tried to cover my traces, including deceiving close friends, in order to protect its identity. I have also left a considerable period of time between the collection of the staffroom data and publication, something for which, given the nature of the staffroom talk, I have been criticized on the grounds that it involves covering up racism. Complex issues are involved and it seems to me that no hard and fast rules can be laid down about whether secret research is or is not legitimate. This is not to say, of course, that my judgements in this case were correct, though I still believe them to have been so.

9 Had I taken more careful note of the circumstances of each exchange, some kind of analysis of the data produced when I was playing different roles could have been undertaken. See Becker and Geer (1960), though their distinction between solicited and unsolicited data is too crude (Hammersley and Atkinson, 1983).

10 Riess (1968) and Manning (1977) report this tendency in the case of research on the police.

11 See Sharp and Green (1975) for a piece of research noticeably produced in this kind of climate.

12 This reinforced earlier experiences at National Deviancy Symposium conferences where interactionist approaches were coming under increasing attack from representatives of 'the new criminology' (Taylor, Walton and Young, 1973).

13 See Lofland (1974) for discussion of some of the criteria underlying the evaluation of ethnographic research reports.

References

ATKINSON, M. (1977) 'Coroners and the categorisation of deaths as suicides: Changes in perspective as features of the research process', in BELL, C. and NEWBY, H. (Eds) *Doing Sociological Research*, London, Allen and Unwin.

BARNES, B. (1974) *Scientific Knowledge and Sociological Theory*, London, Routledge and Kegan Paul.

BAUMAN, Z. (1978) *Hermeneutics and Social Science*, London, Hutchinson.

BECKER, H.S. and GEER, B. (1960) 'Participant observation and the analysis of qualitative field data', in ADAMS, R.N. and PREISS, J.J. (Eds) *Human Organization Research*, Homewood, Ill., Dorsey.

BELL, C. and NEWBY, H. (Eds) (1977) *Doing Sociological Research*, London, Allen and Unwin.

BERLAK, A. *et al.* (1975) 'Teaching and learning in English primary schools', *School Review*, 83, 2, pp. 215–43.

BLOOR, D. (1976) *Knowledge and Social Imagery*, London, Routledge and Kegan Paul.

COHEN, A.K. (1955) *Delinquent Boys*, New York, Free Press.

COHEN, A.K. (1974) 'The elasticity of evil: Changes in the social definition of deviance', Oxford University Penal Research Unit, Occasional Paper, No. 7, Blackwell.

COSIN, B. *et al.* (Eds) (1971) *School and Society*, London, Routledge and Kegan Paul (2nd ed. 1977).

DAWE, A. (1970) 'The two sociologies', *British Journal of Sociology*, 21, 2, pp. 207–18.

ERIKSON, K.T. (1967) 'A comment on disguised observation in sociology', *Social Problems*, 14, 4, pp. 266–73.

FREIRE, P. (1972) *Pedagogy of the Oppressed*, Harmondsworth, Penguin.

GARFINKEL, H. (1967) *Studies in Ethnomethodology*, Englewood Cliffs, N.J., Prentice Hall.

GLASER, B. and STRAUSS, A. (1967) *The Discovery of Grounded Theory*, Chicago, Aldine.

GOODMAN, P. (1971) *Compulsory Miseducation*, Harmondsworth, Penguin.

GOULDNER, A.W. (1970) *The Coming Crisis of Western Sociology*, New York, Basic Books.

HAMMERSLEY, M. (1971) 'Classroom learning, school interaction and the concept of cultural deprivation', unpublished MA thesis, University of Manchester.

HAMMERSLEY, M. (1974) 'The organization of pupil participation', *Sociological Review*, 22, 3, pp. 355–68.

HAMMERSLEY, M. (1976) 'The mobilization of pupil attention', in HAMMERSLEY, M. and WOODS, P. (Eds) *The Process of Schooling*, London, Routledge and Kegan Paul.

HAMMERSLEY, M. (1977a) 'Teacher perspectives', units 9–10, Open University course E202, Schooling and Society, Milton Keynes, Open University Press.

HAMMERSLEY, M. (1977b) 'School learning: The cultural resources required to answer a teacher's question', in WOODS, P. and HAMMERSLEY, M. (Eds) *School Experience*, London, Croom Helm.

HAMMERSLEY, M. (1979) 'Review of Marsh, Rosser & Harre: The Rules of Disorder', *Sociological Review*, 27, 3, pp. 607–12.

HAMMERSLEY, M. (1980a) 'On interactionist empiricism', in WOODS, P. (Ed.) *Pupil Strategies*, London, Croom Helm.

HAMMERSLEY, M. (1980b) 'A peculiar world: Teaching and learning in an inner city school', unpublished PhD thesis, University of Manchester.

HAMMERSLEY, M. (1981) 'Ideology in the staffroom: A critique of false consciousness', in BARTON, L. and WALKER, S., (Eds) *Schools, Teachers and Teaching*, Lewes, Falmer Press.

HAMMERSLEY, M. (1982) 'Staffroom racism', unpublished paper.

HAMMERSLEY, M. (1983) 'The paradigmatic mentality: Science versus critique in the sociology of education', paper given at Westhill Sociology of Education Conference, Westhill College, Birmingham.

HAMMERSLEY, M. AND ATKINSON, P. (1983) *Ethnography: Principles in Practice*, London, Tavistock.

HAMMERSLEY, M., SCARTH J. and WEBB S. (1983) 'Thick description versus grounded theorizing? The case of research on student learning and examinations', paper given to BSA Ethnography Study Group Seminar.

HARGREAVES, D.H. (1967) *Social Relations in a Secondary School*, London, Routledge and Kegan Paul.

HARGREAVES, D., HESTER, S. and MELLOR, F. (1975) *Deviance in Classrooms*, London, Routledge and Kegan Paul.

HARRIS, E. (1970) *Hypothesis and Perception*, London, Allen and Unwin.

HERITAGE, J. (1975) 'Community and practicality in sociology and beyond', *Sociology*, 9, 2, pp. 329–39.

HITCHCOCK, G. (1983) 'Fieldwork as practical activity', in HAMMERSLEY, M. (Ed.) *The Ethnography of Schooling*, Driffield, Nafferton.

HOCH, P. and SCHOENBACH, V. (1969) *LSE: The Natives Are Restless*, London, Sheed and Ward.

HOLT, J. (1969) *How Children Fail*, Harmondsworth, Penguin.

JOHNSON, J. (1975) *Doing Field Research*, New York, The Free Press.

KAPLAN, A. (1964) *The Conduct of Inquiry*, New York, Chandler.

KUHN, T. (1962) *The Structure of Scientific Revolutions*, Chicago, University of Chicago Press.

LACEY, C. (1970) *Hightown Grammar*, Manchester, Manchester University Press.

LEIBNIZ, G.W. (1887) *Philosophischen Schriften*, C.I. Gerhardt (Ed.), Berlin.

LOFLAND, J. (1974) 'Styles of reporting qualitative field research', *American Sociologist*, 9, 3, pp. 101–11.

McHUGH, P. et al. (1974) *On the Beginning of Social Enquiry*, London, Routledge and Kegan Paul.

MACKINNON, D. (1977) 'Sociology and political choice', E202 Schooling and Society, Unit 24, Milton Keynes, Open University Press.

MANNING, P. (1977) *Police Work*, Boston, Mass., MIT Press.

MERTON, R.K. (1967) 'On the history and systematics of sociological theory', in MERTON, R.K., *On Theoretical Sociology*, New York, Free Press.

MERTON, R.K. (1972) 'Insiders and outsiders: A chapter in the sociology of knowledge', *American Journal of Sociology*, 78, 1, pp. 9–47.

NEWBY, H. (1977) 'In the field: Reflections on the study of Suffolk farm workers', in BELL, C. and NEWBY, H. (Eds) *Doing Sociological Research*, London, Allen and Unwin.

PAYNE, G. (1976) 'Making a lesson happen: An ethnomethodological analysis', in HAMMERSLEY, M. and WOODS, P. (Eds) *The Process of Schooling*, London, Routledge and Kegan Paul.

POLANYI, M. (1959) *Personal Knowledge*, London, Routledge and Kegan Paul.

POLLNER, M. (1974) 'Sociological and commonsense models of the labelling process', in TURNER, R. (Ed.) *Ethnomethodology*, Harmondsworth, Penguin.

RIESS, A.J. (1968) 'Stuff and nonsense about surveys', in BECKER, H.S. et al. (Eds) *Institutions and the Person*, Chicago, Aldine.

ROTH, J. (1961) 'Comments on "secret observation"', *Social Problems*, 9, 3, pp. 283–84.

SACKS, H. (1963) 'Sociological description', *Berkeley Journal of Sociology*, 8, pp. 1–16.

SACKS, H. (1972) 'On the analyzability of stories by children', in GUMPERZ, J.J. and HYMES, D. (Eds) *Directions in Sociolinguistics*, New York, Holt, Rinehart and Winston.

SCHWARTZ, M.S. and SCHWARTZ, C.G. (1969) 'Problems in participant observation', in McCALL, G.J. and SIMMONS, J.L. (Eds) *Issues in Participant Observation*, Reading, Mass., Addison-Wesley.

SHARP, R. and GREEN, A. (1975) *Education and Social Control: A Study in Progressive Primary Education*, London, Routledge and Kegan Paul.

TAYLOR, I., WALTON, P. and YOUNG, J. (1973) *The New Criminology*, London, Routledge and Kegan Paul.

TORODE, B. (1977) 'Interrupting intersubjectivity', in WOODS, P. and HAMMERSLEY, M. (Eds) *School Experience*, London, Croom Helm.

TURNER, R. (1960) 'Sponsored and contest mobility and the school system',

American Sociological Review, 25, pp. 855–67.
WATSON, J.D. (1968) *The Double Helix*, London, Weidenfeld and Nicolson.
WILLIS, P. (1977) *Learning to Labour*, Farnborough, Saxon House.
WOODS, P. (1979) *The Divided School*, London, Routledge and Kegan Paul.
YOUNG, M.F.D. (Ed.) (1971) *Knowledge and Control*, London, Collier-Macmillan.

3   Beachside Reconsidered: Reflections on a Methodological Apprenticeship

Stephen J. Ball

Editor's Commentary. Although case studies of schools have been in vogue for some years, Stephen Ball's *Beachside Comprehensive* published in 1981 was the first detailed study of a comprehensive school based upon the work of a participant observer. Stephen Ball spent three years in the school, teaching classes and collecting data for his study. In this chapter he provides an account of the fieldwork, the writing up period and the reception of his published work.

Stephen Ball locates his research within that sociological tradition of empirical study which is founded upon symbolic interactionism and the use of participant observation alongside other methods. Many researchers who work in this tradition emphasize its advantages in examining subjective elements of social life and the meanings which participants attribute to social situations. However, its critics are quick to raise questions about principles of selection, together with reliability and validity of data. Here, Ball demonstrates that these concerns are not absent from fieldwork. His discussion of the selection of a school, of classes and of teachers addresses the question: what principles of selection are involved in an ethnographic study? In the latter part of his chapter he deals with the politics and practice of respondent validation and the reception that his study received from the media.

In this chapter Stephen Ball demonstrates how the researcher begins with a 'good idea' (the study of mixed ability grouping in a comprehensive school), locates a school where the work can be done and gradually shifts from unsystematic observation and data recording to more systematic forms of study. He also demonstrates how the researcher has to deal with such diverse concerns as: conducting interviews, informed consent and confidentiality. Many of these issues have been discussed by methodologists in abstract, while Ball shows how they can be handled by the researcher while conducting ethnographic work in an educational setting.

I began my fieldwork at Beachside in the autumn of 1973 and the book *Beachside Comprehensive* was published almost eight years later in April 1981. For most of the time during those eight years Beachside, in one form or another — Beachside the school, Beachside the thesis, Beachside the book — was a major personal preoccupation. During this time my actual period of fieldwork in the school lasted for three years, three days a week in the first year, four days a week in the second, and about one day a week in the third. This was my second experience of fieldwork, having spent the summer term of 1973 working in a comprehensive in London collecting material for my MA dissertation. That prior experience was important in two ways as far as Beachside was concerned: first it led me to a total reorientation of my main research interest, and secondly it confirmed my commitment to participant observation methods and symbolic interactionist theory.

I began my MA fieldwork with a primary concern with racial mixing in pupil friendship groups and chose to work in a multi-racial comprehensive in order to observe and record the structure and meaning of such friendships. I emerged from that field experience with a wish to investigate the nature of comprehensive schooling and in particular the role of and importance of mixed ability grouping in the comprehensive school. Thus the idea of Beachside was born. But in addition, my MA study had convinced me that participant observation provided the most appropriate and rigorous basis for an investigation of comprehensive schooling inasmuch that I felt it was the practice rather than the rhetoric or structure of comprehensive education that directly affected the school experiences and life chances of the pupil. I was lucky enough to be nominated for an SSRC studentship to do a piece of research on these lines in the Education Area, at the University of Sussex.

My original research proposal suggested a comparative study of two comprehensive schools both of which were in the process of introducing mixed ability grouping. Indeed I went as far, with Colin Lacey's help, as contacting and receiving approval to work in two schools. However, it only took two or three visits to Beachside for me to realize that two full-scale, long-term ethnographies of large schools more than forty miles apart were beyond the capacities of a single research student. I decided, therefore, with the approval of my supervisor to concentrate on Beachside exclusively.

'Riding the Bike'

A colleague at Sussex recently suggested that doing ethnographic fieldwork is in many respects like riding a bicycle: no matter how much theoretical preparation you do there is no real substitute for actually getting on and doing it. Indeed, I feel that this dictum applies not only to the social and technical processes of doing fieldwork but also to its theoretical underpinnings. Some writers in the tradition argue that the realities and complexities of the theory and method of symbolic interactionism cannot, and in some respects should not, be fully worked out prior to or outside the fieldwork experience of participant observation. Thus Rock (1979, p. 213) comments

> I feel that the fieldworker needs only a minimum of theoretical orientation before he begins his observations ... he may be positively handicapped if he postpones his fieldwork until he feels that he has a thorough grounding in theory.

My own grasp of participant observation techniques, even after my MA work, was hazy to say the least as I began work at Beachside. None of my reading on research methods seemed to turn up a model of fieldwork practice which I could translate straightforwardly into a structured routine of data collection at my school. I was left very much to my own devices to arrive at a set of working methods which, as I refined them over time, began systematically to build up various sets and categories of data. My methods were devised to respond to the specific demands and contours of the various situations under study — classrooms, staffroom, playground and so on — and in a similar way my research relationships evolved to take account of the complexities of a hierarchical institutional setting. As Rock (1979, p. 215) asserts, 'fieldwork is accomplished chiefly in action, it cannot be mastered by speculation.'

However, such statements do little to calm the fears or assuage the insecurities of the novice ethnographer. The experience of fieldwork, even in relatively familiar settings like schools, can be stressful and lonely (Wintrob, 1969). These feelings were certainly to the forefront in my first weeks in the field and they recurred at frequent intervals throughout my fieldwork experience. This is not only a result of being thrust into a strange institution to face people who may be suspicious or initially hostile, but also derives from the fear of failure. In particular the new entrant into the field is constantly confronted with the question: 'am I really getting the data I need?' (Wintrob, 1969, p. 67). In effect the fieldwork experience may be thought of as a *rite of passage*. It involves a personal confrontation with the unknown and requires that the aspirant come to grips with the use of theory and method in the context of a confused, murky, contradictory and emergent reality. That is light years removed from the systematic theories and pristine research reports read in preparation for 'research seminars'. Wax paints a similar picture in the case of anthropology, where

> ... young anthropologists often embarked on a first field trip in a spirit not unlike that of adolescent primitives facing initiation into the tribe. In solitary agony, supported only by the wise sayings of their anthropological ancestors, they met their crucial and mysterious ordeal. (Wax, 1952, p. 34)

In this respect participant observation probably differs fundamentally from other research methods. The lack of prescription and specificity as to its conduct is both inevitable and necessary. What is being attempted is the implementation of a set of theoretical, rather than technical, precepts. To wit:

> The study of action would have to be made from the position of the actor. Since action is forged by the actor out of what he perceives, interprets and judges, one would have to see the operating situation as the actor sees it. (Blumer, 1977, p. 16)

Thus most definitions of participant observation are unable to go beyond a minimal elaboration of 'me and my notebook and writing everything down'. The Becker *et al.* (1968) definition is the one I prefer:

> For our purposes we define participant observation as a process in which the observer's presence in a social situation is maintained for the purpose of scientific investigation. The observer is in a face-to-face relationship with the observed, and, by participating with them in their natural life setting, he gathers data.

The participant observer is committed to becoming embedded in the perspectives of those who inhabit the socio-cultural world that is to be described and analyzed. The prime concern is to share in a direct, immediate and non-presumptive sense the phenomenal givens of these actors in order to construct an account of their cultural setting.

That's all well and good but it brings us back to the question: how does that work out in practice? The folklore suggests that the participant observer begins by working in two ways. First, there is the process of familiarization, making oneself aware of the different settings and events within the research scene. This reflects two aspects of Becker *et al.*'s definition: (i) is 'being there', actually being present in those action contexts that one seeks to understand; (ii) is 'sharing', working alongside or questioning the actors about their actions. I was actually involved in teaching at Beachside.[1] Secondly, there is the collection of background materials. Malinowski used to suggest to his students that they begin by doing a household survey of their village; the collection of genealogies can serve a similar purpose in anthropological research.

These two aspects of the first phase of fieldwork were represented in my own activities at Beachside. First, my 'being there' involved a whole range of types of attendance and observations in the school, which I will describe in more detail below, and my teaching provided a very immediate sense of 'sharing' (at least with the staff). Secondly, I began by collecting material on the age, experience and training of the Beachside teachers, I had access to pupils' files and read through two whole year groups, I visited each of the 'feeder' schools and I began to analyze registers and the school detention book. This latter material was fairly easy to handle and was to prove useful later in my writing up of Beachside. But the earlier observation material was to prove much less useful. For one thing, looking back at my earliest fieldwork notebooks and entries in my fieldwork diary the comments, descriptions and quotations to be found there are both sketchy and poorly referenced. At a variety of levels these early attempts at capturing and recording material demonstrate my lack of fieldwork skills. I had yet to develop that fluency of virtually indecipherable notetaking which would allow me later to record whole sections of conversation verbatim or describe classroom and staffroom incidents in elaborate detail. Neither was I yet aware of the importance of the careful identification of speakers, settings and forms of initiation that was to prove so crucial in handling some of the subtleties in the data in my analysis of events. The first diary has long lists of quotations from 'band 2 pupil', 'history teacher', 'year tutor', etc., without any other form of identification or referencing. In many respects, inevitably of course, I had little idea of what kind of material would actually come to constitute 'data' later in my work; what details of staffroom talk, or classroom exchanges or playground incident were to be of value in constructing accounts of the school lives and experiences of my case study classes; what sorts of systematic recording would provide useful comparative material.

One of the major themes of the analysis of the pupils' experiences at Beachside is change over time in their attitudes, behaviour and commitment to school. One way of plotting, triangulating and illustrating these changes was to compare at different points in time things like: attendance at extracurricular activities; membership of school clubs; reference of pupils to the year tutor; informal detentions held by subject teachers; failure to bring books to lessons; alterations or deviations from official uniform; and so on and so forth. However, in my first few months in the field I recorded few of these 'naturalistic' indices in any systematic way and thus lost out entirely on one comparative dimension with data collected at a later time.

Clearly, in the early weeks or months in the field that which is to be 'important' is the object of the discovery process not its organizing principle. One result of such an orientation to the field, indeed it is an expectation of ethnographic study, is that the process of fieldwork is marked by changes in the direction, focus and scope of the research objectives. These changes, some short-lived and unprofitable, some profound, are accompanied by the problem of false trails, dead-ends and the collection of much useless or irrelevant data. Several such reorientations, some major some minor, occurred in my fieldwork at Beachside.

For example, a comment in my fieldwork diary[2] for Wednesday 20 February 1974 marks the beginning of the end of the first phase of my fieldwork. It reads:

> I've really got to the stage when uninformed observation from the outside has been pushed to its limit, the rough operational design of the actual progress of the research should be expounded now and intensive observation of classes should begin.

This rather obscure remark, written in capitals, indicates my intention to cease my haphazard observation of classes and to select and begin to observe a number of case study form groups. I chose two band 1 forms, two band 2 forms and two mixed ability forms and approached their form tutors to obtain their support and cooperation. All agreed. I intended to concentrate primarily on one band 1 and one band 2 form, using the others for comparison and to collect back-up data. In the terminology of my diary I would be 'following' these forms, dogging their footsteps through the school through the next two and a half years. I discussed the choice of these particular forms with their respective year tutors but my diary is not very forthcoming on the reasons for choosing these forms rather than any others.

A decision to select or focus is of course also a decision to set aside or exclude other issues or contexts. Taken together the decisions made at choice points like this are of major significance in shaping the overall topography of a study. Despite the understandable reluctance

of ethnographers to use the term, those decisions constitute a form of
sampling. In studying a large, complex institution like a secondary
school a single-handed researcher must of necessity sample, whether
aware of it or not. Smith (1978) writes of sampling:

> In our view it lurks behind every decision the investigator
> makes when he elects to be here vs. there, to spend more time
> here rather than there, what array of documents to read, of
> people to interview, of settings to hang around. At the data
> level, the question is always, 'Has one seen the nooks and
> crannies of the system as well as the main arenas to give a
> valid picture of the system.

Sampling in a Complex Institution

Sampling is not something that is normally talked about by ethnographers — except for theoretical sampling. It carries with it a set of
working assumptions about the nature of social reality in general
which are alien to ethnographic methodologies. Yet in studies of
complex institutions, like schools, the field worker is engaged in both
explicit and implicit forms of sampling. I do not refer here to
sampling in any statistical sense but in terms of naturalistic coverage
and the problems of selectivity (see Burgess, 1982 for a discussion of
sampling in field research).

The first and probably most important point of selection in my
research was the choice of school — why Beachside? To be frank a
number of factors played a part. I would like to think, and indeed
have argued in the book, that Beachside was a critical case for
comprehensive education. I wanted an innovative school that was
attempting to go beyond the givens of the tripartite system. As I saw
it, mixed ability grouping was crucial in this. Both of the schools that I
made contact with were chosen deliberately because of their interest
in mixed ability and both were regarded in their locality as somewhat
avant garde in this respect. They certainly presented a view of
themselves couched in a rhetoric of innovation. My attention was
first drawn to Beachside by my thesis supervisor, who had heard
about the school, but it is difficult to reconstruct with total reliability
the original thinking that attracted me to the school. My supervisor
recalls that I had a number of things in mind:

> First of all you'd want some working class kids and Beachside
> had them. Secondly you'd want a fairly liberal regime.... I

certainly knew that the Head there was a liberal guy.... I may have heard him give a talk.... I knew that while you would get working class kids in Brighton, but I knew you wouldn't get any relaxing of the streaming system, at that stage, I knew that Brighton was very conservative, so you had to go out of the county.

The search then was for a 'likely' school, a school that fitted certain minimal criteria. But other personal factors must be added to this: first, Beachside was relatively accessible to me, I had a car and the school was within reasonable driving distance of my home. The alternative would have been to return to London where I had done my MA fieldwork. Secondly, Beachside was both officially and unofficially welcoming and cooperative. One of the comments which I recorded in my field notebook after my first visit to the school, to discuss the possibility of doing my study there, was made by the headmaster. 'I think we need to be studied', he said. This openness was immediately reinforced on the occasion of my first field visit. I called into the headmaster's secretary's office and announced my arrival and she disappeared into the head's room. 'He says you should go into the staffroom and make yourself at home and carry on', she said when she returned. So I did. I sat in the staffroom and remember thinking, 'carry on with what'. But I had been sitting for less than two or three minutes, waiting for something to happen so I could write it down, when I was joined by a teacher — who I later discovered to be the head of English — 'Who are you then?' he said. I attempted gamely to explain. 'So you'll be wanting to see some lessons then?' Dare I ask? I did. 'No problem anytime. I've got a mixed ability group after break. Why don't you come along then? And I'll introduce you to some other staff as well.' I was off. Perhaps it wouldn't be so bad after all.

Within the school I was also making important selection decisions at various points in the research. Very soon I decided that I would concentrate upon the academic teaching in the school. I certainly observed my share of art, PE and craft lessons, plus a few music, but I have no record of attending any metalwork, needlework, PE or domestic science lessons, although I was given 'covers' for these. (Hammersley, in this volume, describes his attempts to systematically attend these subjects on the periphery of the curriculum.) Also Mode 3 CSE, remedial and sixth form classes are underrepresented in my observation records. The focus of my study on mixed ability and banding led, in part at least, to a systematic neglect of these other areas of pupil experience. If one looks at other comparable studies it is clear that this neglect extends across the whole range of classroom-based, school ethnographies; Lacey (1970), Hargreaves (1967) and Woods (1979) also have little or nothing to say about the 'non-academic' curriculum and they quote few observations made in teaching situations that are not literally classrooms (or laboratories). The dark recesses of workshops, domestic science rooms, gyms, and needlework rooms have been rarely penetrated by the fieldworker.

The decision to concentrate on the academic, while it did coincide with the 'central value system' of the school, had further sampling consequences of which I was not fully aware at the time and which served to devalue my work in the eyes of at least some of the readers of my work within the school. I gave little direct attention to either the work of the pastoral staff (except where this was related to the 'behaviour' of the pupils I was observing) or the wealth of extra curricular activities offered by the school. That is not to say that I totally ignored these things, I attended school concerts and plays, sports events, open evenings and parties as part of my general familiarization with and sharing of the whole cultural life of the school, but I did not systematically record or observe these events or school clubs or the Youth Wing or sports practices, and then subject them to careful analysis, as I was doing with classroom work and staffroom politics.[3] My account of the school is as a result profoundly distorted. Although, again I was always keen to collect indirect material referring to these non-academic activities, for example, the pupils' participation in clubs and teams; their perception of school events; accounts of their behaviour on trips or at discos. These aspects of the life of the school were within my peripheral vision while my gaze was fixed elsewhere.

Once focused upon academic classroom lessons I was still making a number of sampling decisions. In the initial three months of my fieldwork I decided to observe any and all lessons to which I could gain access. (It was mainly during this period that I observed a variety of non-academic lessons.) I asked to observe almost everyone I came into contact with, quite haphazardly. I wanted to find out as much as I could about the school, the pupils and the teachers, in the shortest possible time. I wanted to get 'a feel' for the place. I wrote down anything that came to mind while I observed in lessons and elsewhere, talked to teachers or pupils, or listened while others talked. Much of this did not at the time make much sense to me[4] and I certainly did not know how much of it was to be of relevance to what I would eventually write about the school. This reflects my 'orientation toward discovery', referred to above, my concern was 'to actively explore the social world, a process in which one's normal routine preconceptions should, as far as possible, be suspended and thus left open to challenge' (Hammersley, 1980). This openness, I would argue, provides one of the important bases of the value and power of participant observation research, and brings it 'nearer than any other social science method to capturing patterns of collective actions as they occur in real life' (Becker *et al.*, 1968). But even here the distortions inherent in any kind of observation must be admitted. Access to a world of fleeting, overlapping, contradictory, murky, incoherent realities demands selective attention from the fieldworker. For everything that is noticed a multitude of other things go unseen, for everything that is written down a multitude of other things are forgotten. Great parts of the real world experienced by the participant observer, probably the greater part, is *selected out* (see Cottle, 1982). Even those aspects of the world of the observed to which specific (and unusual) attention is paid are subject to the distortions of abstraction, reification, and temporal freezing. Over and above these perceptual and recording distortions my fieldwork relations with staff were marked by my involvement in particular *social networks*, 'defined by the patterns of interaction which run through the formal channels of communication' (Cockburn, 1981, p. 3). I had no fixed base in the school but I certainly became quickly aware of the way in which the seating arrangements in the staffroom tended to affect the pattern and nature of my social contacts with staff. I was most 'at home' sitting with the English department and often felt the need to make a deliberate decision to sit elsewhere in the staffroom. This may have tended to distort the range and variety of my observations particularly in the early part of my fieldwork, although the analysis of my fieldnotes does not suggest any obvious subject biases, over and above those mentioned already. But over the whole period of my fieldwork there is clearly a pattern to my contacts with teachers, of which I was not fully aware at the time. This is probably most obvious in my relationship with a number of 'informants'.

Anthropologists have long been aware of the crucial role played by informants in their research (Casagrande, 1960), and Whyte's (1955) 'Doc' is a familiar character to most ethnographers, but ethnographic educational research does not appear to have had the same reliance on these intriguing people. At Beachside informants were of considerable importance to me throughout my fieldwork. Five of the Beachside teachers acted in this capacity — Mike, Roger and Gloria were a source of major help and support for virtually the whole of my time in the school, Dan and Terence provided help and information at specific points in my research.[5]

Mike — a humanities teacher in his early thirties, also held a pastoral care post working with the banded cohort on which I chose to concentrate. He gave me complete access to pupils' records, provided other information on pupils' backgrounds, parental involvement with schools and pupils referred to him by subject teachers. He often allowed me to attend pastoral meetings and discussions with pupils concerning option choices. He made available to me all the records and forms connected with the option choice process including the notes 'rejecting' certain pupils, sent back by staff. He discussed every stage of the process with me and candidly described his dealings with other teachers. Mike also read and commented upon a number of the working papers I produced during my fieldwork, although he was rarely very critical of my analysis. It is significant I think that we often discussed his future career and the fact that he was uncertain about what prospects he might have at Beachside. The internal routes of promotion seemed blocked and in the last year of my fieldwork he obtained a post at a brand new comprehensive as Head of Humanities and the sixth form. He was a very competent teacher and I observed a number of his lessons. He was clearly respected by his colleagues both for his teaching skills and his efficiency in pastoral work. He is virtually the only Beachside teacher with whom I am still in contact.

Roger — a history teacher in his late twenties and a very strong supporter of mixed ability teaching, he said in one of several interviews I had with him: 'When I came for an interview I asked about mixed ability.' He taught one of the mixed ability classes I was 'following' and I observed his lessons with them regularly for several months. I recorded a number of these lessons and he commented upon and wrote notes on the transcripts. On a couple of occasions I taught his classes while he sat at the back of the room and watched me. He also read and commented upon other written material which I produced during my fieldwork. Later he also obtained a pastoral post and was able to help me considerably with my work with a 'gang' of disruptive pupils in the fourth and fifth years. I recorded a number of interviews with him discussing the activities of this gang and the attitude of the rest of the staff towards them. After my fieldwork was completed I was able to involve Roger in some teacher training work at the university.

Gloria — a social science teacher in her early thirties. I shared some social science teaching with Gloria for a period during my fieldwork and was involved with her in the ordering of books, and discussions about the syllabus and teaching methods. I was able to bring resource materials into school from my other college teaching. On a number of occasions I attended school social events like plays and concerts and speech day with her. Also I recorded a number of interviews with her on mixed ability and the gang of pupils in the upper school in whom I was interested; she had several members of the gang in her tutor group and she was thus able to keep me informed about their behaviour and the trouble they tended to get into around the school. Gloria had previously taught in a middle school and often found her educational views to be at odds with those of many other members of staff. She left the school to get married in the last year of my fieldwork.

It is misleading to talk about typical and untypical teachers at Beachside, probably at most schools, but it probably is significant that all three of these people were 'young' staff and that in different ways Mike and Gloria were 'distanced' from the mainstream of school life. As it does for the researcher, this distancing allowed them to maintain a reflexive stance towards their own work and their involvements with colleagues. Furthermore, over and above the specific help they were able to give me, all three provided a constant source of feedback on and correction to my evolving grasp of the culture and 'ethos' of Beachside. At times, as Lacey (1976) suggests, each of them was 'brought into the analysis as a positive contributor — almost as a research assistant'. My gravitation towards these three teachers also probably owes something to what Cockburn (1981, p. 32) calls experiental commonality:

> The fundamental backcloth to which the forms of gravitation are pinned is essentially social in nature, textured by an inter-weaving of experiential commonalities between field-worker and participants. Epistemic and comparable status gravitation can be reduced to social gravitation.

My relationship with the other two teachers I have named as informants was rather different and the 'services' they provided were also different.

Dan — a head of department in his early 40s who strongly supported mixed ability. We had many long discussions about the concept of mixed ability and its particular role in his subject area. I also recorded a number of long interviews with Dan and participated in some extracurricular activities which he organized for the school. He provided a channel of information from the senior management of the school. At one time he arranged for pupils in several of his classes to write essays for me on the topic of 'comprehensive education'. I often watched him teach and talked to him at length about his teaching methods.

Terence — a senior member of the pastoral staff in his early 40s. Terence solicited my help on a couple of occasions while he was on secondment for a year on an in-service BEd course. He later enrolled on a course at the university and I taught him in a component called 'The Analysis of Classroom Transactions'. He was always keen to discuss research methods and often asked me how my research was 'going'. In return Terence frequently provided me with feedback on the way I was perceived and received by other members of staff.

The involvement of these informants in my research certainly differs or diverges from the careful selection of such people that is advocated in some of the anthropological commentaries on fieldwork method (see Honigmann, 1982 and Tremblay, 1982). These individuals were not chosen by me according to any carefully worked out criteria, rather they emerged from the relationships I made in the school or were self-selected in some cases, on the basis of an interest in my research. Nonetheless, Mead's prescriptions concerning the need to evaluate 'an individual informant's place in a social and cultural whole' (1953, p. 646) were well taken. As indicated above, I was aware of their untypicality and in some cases their marginal position within the school.

My research relationships with my informants also raises the question of the different types and the quality of the data elicited from teacher respondents at Beachside generally. For example, the category of data glossed in the published version of Beachside as 'interview' embraces a set of widely differing situations and relationships. In the case of my informants, and a number of other respondents, 'interviews' were definitely not formal 'one-off' events. Data were collected from repeated 'interviews' which varied from taped, single-topic, question and answer sessions to the most informal of 'chats'. Rather than simply 'interviewing' this is what Laslett and Rapoport (1975) refer to as 'interactive research' within which the hierarchical nature of the researcher-respondent relationship is broken down and 'an attempt is made to generate a collaborative approach to the research which engages both the interviewer and respondent in a joint enterprise' (p. 968). In this mode of research there is no attempt to maintain the formality of a uni-dimensional researcher-respondent relationship, indeed it relies 'very much on the formulation of a relationship between interviewer and interviewee as an important element in achieving the quality of information required' (Rapoport and Rapoport, 1976, p. 31). Neither the interviewer nor the interviewee 'are thus depersonalised in the research process' (Oakley, 1981, p. 37). However, there was a still larger group of respondents among the staff with whom my research relationships tended to be much more depersonalized and formal. In some cases data were collected from them in a single formal interview. These respondents were known to me primarily as 'a geography teacher', 'a year tutor', 'a probationer', or whatever, the way in which their contributions are designated in the book. If I may play fast and loose with Schutz's work for a moment, my field relationships ranged on a continuum from respondents as 'contemporaries' whereby 'I grasp the factual existence and being-thus-and-so of a contemporary only by means of derived typifications' (Schutz and Luckmann, 1974, p. 74) and 'the experiences of mere contemporaries appear to me as more or less anonymous events' (p. 75), to respondents as 'consociates' based upon 'concrete social relations' (p. 64) within which 'we can live in each other's subjective contexts of meaning' (Schutz, 1972, p. 166). But even in the case of the 'consociate' we-relationship Schutz notes that 'the extent of my knowledge of the other can naturally be quite varied' (1974, p. 64). In practice my relationships with teachers at Beachside were grouped towards the consociate end of this continuum, those with pupils towards the contemporary end.

Altogether what I have referred to as 'interviewing' in my work at Beachside, with some exceptions, resembles the long-term conversations employed by Cottle (1982) in his life studies of working-class families in the United States. My entry into the teachers' lives was not unlike his entry into the lives of families he studied, 'another person coming into their home uninvited, ready to *take* something from them. In another sense, they may feel that my presence, like that of any researcher, means a chance to talk and be heard, to be recognized ...' (p. 123). My basic concern was to hear the teachers talk on topics that concerned them as these arose in the course of everyday work, 'one encounters people, listens to them speak about what matters to them, hears the attitudes and opinions they only naturally cultivate and then records what they say' (p. 123). On the other hand, like Cottle, I must recognize that my presence stimulated talk, produced response, encouraged concern, 'what I observe and record is not only the material experienced by me, it is in part, generated by me' (p. 125). But the biases involved in this kind of confrontation between selves are very different to the problems which attend formal interviewing, 'in a sense the structured interview becomes a barrier between people, albeit a porous one, as well as a means of keeping responses of all kinds under control' (p. 127). The conversations I was engaged in at Beachside were conducted in the staffroom, in classrooms and corridors, on the playing fields, in the pub, teachers' homes, on school trips, in the car to and from school, and at casual meetings in the town, they are slices of my life and slices from the lives of the teachers and pupils. Clearly, these social relationships were subject to the same constraints as any others, we 'hold back, and recognize that certain issues and the emotions connected to them, are better left unsaid' (p. 125). But, at the same time, as a researcher, an outsider, I was privileged with confession, the otherwise unsaid, the heart-felt and the bitter.

Feedback and Respondent Validation

With one or two exceptions,[6] ethnographic studies have not given much attention to the processes or outcomes of feedback of data and analysis to respondents. As a result we have little insight into either the responses of the researched or the problems or possibilities of *respondent validation* techniques. In the Beachside study I did attempt some feedback to my respondents and did employ this feedback in a variety of ways to amend and redirect parts of my description and analysis of the school.

Four types of feedback were involved: (1) as mentioned above, I used my relationship with 'informants' as a vehicle for checking facts, interpretations and analysis. This was done informally in discussions and more formally when I handed over papers or chapters for comments; (2) discussions with other staff also gave opportunities for informal validation; (3) towards the end of my fieldwork period I held two seminars after school which were open to all staff; on each occasion I made copies of a draft chapter available in advance in the secretary's office; both seminars were attended by between twenty and twenty-five members of staff and both were tape recorded; (4) when a complete draft typescript of my thesis was ready I made a copy available to the headmaster. He then circulated this to several heads of department for comment and I met with him to discuss his and their reaction.

These procedures of feedback and respondent validation were not without their problems. I believe that the responses of the Beachside staff provide some insight into both the political nature of doing school ethnography and the complexities of the concept of respondent validation in relation to institutional analysis. Bloor (1978) outlines the methodological basis of respondent validation as follows:

> the truth of our analyses, their validity, is constituted by establishing some sort of correspondence between an analyst's and collectivity member's view of their social world ... one can only establish a correspondence between the sociologist's and the member's view of the member's social world by exploring the extent to which members recognize, give assent to, the judgements of the sociologist.

It also needs to be said that Bloor's use of respondent validation, in the context of a study of medical diagnosis, was limited to one-to-one exchanges of views between himself and individual doctors. His problems were mainly procedural and concerned the lack of interest or commitment on the part of the respondents. This is paralleled in my categories 1 and 2, which were also marked in some cases by a lack of interest by respondents in my work. However, my categories 3 and 4 constitute very different validation processes from those outlined by Bloor and throw up very different problems.

Clearly, my chapters were not aimed at or concerned with individuals or homogeneous groups of the actors at Beachside. The subject of the first seminar, a chapter on banding and the attitudes and behaviour of banded classes and teacher-pupil relations in the bands, addressed the experiences of virtually the whole staff. The twenty-odd who turned up (I wish now that I had made a more careful record of attendance) represented a full cross-section of subject departments and pastoral staff. I was faced by the realities of the precept that 'an individual's statements and descriptions of events are made from the perspective that is a function of his position in the group' (Becker and Geer, 1960, p. 273). Perhaps it should be added that an individual's statements will also reflect the vested interests of their position and their values. The chapter on banding began with a long description of a band 2 French lesson based on my observation notes. This illustration was intended as a dramatic example of the extremes of band 2 behaviour in lessons and the resulting problems faced by some teachers. Two senior members of the languages department attended the seminar specifically to ask me why I had 'picked on' French this way. (One is quoted below as T2.) This led to a discussion of the use of pseudonyms and the extent to which individual teachers could be identified in my material. One of the French staff commented, 'we all know who this is'. I was unable to convince the French delegates that I had no particular reason for choosing an illustration from their subject or that this would not create a poor impression of their subject in the school if it remained. Another contributor, an English teacher (T1), was concerned not about the particular ramifications of the lesson sequence for French but for the teacher described. He said:

> T1: I enjoyed reading it. But my first impression is, have you or anyone or should you have the right to do a sort of carve up job on a teacher.... You know. I question the right to do it on a teacher. Now you could answer that by saying we don't recognize that teacher. Am I right?
>
> SB: I think there are two things, important things — one I don't think you should be concerned to try and identify the teacher....
>
> T1: ... except I do think ... this kind of research, for teachers, who are indeed in the job as a career and however much you will try and do your damndest not to harm them, it may be that you might. Now, could I ask you a question? We don't know who this teacher was — does the headmaster know who this teacher was? You don't think so. I think these are important questions, not for your research but for teachers generally, if you get their help and cooperation and you want it in the future, you and other people.
>
> SB: The alternative to that is to say, well all teachers are good teachers. We'll put them on the side for the moment — which has been the way its normally been done.
>
> T2: You say that you altered the name of the teacher ... so why must the heading state that its a French lesson?

As the meeting continued the whole issue of the disruption caused by band 2 classes was increasingly called into question. One teacher argued that problems were confined to the lessons of inexperienced teachers or those whose control was poor in any case. Another commented that

> insofar as your case stands we've all got to be concerned we are failing large numbers of children by neglecting to take

account of these informal groups, those diverse motivations and attitudes. But before I take myself to task I want to question some of the points raised by your research.

But this direction of argument and the whole tenor of the meeting changed when one head of department stated, 'Come on. We all know that band 2 classes are a problem area we've all had difficulties with band 2 kids. We're fooling ourselves if we say we don't.' In a sense this head of department spoiled the emergent 'team performance' (Goffman, 1971, p. 88) by giving the show away. My initial reaction to the meeting was one of considerable confusion. Over the next few days I discussed the reactions of my 'opponents' with most of my informants (perhaps I should have been talking to the French teachers instead). A number of important points seemed to be raised by the discussions at this meeting.

    1   As the quotation above, from Becker and Geer, suggests, many of the staff had apparently read my chapter solely in terms of what it had to say about them or their subject. There was little or no discussion of the general issues I was trying to raise or the overall arguments of the chapter. My expectations of the seminar and those of the teachers were obviously quite different. In part at least this may be explained not only in terms of the different vested interests but also in positional terms. I had taken as my task as ethnographer the description and analysis of large-scale trends which extended as I saw them across the whole school, an overview. The staff responded from their particular view of the school, from the vantage point of the position they held. None of the staff had the opportunities I did to observe in a variety of lessons, across a range of subjects or to talk at length with individual staff about their practices and experiences in the classroom. In one sense I witnessed and wrote about Beachside from a position of privilege. Hopefully, without sounding too arrogant and patronizing it would seem that the majority of staff responded to my work from a narrow viewpoint of immediate personal concerns and experience.

    2   In symbolic interactionist terms, it is important to recognize the possible significance of the contextual determination of meaning, that is, to recognize the social nature of the seminar as an event. It was constituted as a fairly formal, public situation and gave rise almost exclusively to forms of 'third party talk' (Hargreaves, 1977). In Keddie's (1971) terms we were operating very much within the educationalist context rather than the teacher context. The set-up of the seminar (indeed the use of the term itself) made my status as an

outsider very visible. After years of fieldwork I was normally very much a seen but unnoticed feature of school life. Furthermore, meetings of this kind were not usual at Beachside, staff only came together for discussions of this kind in occasional staff meetings.

3   The discussion of band 2 classes may be seen as a concerted effort (although not consciously concerted) to re-establish what Bailey (1981) calls the 'preferred view' in the face of my attack upon or undermining of the school's normally confident self-image. Becker (1964) talks about the 'irreducible conflict' that exists between 'the researcher and those he studies', as well as noting that 'as men of goodwill, the researcher and those he studies will be able to find some common ground for decision' (p. 272). Nonetheless, 'the sociological view of the world — abstract, relativistic, generalizing — necessarily deflates people's view of themselves and their organizations' (p. 273). My work set in the public context of the feedback seminar provided just such a deflation.

4   The conduct of these sessions revealed another problem of which I should perhaps have been aware at the time, and if I had been, should have taken steps to remedy. Despite the formalities of a kind of 'informed consent' and numerous and repeated explanations of my work in the school (as far as this is possible set against the 'orientation to discovery' of ethnographic research), the majority of the staff clearly had little idea of what sociological research was and the sort of outcomes it might produce. This has been noted by several other participant observers; Gusfield (1960, p. 106), studying the Women's Christian Temperance Union, wrote that 'they didn't seem to see how much I was discovering about them. Their conception of a sociological study was rather naive and at a highly formal level.' Similarly, from a study of a laundry, Bain (1960, p. 145) records that 'one of the biggest mistakes was assuming that the workers knew what "research for a master's thesis" meant.' The only discussion I had of this 'reality gap' and its implications came in the meeting I had with the headmaster when we discussed his reaction, and that of heads of department, to my complete typescript. He commented: 'I don't think that many of the staff realize the critical nature of sociology as a discipline.'

5   My final point requires some reference to the second of the feedback seminars. This one was based on a chapter which examined the mixed ability innovation and the responses of the various departments to the problem of mixed ability teaching. In my mind the session was dominated by a single issue, again based upon a 'partisan' response. The discussion was opened by the head of science

who felt that his department had been portrayed unfairly:

> HoS: Now that to me was quite shocking because it seemed that you were criticising ... and I'm not objecting to any kind of criticism but I do object to criticism from people who are not qualified to criticize about such things and I don't think you are. You never taught a science lesson in your life — you don't know anything at all about science teaching and the difficulty of teaching mixed ability classes or science to older kids. You have absolutely no idea about any of that. And yet this is to be published.

In particular the head of science objected to my 'accusation', as he saw it, that chemistry was taught to mixed ability classes on the basis of 'chalk and talk methods'.

> HoS: I'm not objecting to the fact that you're doing research on interaction between kids. I am objecting to the fact that you're criticizing teaching methods....
>
> SB: The times you've said to me that there are problems with your syllabus and how you would like to change it, that there are certain problems with it. In a' sense I'm reporting what you told me....
>
> HoS: Well certainly I'm not aware I said that — actually I'm not particularly objecting to a good two-thirds of that paragraph ... but what about this 'chalk and talk'. How can you make comments like that.

The head of science continued with queries about the 'scientific' adequacy of my work. He asked what 'measures' I had used and what 'tests of significance' were employed, adding '... well I think it comes back to what I said originally. Your sample is so very tiny that you can't hope to make comments like that.' The remainder of the session consisted of my attempts to explain the epistemological basis of ethnographic research and the conflicts between positivist and interpretative sociologies. The head of science remained quite unconvinced by my arguments and finally dismissed my account as 'honestly, absolute drivel'. Vidich, Bensman and Stein (1964, p. 157) make the important point that:

> above all in 'reporting' — though not only there — the sociologist is functioning supremely socially. What he tells —

how, with what emphases and shadings intuitively calculated towards achieving what effects — is a function of nothing so thin as 'role' and 'social structure', but rather a function of his *inclusion* as an actor in a full-scale social drama.

My exchanges with the head of science were at times quite heated and there was little in the way of contributions from the other staff at the meeting. The rest of the session was rather an anti-climax after the 'paradigmatic confrontation' between the canons of natural science and the epistemic quibbles of interpretive sociology. The head of science could not recognize my 'findings' as such because, as he saw it, they lacked any scientific validity. This validity, it seemed, would have had to have been established upon numerical data to be acceptable. Although what exactly would be counted and measured was not made clear in the discussion. In the absence of these data my analyses and arguments were dismissed. Again, as in the first seminar, the issues raised by the chapter as a whole were never addressed. The main concern, at least of the head of science, was perhaps understandably to deflect or emasculate the critical tenor of my 'findings' by destroying the credibility of my methods, possibly in the same way that my work involved a challenge to the credibility of his department in the school. The confrontation perhaps again highlights the 'irreducible conflict' between researcher and researched and once again points to the political nature of my research when it was exposed in a public arena; 'the research process is bound up with the exercise of power' (Lacey, 1980).

Several of these issues arise once again in relation to my discussions with the headmaster over the completed draft typescript. In particular he and several of the heads of departments were unhappy about the focus of my analysis being exclusively upon the academic system of the school. They felt that I had neglected the pastoral work and the range of extra curricular, especially drama and music, activities in which the school was engaged. In other words, that my portrayal failed adequately to reflect the expressive culture of the school. There were and still are a number of grounds on which I would want to respond to the substance of that criticism but I will not rehearse those here. Again my work was threatening an important aspect of the public and communal presentation of the self by the school. Also the head was worried about the extent to which my account gave too great a credence to and relied over much on the views of staff who were marginal or transient. Two staff in particular were named, who were described as 'out of sympathy with what the school was trying to do'. I had had little contact with either in fact and some specific comments attributed by the head to one of them had been made by a head of department (at least my use of pseudonyms seemed to be working). The chapter on the fourth year option system received a great deal of attention in this discussion and was seen as the most critical of the school. The head objected to a term 'sink', as applied to pupils and subjects, used by staff in interviews and asked me to change or remove these references (I did the former).[7] But the heads of department also commented that the system '*does* not work like that' (my emphasis). In a number of respects my account of how the school *was* at particular points in time was being read as an account of how the school *is*. Again in terms of symbolic interactionist orthodoxy I view my account of Beachside as an historical document, but for the staff it was being related directly to current practice two years later. Footnote 3 (p. 299) in the book says: 'It is important to note that in the year following the one dealt with here the option-allocation system was revamped to increase the amount of counselling received by the pupils....' I responded to the discussions with the headmaster by rewriting several pages and sections in the typescript and adding material to the first chapter, which introduces the school. I sent copies of these to the head and we arranged another meeting.

Elliott (1980, p. 17) takes a hard line on the role of respondent validation in case study research and argues that:

> Mismatches between observational and participant accounts do not render the latter invalid. But they do call for *free and open dialogue* between observer and participant. And I would argue that it is only when an account has been agreed under these conditions of dialogue that its validity can be considered to be demonstrated.

It is not clear to me whether the accounts discussed in my meetings with the Beachside teachers were agreed or not or whether indeed the substance of the accounts was very often addressed in these discussions. It seems to me that Elliott's account of validation, at least in terms of my experience, fails to address the *political* aspects of dialogue. It may not be in the interests of the participants to 'arrive at a consensus under conditions of free and open dialogue with the researcher and each other' (p. 18). Schools are political arenas where opposing ideologies and competing vested interests are played out. Any case study which taps into these facets of institutional life would seem to stand little chance of consensual agreement.

Completion and Publication

The book, *Beachside Comprehensive*, was published almost five years after my fieldwork at the school was concluded. In the meantime the manuscript had gone through numerous drafts and versions. My first complete draft was over 120,000 words in length. The regulations for DPhil submission at the University of Sussex state a maximum wordage of 80,000. I have always felt that this is a ridiculous rule. A DPhil should not, by its very nature, have any arbitrary word limit attached to it. The length of an individual thesis should be determined by intrinsic criteria related to the nature and scope of the work undertaken. A supervisor and examiners should be capable of making rational decisions about the extent to which a particular thesis is over-long. Word limits are of course a particular problem for ethnographers and they are imposed not only by universities but also by publishers and book and journal editors (for very different reasons).

The Sussex regulations had a number of consequences for my DPhil. In effect the greater part of three chapters was removed in order to get the wordage to just below 100,000 (which was an acceptable breach of the word limit rule). The research method section was cut almost entirely, although I was able to publish this separately under the auspices of the Education Area. The theory chapter which attempted a conceptualization of classroom interaction based on symbolic interactionist precepts was cut out (see Ball, 1980). And a long exposition of my mixed ability case study classes was also cut. The alternative to these particular decisions, in particular if I had kept in theory and method, would have involved me in cutting data and substantive material which I considered to be more important to the basic objectives of my thesis. I think that this was justified in that I have been able to write and publish my views on interactionist theory and method elsewhere (see Ball, 1982a; 1982b; 1983). My publishers, however, required further cuts to reduce the book to an economically viable 80,000 words. I am certainly not unsympathetic to their financial concerns and both my selfish and more principled investments in wanting the book published certainly outweighed my feelings at the time about the requirements of methodological rigour. However, these cuts were to have a more significant impact on the technical adequacy of the study. I think it is worth noting here, if only briefly, some of the ways in which cuts were made and the subtle changes that this effected in the role of some of the data presented in the text. After the removal of all appendices, the further reduction of the theoretical discussion in the introduction, the amalgamation of two chapters into one and the almost entire removal of another chapter dealing with the social lives of fourth and fifth year pupils, the rest of the cuts were achieved by paring the data presented. Typically, the number of instances quoted in support of arguments was reduced; some transcripts were shortened and edited; all of the desk plans of classroom seating arrangements were removed; several tables showing test scores and the further analysis of sociometric data were cut; other tables were compressed. Subtley, there was a shift from a concern with the use of data as evidence and proof and conceptual elaboration to the use of data as illustration. Again this is a problem which is specifically acute in the case of ethnographic research where there is a reliance on qualitative data. I recognize, however, that this is a concern that is not necessarily shared by all those who engage in or read ethnographic research. It would seem that greater credence and emphasis is often given to the theoretical and interpretive sophistication of the research than to its technical rigour (Willis, 1977 and Sharp and Green, 1975 might be good examples); (see Delamont, 1981). As ever, the craftsman is of lower status than the theorist.

Needless to say, when Beachside was eventually published these methodological concerns were not the issues which seemed to be of most significance to readers in the media. A couple of weeks after the book appeared I received messages at my university that the local radio station wanted to contact me urgently. When I rang the station I discovered that they wanted me to be interviewed about my research on their news programme that evening. I also discovered subsequently that they had been ringing local schools to ask if they were Beachside and whether they wanted to comment on the book. (All this was happening while our university telephone exchange was occupied by the students.) I refused to be interviewed for a news programme but said I might be willing to take part in a discussion of the educational issues raised by my book. I then received a number of telephone calls at my home from two different news editors at the radio station who tried to persuade me to be interviewed. The more telephone calls I received the more convinced I became that I did not want to cooperate. I finally refused to contribute to any programmes. Back at the university another series of messages began to arrive from local schools to the effect that a national newspaper was ringing up to ask if they were Beachside. I am pleased to say that none of them was. When I telephoned the newspaper named by the schools everyone I spoke to denied any knowledge of making the calls.

During the summer of 1981 a news report on Beachside appeared in a national Sunday paper, *The Sunday Times*, and I appeared on two television programmes to talk about the book — a live discussion on comprehensive education for a BBC Wales current affairs programme, with Neil Kinnock and Mike Sullivan, and a London Weekend Television series 'Starting Out: An Inquiry into London Schools', to talk about the effects of streaming. But in each of these cases the people concerned were interested in the general issues about comprehensive education raised in the book rather than identifying and discussing the school itself. Even so my experiences with Beachside would certainly affect the way in which I presented any future ethnographic work for publication. Apart from careful use of pseudonyms I fully intend to ensure that I actively mislead any readers as to the location or identification of the school or schools concerned.

The distinction between Beachside as a particular school and Beachside the case seems to me to be an important one. The local radio station was not, it seemed to me, interested in the latter, but was interested in making trouble for the school. Schools have become fair game and easy pickings for the media over the last ten years and ethnographers should not be casually providing more ammunition for the barrage of criticism which is faced by those schools that want to do things a little differently from the rest. The innovative school has always been of interest to researchers but if we are not careful we are in danger of helping to kill off those innovations that we wish to study. Happily the reviewers of *Beachside* have concerned themselves without exception with the issues raised by the study, comments on the school itself have been few, and when they have been made, in contrast to the predictions of the headmaster, they have cast the school in a positive light. Thus, J.D. Wilson reviewing the book for *British Book News* (August 1981) writes that, 'Beachside emerges as a remarkably harmonious institution with a progressive head supported by a young staff' (p. 466). I agree.[8]

Notes

1 In the first year of fieldwork I agreed to work as a 'cover' teacher, to fill in for staff who were absent. I also taught some O-level sociology. In the second year of fieldwork I was timetabled for four periods of sociology a week and three periods of mixed ability history.
2 I kept a notebook with me at all times in the field and wrote up my notes from this each evening into a hardback research diary. Also in the diary I

wrote my 'interpretive asides' and comments on the development of my fieldwork.

3 It could be argued that this concentration on the academic system would tend to exaggerate the fixed and polarized nature of the pupil subcultures I describe in *Beachside*. More attention to the non-academic might have indicated greater variation in pupils' commitments (cf. Measor and Woods, forthcoming).

4 Clearly, the interpretation of ethnographic data is prospective and retrospective, that is to say, much of social action can only be made sense of in relation to what came before and what comes after.

5 There was also a small number of pupils who could be described as my informants but I do not have the space to discuss them here.

6 Whyte discusses the responses of Doc and others to his work in the Appendix to *Street Corner Society*, and Willis had some of 'the lads' read drafts of *Learning to Labour* (pp. 194–9), but most of the work on problems of feedback has been done in evaluation research.

7 This, of course, raises another set of questions about the politics of respondent validation. It was the headmaster who spoke for the school at this stage, rather than the teachers I had been working with, although to be fair his responses to my work were always couched in terms of comments and requests. He made it clear that he recognized the importance of the research to my career.

8 I am grateful to John Burke, Scilla Furey, Alan MacGregor and Bob Burgess for their useful comments on a previous draft of this paper.

References

BAILEY, A.J. (1981) 'The school as a social arena', unpublished paper, Education Area, University of Sussex.

BAIN, R.K. (1960) 'The researcher's role: A case study', in ADAMS, R.N. and PREISS, J.J. (Eds) *Human Organization Research*, Homewood, Ill., The Dorsey Press.

BALL, S.J. (1980) 'Initial encounters in the classroom and the process of establishment', in WOODS, P.E. (Ed.) *Pupil Strategies*, London, Croom Helm.

BALL, S.J. (1981) *Beachside Comprehensive: A Case Study of Schooling*, Cambridge, Cambridge University Press.

BALL, S.J. (1982a) 'Participant observation as a method of research', in University of Deakin, Australia, *Case Study Methods 6, The Conduct of Fieldwork*, Readings 36–44, University of Deakin Press.

BALL, S.J. (1982b) 'The verification and application of participant observation case study', in University of Deakin, Australia, *Case Study Methods 5, Ethnography*, Readings 26–33, University of Deakin Press.

BALL, S.J. (1983) 'Case study research in education: Some notes and problems', in HAMMERSLEY, M. (Ed.) *Ethnography and Schooling*, Driffield, Nafferton.

BECKER, H. (1964) 'Problems in the publication of field studies', in VIDICH,

A.J. BENSMAN, J. and STEIN, M.R. (Eds) *Reflections on Community Studies*, New York, John Wiley.

BECKER, H. and GEER, B. (1960) 'Participant observation: The analysis of qualitative field data', in ADAMS, R.N. and PREISS, J.J. (Eds) *Human Organization Research*, Homewood, Ill., The Dorsey Press.

BECKER, H. *et al.* (1968) *Making the Grade*, New York, John Wiley.

BLOOR, M. (1978) 'On the analysis of observational data: A discussion of the worth and uses of inductive techniques and respondent validation', *Sociology*, 12, 3, pp. 545–7.

BLUMER, H. (1976) 'The methodological position of symbolic interactionism', in HAMMERSLEY, M. and WOODS, P. (Eds) *The Process of Schooling*, London, Routledge and Kegan Paul.

BURGESS, R.G. (Ed.) (1982) *Field Research: A Sourcebook and Field Manual*, London, Allen and Unwin.

CASAGRANDE, J.B. (Ed.) (1960) *In the Company of Man: Twenty Portraits of Anthropological Informants*, New York, Harper.

COCKBURN, J. (1981) 'Social and methodological processes in condensed fieldwork: Some conceptualization from the LASS fieldwork experience', Centre for Applied Research in Education, University of East Anglia.

COTTLE, T.J. (1982) 'The life study: On mutual recognition and the subjective inquiry', in BURGESS, R.G. (Ed.) *Field Research: A Sourcebook and Field Manual*, London, Allen and Unwin.

DELAMONT, S. (1981) 'All too familiar? A decade of classroom research', *Educational Analysis*, 3, 1, pp. 69–83.

ELLIOTT, J. (1980) 'Validating case studies', paper presented at the Annual Conference of the British Educational Research Association, University College, Cardiff.

FICHTER, J.H. and KOLB, W.L. (1953) 'Ethical limitations on sociological reporting', *American Sociological Review*, 18, October, pp. 96–7.

GOFFMAN, E. (1971) *The Presentation of Self in Everyday Life*, Harmondsworth, Penguin.

GUSFIELD, J.R. (1960) 'Fieldwork reciprocities in studying a social movement' in ADAMS, R.N. and PREISS, J.J. (Eds) *Human Organization Research*, Homewood, Ill. The Dorsey Press.

HAMMERSLEY, M. (1980) 'Ethnography and education', paper presented at the British Educational Research Association, Annual Conference, 2–4 September.

HARGREAVES, D.H. (1967) *Social Relations in a Secondary School*, London, Routledge and Kegan Paul.

HARGREAVES, D.H. (1977) 'The process of typification in the classroom: Models and methods', *British Journal of Educational Psychology*, 47, pp. 274–84.

HONIGMANN, J.J. (1982) 'Sampling in ethnographic fieldwork', in BURGESS, R.G. (Ed.) *Field Research: A Sourcebook and Field Manual*, London, Allen and Unwin.

KEDDIE, N. (1971) 'Classroom knowledge', in YOUNG, M.F.D. (Ed.) *Knowledge and Control*, London, Collier-Macmillan.

LACEY, C. (1970) *Hightown Grammar*, Manchester, Manchester University Press.

LACEY, C. (1976) 'Problems of sociological fieldwork: A review of the methodology of Hightown Grammar', in SHIPMAN, M. (Ed.) *The Organization and Impact of Social Research*, London, Routledge and Kegan Paul.

LACEY, C. (1980) Research seminar, Education Area, University of Sussex.

LASLETT, B. and RAPOPORT, R. (1975) 'Collaborative interviewing and interactive research', *Journal of Marriage and the Family*, November, pp. 968–77.

MEAD, M. (1953) 'National character', in KROEBER, A.L. (Ed.) *Anthropology Today*, Chicago, University of Chicago Press.

MEASOR, L. and WOODS, P. (forthcoming) *Adapting to the Comprehensive School: The Negotiation of Pupil Identities*, Milton Keynes, Open University Press.

OAKLEY, A. (1981) 'Interviewing women: A contradiction in terms', in ROBERTS, H. (Ed.) *Doing Feminist Research*, London, Routledge and Kegan Paul.

RAPOPORT, R. and RAPOPORT, R. (1976) *Dual Career Families Reexamined*, London, Martin Robertson.

ROCK, P. (1979) *The Making of Symbolic Interactionism*, London, Macmillan.

SCHUTZ, A. (1972) *The Phenomenology of the Social World*, London, Heinemann.

SCHUTZ, A. and LUCKMANN, T. (1974) *The Structures of the Life World*, London, Heinemann.

SHARP, R. and GREEN, A. (1975) *Education and Social Control*, London, Routledge and Kegan Paul.

SMITH, L.M. (1978) 'An evolving logic of participant observation, educational ethnography and other case studies', in SHULMAN, L. (Ed.) *Review of Research in Education*, Chicago, Peacock Press.

TREMBLAY, M.A. (1982) 'The key-informant technique: A non-ethnographic application', in BURGESS, R.G. (Ed.) *Field Research: A Sourcebook and Field Manual*, London, Allen and Unwin.

VIDICH, A.J., BENSMAN, J. and STEIN, M.R. (1964) *Reflections on Community Studies*, New York, John Wiley.

WAX, R. (1952) 'Reciprocity in fieldwork', *Human Organization*, 11, 3, pp. 34–41.

WHYTE, W.F. (1955) *Street Corner Society*, 2nd ed., Chicago, University of Chicago Press.

WILLIS, P. (1977) *Learning to Labour*, Farnborough, Saxon House.

WINTROB, R.M. (1969) 'An inward focus: A consideration of psychological stress', in HENRY, F. and SABERWAL, S. (Eds) *Stress and Response in Fieldwork*, New York, Holt, Rinehart and Winston.

WOODS, P.E. (1979) *The Divided School*, London, Routledge and Kegan Paul.

4   Dimensions of Gender in a School: Reinventing the Wheel?

Mary Fuller

Editor's Commentary. This chapter continues to discuss some issues that have been considered in earlier contributions while developing particular aspects of the research process in relation to a specific research problem. Mary Fuller's work, like that of Martyn Hammersley and Stephen Ball, was conducted in a state secondary school. However, she was not concerned with studying the school but with using the school setting to examine social divisions based on sex and race. In this sense, her work breaks new ground. In turn, like Sara Delamont, she focuses on some of the issues and problems that surrounded writing a PhD thesis. She points out the way in which the themes of her thesis developed out of her own social, political and personal perspective and out of her changing interests in research methodology.

In this chapter, Mary Fuller demonstrates how the focus of her research changed over time and how this resulted in the design and redesign of her project. Indeed, she discusses the way in which her changing interests not only influenced the collection of data but also had an impact upon the analysis and the way in which she wrote up her thesis. Among the issues that her account addresses are: the problems associated with starting and restarting a research project; the influence of feminism on her research design; the ethics and politics of gaining research access; and the way in which a researcher attempts to handle the relationship between quantitative and qualitative methodology. Mary Fuller's work considers such questions as: how is access negotiated and renegotiated with teachers, pupils and parents? What is the relationship between data collection, data analysis and writing up? Her discussion indicates the ways in which a researcher can attempt to come to terms with such problems in the course of doing research and how it is possible to blend together quantitative and qualitative data in a research project.

'Dimensions of Gender in a School' is the title of the PhD thesis I successfully submitted to the University of Bristol in 1978. It is an account of the salience of two major social divisions — those based on biological sex and on 'race' — within the school which I call Torville. It is based on research involving five fifth year classes (142 pupils) and the forty teachers who taught them. Torville was a ten-form entry mixed, multi-racial comprehensive in the London borough of Brent. Although the study involved research with male and female pupils and with three distinct groups — white British, Afro-Caribbean and Indo-Pakistani pupils — this would not be especially obvious from the parts that have been published, since the only aspect of the research to have been published so far concerns the educational and vocational aspirations of the 'Asian' and 'West Indian' girls (Fuller, 1980a; 1980b; 1982; 1983), these being apparently considered more interesting or topical than the experiences of boys or white girls.

The thesis is written up as a case study of the extent to which, and the circumstances in which, gender and race mattered to the pupils and teachers in a particular school. The written account diverges considerably from the project as originally envisaged, because the research focus (though not the methods) underwent some large changes in the early days of doing the research. Though by no means a thoroughgoing ethnography of Torville School, the thesis is nevertheless nearer to that than to anything I had started out to produce. To make this clearer I shall need to go back to my original intentions and to give in some detail the research strategy I had mapped out. Since what I wanted to research and how I wanted to do the research are themselves linked to my professional, personal and political biography up to that point, I shall start from there.

When I was offered a research post after a year's unemployment and searching for work, I did not really think twice about accepting the condition that I also register for a higher degree. I had not actually been seeking the opportunity to do one, but like many research assistants before and since I was assured that it would be simply a matter of settling on a particular aspect of the research I was being engaged to carry out, 'carving out' that part for myself and in due course I would have the data to write up a PhD in my spare time. At the time I knew no-one contemplating or working on a higher degree by research, so made my decision in ignorance of what it would entail. Choosing the topic was less a matter of chance. My interest in the social position of women dated from undergraduate days when I had written a dissertation on the underrepresentation of women in science, and as a feminist I was becoming particularly interested in the ways in which gender is socially constructed. Working now in a project designed and directed by a social psychologist, I began to encounter some of the psychological literature on sex differences and on cross-cultural studies of gender. I was sceptical of the claim that some of this literature made that there are 'universal features' to notions of masculinity and femininity, and so decided that I would use this as the starting point for my thesis. I duly registered a topic which reflected this interest in gender. The stipulation that the topic be compatible with the research project I was working on did not feel like a constraint — in fact to investigate the supposed universal features of gender would require my comparing perceptions of gender and self-definitions in people of diverse backgrounds, a requirement which could be well met in a research project concerned with adolescents from three ethnic groups.

However, as others have also found, there are inherent problems in obtaining satisfactory material for one's own purposes from a piece of research which is not explicitly designed with those purposes in mind. After about two years these problems became more pressing and I started again. Retaining the intention to study conceptions of gender, I would design a more appropriate way of going about researching the topic. By the time I drew up a second PhD proposal late in 1974 I came to the task with something of a prepared mind. I had read fairly widely, both feminist and psychological literature dealing with gender. I had extended my experience of interviewing to include interviews with young adults from three ethnic groups, which gave me a much clearer view of the potential problems in cross-cultural interviewing; and I was now in a position to make a choice about how I would go about researching the topic.

So far my research experience (with the exception of my undergraduate dissertation) had been restricted to implementing someone else's research design. In this way I had accumulated experience of a study involving large samples contacted by postal questionnaire; I had been involved in interviewing fourth and fifth form pupils (at school and later in their homes) as a first stage in obtaining their personal constructs about themselves and others. This project had also given me considerable experience of computing and analysis of computer printout. I had received my first degree from a sociology department where the predominant view was of sociology as a science, with all that that implies in terms of training in quantitative research methods and in statistics.

While little of this experience actually prepared me for participation and observation as a research method, it had been sufficient to convince me that the simple logic or common sense to which quantitative researchers seemed to resort in explaining their findings were inappropriate for understanding and interpreting processes. It had also taught me that I was not comfortable with research which kept a distance between me as the researcher and the research 'subjects'. My discomfort with rushing into schools, grabbing 'data' from interviews and questionnaires and having no opportunity to discuss anything with teachers or pupils was given some focus by my reading of certain feminist researchers such as Carlson (1972), who described such methods as 'agentic', and Bernard (1973), who suggested the distinction between 'hard' (quantitative) and 'soft' (qualitative) data might also have some interesting (sexual) political overtones since, in America at any rate, the gathering of 'hard' data seemed to be a predominantly male activity; she suggested also that more participatory methods of carrying out research were more consistent with a feminist perspective, because they did not necessarily involve the researcher standing aloof from those being researched. (These and other issues to do with doing feminist research are discussed in Roberts, 1981). I was also aware that my skin colour (white) could affect the extent to which some pupils would willingly or readily talk to me. In fact, my own and others' experience suggested that, as a white person, I might have considerable difficulty in engaging black teenagers in my PhD research. It also seemed likely that my being a woman would affect the willing cooperation of some pupils, though at the time when I was writing my proposal I did not know of any work which indicated in what way this might be a factor. In other words, I believed that I would have to work to establish a trust which could not be assumed to exist, before even inviting pupils to be involved in my research. To work to this end and to enable pupils to have something on which to base their decisions meant building in time at the beginning of the project to explain the research to them and finding a way for me to be available so that they could get to know me.

Original Intentions

In some respects my research aims were straightforward and limited. I wanted to administer the Bem Sex Role Inventory (Bem, 1974; Bem and Watson, 1976) to a sufficiently large cross-section of young people that I would be able to make statistical inferences about group differences. I might have been sceptical about quantitative research, but I was not about to abandon it completely for the unknown! I wanted to discuss the claimed universals in masculinity/femininity by having a sample which included males and females from a variety of distinct cultural backgrounds. I wanted to compare the test results with people's own perceptions of themselves as male or female and with their perceptions of social norms concerning gender. I decided very early that locating the research in school would provide me with a reasonable cross-section, providing that I restricted myself to pupils below the statutory leaving age. This decision was treated at the time as essentially a technical one, though it was to change the nature of my project in some fundamental ways. The decision to work in one rather than several schools came later, as the result of decisions about the most appropriate research role to be adopted.

The research aims may have been simple, but the means of going about achieving them would have to be less simple. In deciding what I would need to do, I started from what I saw as the core of the research (the 'real research') — administration of the Bem Sex Role Inventory (BSRI) and interviews — and worked backwards from there. As I would be interviewing only a sample of the pupils, I would want some basic information about them (for example, socio-economic status, place of birth, and certain other information such as number and sex of siblings, which the literature suggested had a bearing on how people perceive sex roles) to provide the basis of accurate sampling. This indicated that I would need to give a questionnaire to all pupils who would also be completing the BSRI, and access to school records would also be required. Since I did not wish to influence more than necessary how the sample who would be interviewed would discuss gender, the interviews should be completed before I began administering the BSRI. To be in a position to be sampled accurately, all pupils should have completed a questionnaire and I should have completed my recording of the school's documentation about each pupil prior to the first interview. I wanted to record forty-eight individual interviews. Working on two assumptions I calculated that interviews, questionnaires and the Inventory could not be completed in less than a full school term. My assumptions were that I would have more chance of getting into a suitable school if I did not ask for normal routine to be disturbed so that I could carry out my work — this seemed to suggest that I would do my interviewing and related research activities during lunch breaks; and secondly, that I would administer questionnaires and the BSRI in small groups only, rather than to a class at a time — to avoid a high rate of uncompleted questionnaires. Since these tasks would take up virtually all non-teaching school time for a term, I would only be available to the pupils during lesson time. Consequently I decided that the best way I could ensure being available was to build in a term in the school immediately before that in which I would carry out the 'real' research. I thought of this as a period of 'hanging about', of marking time, necessary but productive mainly as a means to an end. As I have said, though, it was not only for pragmatic reasons (to do with the location of the research and the nature of the sample) that I adopted a research role which reduced the distance between me and the pupils, it also accorded with my preferences. Again, at the time, I thought of this as mainly a technical decision, although spending a fairly lengthy period of time in the school, especially that first term of 'doing nothing', substantially altered the direction I took when I began writing up the thesis. In particular I accumulated a considerable amount of information about the school and its organization (from various documents routinely generated in the school) and about classroom life (from the notes I kept about each lesson I observed), sources of information to which I shall return later in this chapter.

The Research Role

Although, as I thought of it at the time, the research only 'happened' to be in a school, I knew that I would need to think carefully about what my role would be for the two terms I was going to spend there. I wanted to be able to observe and participate as a way of being available to pupils. I wanted to avoid being placed in a position of 'authority' in relation to the pupils — in particular I wished to avoid, as far as possible, being categorized prematurely by them as a teacher. If the school I selected were one in which relations between staff and pupils were strained, it would not have helped my case to be seen as a teacher. (The possibility of entering the school as a teacher did not arise as I am not qualified to teach in school). I was equally certain that I wanted to be free to carry on with my work without the strain of lying to either pupils or teachers about my research. Wolcott (1975) neatly summarizes the dilemma for the researcher in a school:

> ... the widely used technique of participant observation runs afoul of that organization's own traditon. There are relatively few formal roles in schools, and the roles available are not necessarily attractive for accomplishing research that must be based on limited rather than on total involvement. Schools do entertain hordes of 'observers' but ... unless one places himself behind a podium, a typewriter, a broom, or the

principal's desk, there simply are no other roles.... The only alternative in the school setting appears simply to resign oneself to becoming an observer.... Perhaps in time one can find additional avenues for enlarging one's perspective. (Wolcott 1975, p. 122)

I would enter the school as a researcher, not pretending to be anything different, and I would give both staff and pupils the same 'true' account of why I was there. Obviously people would try to make sense of my presence and maybe slant their behaviour accordingly, but the advantage of everybody having been told the same story was that I would have some idea of what bias my presence might have introduced, and indeed that could be (and was) a subject to be discussed with both pupils and teachers.

During the first term at the school (approximately fifteen weeks) I observed teachers and pupils in lesson time, making a record of information on a prepared data sheet (a copy of this can be found in the Appendix to this chapter), one or more for each lesson attended. I believed that having something of this sort would be a prop for me in the classroom, evidence for myself that I was 'doing something', as well as a convenient way for me to jot down information about pupils so that I could more easily fit names to faces. Apart from these uses I had no fixed idea at the outset what, if anything, else I would use them for. At various times I used these forms to collect such material as seating plans, friendship groups, types of classroom activity, information about a specific pupil or group of pupils, descriptions of the classroom. I began the collation and preliminary analysis of various school documents (pupils' records, set lists, timetables, school rules, lists of teachers, the subjects each taught and so on). Much of this work was aimed at providing me with sufficient information to be able to sample accurately school subjects, sets, and forms, so that I would be equally available to all pupils. So though my role in that term was, in a sense, that of an honorary pupil and the major part of each day (as for the pupils) was spent in lessons, observing and participating where possible, I was incidentally building up systematic information about classroom interaction and school organization, recorded at the time, together with a note of any special circumstances that might affect the observations made. During this term I also systematically sampled the activities and places where pupils went at break times. The major omission in this sampling was that I decided not to hang around the lavatories, since I could think of no acceptable way of doing this in the boys' lavatories.

During the second term research 'proper' began. When I was not engaged in this — administering the questionnaire or BSRI, or carrying out interviews — I continued with classroom observation for part of each day, collated information from pupils' school reports (which incidentally also enabled me to observe the school's 'cooling down' room) and was able, with the pupils' knowledge, to spend time in the staffrooms at different times each day.

In thinking about the research role I should adopt I was influenced by anthropologist colleagues at the SSRC Research Unit where I was working and by a desire to create a situation in which the young people at the school would be able to decide for themselves whether they took part in the research. Unlike Sara Delamont (this volume) I was not trying to do better than Hargreaves and Lacey. I did not at the outset, nor during the time that I was in Torville School, consider that the school was the focus of my research. So, though I knew of Hargreaves' early (1967) study, I did not connect his enterprise with mine — his was *about* a school, mine happened to be using a school for convenience sake. In thinking about the practical and ethical issues of participant observation, I drew on my knowledge of British and American studies in industrial settings (for example Lupton, 1963), since this, rather than education, was an area of sociology where I had encountered the tradition of participant observation.

The Research Process

The new research proposal having been approved, I spent the early part of 1975 researching outer London boroughs, finally deciding on two which seemed suitable, in terms of the type of school and the proportion of black pupils in some schools. I made my first approaches to the LEAs in May. In the first borough the interview with the Education Adviser was brief and simply resulted in my obtaining permission to approach the head of whichever schools I might choose. After discussions with staff at the borough's Teachers' Centre, some of whom I already knew, I wrote to two comprehensive schools, obtaining interviews with, in one case, the fifth year tutor, and in the other, the deputy head. In Brent my interview with the Director of Education was lengthy, resulting in appointments being made for me with heads of suitable schools. In each case in Brent I discussed the research with the headteacher.

Before each interview at LEA or school I sent the person

concerned a brief summary of the research proposal. The purpose of each of these visits was two-fold: firstly, to elaborate and explain the research, indicating the potential problems for staff and pupils which the kind of access I was seeking might create; and further, to discuss the ways in which these problems might be dealt with or avoided. Secondly, I wanted to obtain certain kinds of information about the school, for example, the organization of fifth year teaching, in order to judge whether the school would be a suitable location, and as well, to assess the potential 'sponsor' or 'sponsors' of the research. At the time it seemed to me that I was asking a great deal of the school in wanting to be there for an extended period of time, working intensively and not acting as a teacher nor in any other capacity which might be of use to the staff or pupils. For this reason it seemed likely that in order to gain worthwhile access (which did not unduly restrict my freedom of manoeuvre or place gross restrictions on the type of contact with pupils or the type of students I could work with) I would need to obtain positive backing for my research.

Negotiating access to do research in schools is relatively straightforward and in a sense the researcher's 'choice' of initial sponsor is dictated by established etiquette. That is, it is normal to first contact the LEA and then to negotiate with the head(s) of the chosen school(s). At either stage the negotiations may be delegated to someone lower than the most senior officer, but the route is essentially the same. This does not leave the researcher entirely powerless to exercise choice, however, and I decided that if sponsorship were such a vital feature of the research it was best to ensure some degree of choice by the way I approached the potential sponsors.

For this reason I contacted two LEAs rather than one and also took the decision that I would find it easier to assess these 'sponsors' by explaining fully what the research was about and what it would demand of the school participating. I considered it would be possible, from the type of questions raised and the ensuing discussion, to assess how much the project was understood and the degree to which it interested the sponsor.

I did not feel that I could promise any short-term benefit to anyone as a result of their participation in the research, because I could see none for them. I imagined this would be one, if not the major, hurdle in gaining access to the school, but in the event it was seen as a minor consideration. Similarly, what I had anticipated would be a difficulty, the length of time to be spent in the school, was welcomed and approved.

After these preliminary discussions I rejected the first LEA contacted, partly on the basis that in both schools organization of the fifth year was not particularly convenient for my purposes, but equally because the persons deputed to consider my application fell short of what I hoped to find in a sponsor. In one case, the need for promising confidentiality was not considered legitimate so that onerous restrictions would have been imposed as a condition of entry. In the other case, and despite my best efforts, the teacher who interviewed me could not be moved from his understanding that I would be asking pupils only about their sex lives, and it was as such that he introduced me to several of his colleagues during lunch. No matter whether this was a genuine misunderstanding or a sophisticated ploy to dissuade me from working in the school, it did not seem a propitious start. In the second borough both the Director of Education and the heads to whom I spoke appeared to grasp more readily what the project was about and what it would entail for them. They also seemed to appreciate the reasons why I was proposing to do the work in the way that I had decided. Finally, they were *interested* in the project, a factor which I thought would probably be of help during the fieldwork, and, just as importantly, in the dissemination of my findings.

During my interview with the head of Torville School we went step by step through my proposed timetable so that he should have a clear picture of the shape of the research and how the classroom observation, interviewing and questionnaires fitted into the scheme, both conceptually and in terms of timing. I was examined conscientiously about my intentions, but at no time did the head ask or expect me to submit my questionnaires and other material for him to approve. He decided that it would be good for the pupils to have a non-teaching adult around with time to ask questions and get them thinking about issues, a 'benefit' which justified my presence, though it was one which I would not have dared propose as being sufficient. I raised the question of parental permission and the ethical issues involved in research of this kind and explained why I wanted to introduce the research to staff and pupils myself, rather than expecting him to do so.

I was able to discuss the research with all teachers who attended an ordinary staff meeting for those who taught in the senior part of the school (where the research was to be carried out). Such meetings were held regularly throughout the term and were chaired by the head. I began by telling them briefly about my work history, stressing that I was not a qualified teacher, would not be teaching in the school and was not attempting to assess their performance, even though I would be attending lessons for two terms. I gave a brief resumé of the research and how I intended to use my time at the school, so that they would have some idea what I would be doing in the classroom and why I wanted to spend so much time there. I underlined that my being in the classroom was mainly aimed at getting to know pupils, giving them a chance to know me, trying to understand what classroom life was like, and so on. I gave assurances that they would not be expected to interrupt their normal teaching routine — I would fit in to the class as best I could — nor would I be asking them to release pupils from their lessons to take part in the project. Finally I made it clear that I would be giving an explanation of the work and the reasons for my presence in the school to all pupils who would form the sample for the study. Teachers raised a number of questions concerning the ethics of the research and, specifically, the issue of pupils' and parents' permission regarding participation. These were fielded by the head, whose view was that permission would only be required from parents in the case of activities which could not be regarded as a normal and expected part of a pupil's attendance at school (for example, being interviewed, filling in a questionnaire). There was no question of requiring parental permission for me to observe and participate in the normal school activities of pupils up to the fifth form. He and the staff decided what went on in the school and he would rely on their professional expertise to decide for themselves whether they would allow me to take part in their classes and to exclude me if they had any worries that my presence was affecting their or the pupils' ability to carry on with their ordinary tasks. (In the event one teacher asked me not to attend two of her lessons in the second term, but invited me back as soon as she felt they had settled down — they had, she thought, 'gone a bit wild' during her absence with flu).

A day before the autumn term (and the main period of fieldwork) began I attended a second staff meeting, this time chaired by the deputy head, attended by all heads of department and whose purpose was to bring together all members of staff new to the school that term. Rather more briefly than at the previous meeting, I again explained my presence in the school, but limited my explanations more to the practical implications for them as teachers than to raising the ethical and conceptual problems which had been discussed at the earlier staff meeting.

On reflection and subsequent discussion with teachers it seems that, apart from any inherent good-will towards me and/or the research, three issues helped to obtain the active cooperation rather than passive compliance of virtually all relevant staff. In the first place, that the head actively sponsored and interceded on my behalf; as I later found out, despite differences of opinion among the staff and between head and teachers, staff respected him and his judgement. I was not at the time aware that a significant minority of the staff were what might be categorized politically as 'active radical left'. My insistence on a non-teaching role was something which they approved and averted any potential difficulties that might otherwise have arisen. Thirdly, *because* I was going to be in the school so long teachers felt confident that not only they, but I also, would have to live with any adverse consequences my presence created.

I had only a brief period of time to talk to each of the five classes, during which I covered what the research was about, explained that I was a researcher, not a teacher or student teacher, and told them how long I would be in the school and why I would be attending their lessons. I said there would be time to ask me more about the research in the next two terms and stressed that they were free to decide for themselves whether they wanted to fill in a questionnaire or be interviewed. I also told them that their parents would be receiving a letter from me asking for their permission for their son or daughter to take part in the research, though nobody would be made to take part just because his/her parents had given permission. There would be no sanctions against those who chose not to take part. Two major areas came up in pupils' questions at these meetings — clarification that I was not a teacher, youth employment officer or education welfare officer and reassurance that I was not 'really' interested in who misbehaved in class.

All these meetings took place during the summer term. Once I had talked to head, staff and pupils I was able to do some pilot work in the class and to spend some time learning about the intricacies of the fifth year timetable and option scheme. The main fieldwork began in the autumn term of 1975 and continued until the end of the spring term in 1976.

I returned to the school towards the end of the summer term (1976) to see the pupils who had been involved in the research. We had a morning together and I talked about some of my preliminary and tentative findings. Their constructive and sceptical comments about the Bem Sex Role Inventory were especially fruitful and have informed the way the BSRI is treated in the thesis. I also spoke to the staff at a staff meeting that day to give them an account of how I was using the material I had gathered from their staffroom and classroom talk.

This was supposed to be my final contact with the pupils and teachers. I spent the rest of the summer analyzing some of the material and getting the questionnaire and BSRI information onto computer. In September I returned to my job from which I had had a year's leave, and resumed work on another research project.

Handling the Data

When I came to writing up I had a mixture of qualitative and quantitative material and the thesis reflects this in a way which I had not envisaged when planning and carrying out the research. For example, my original intention had been to analyze the interview material so that it could be presented quantitatively, alongside the results of the BSRI. The BSRI test results, seen as central up to this point, became a minor part of the written account, and the pupils' own discussions of gender have a more important place in their own right. Thus my conclusions about the BSRI information are moderated and informed by observation, interviews and by pupils' comments. Instead of being treated as an accurate reflection of how pupils saw themselves, the BSRI test results are discussed in the thesis as an indicator of the extent to which pupils were aware of and subscribed to essentially American norms of masculinity and femininity. There was often a big discrepancy between pupils' awareness of what they were 'supposed' to think, feel and do as females or males and their self-descriptions as gendered people, a discrepancy which I was able to observe in their school life. I had set out with the intention of exploring the claim that there were universal connotations to masculinity and femininity, suspecting that this might be a case of ethnocentrism. I thought it likely that pupils from each ethnic group, irrespective of sex, might have different definitions of the most important aspects of masculinity/femininity and that those aspects common to all ethnic groups (if there were any) would be relatively unimportant. So I was disposed to concentrating on similarities between the sexes within an ethnic group and on differences between ethnic groups. To some extent the BSRI results supported this distinction. But what was clearer, particularly from my observations, formal and informal interviews, was that irrespective of how pupils defined masculinity/femininity boys were relatively uncritical in their attitudes to gender, whereas girls had a more critical attitude to it.

One of my reasons for acquiring information about the organization of Torville School was the practical one that I would need
such information to find my way round, to sample classroom time
accurately and so on. I also thought it would be necessary, when
writing up the research to describe Torville as a school, in the belief
that pupils' thinking and talking about gender might be affected by
the institutional setting in which that information was gathered. This
meant describing the salient features of its structure and organization
as well as those which could be thought to have some relevance for
my research focus — gender. Partly because of my initial lack of
confidence in my ability to carry out participant observation, but just
as importantly, because of my training and experience in positivistic
research, it was second nature to attempt to 'control' for possible
sources of bias. Treating observational data as potentially suspect on
the grounds of bias, I ensured that my recordings of observations
were systematic, based on accurate sampling and contained notes on
possible sources of bias. So my own experience of coming to terms
with the institution, documented in my fieldwork diary (written each
evening) and in systematic notes of classroom life, together with
documents (set lists, lists of teachers, who taught which subjects, and
so on) and an analysis of pupils' choices of optional subjects,
provided invaluable material in both selecting and documenting the
salient features of Torville School. It was an institution organized
around gender; a mixed school in which there was considerable
segregation of the sexes (both institutionally imposed and as a result
of pupils' choice of subjects and of out-of-classroom activities); an
organization in which female pupils and teachers had very different
experiences from male pupils and teachers. For example, there were
visible differences in the power and status of women and men
teachers: women made up 48 per cent of the staff, yet virtually all
senior posts (head of department upwards in the hierarchy) were held
by men, a state of affairs which I was able to establish (by analyzing
school documents) had obtained for at least as long as the fifth form
pupils had been attending the school. A significantly higher proportion of women was restricted to teaching pupils aged 11 to 14,
teaching on a separate site from the senior part of the school. More
men than women taught only fifth and sixth form pupils. This created
a sense of the lower school as a female domain and the senior part,
where the relatively prestigious teaching took place, as a male
domain. A very high proportion of school subjects was taught solely
or predominantly by one sex (maths, sciences (except biology) and
'technical' subjects were in this sense 'male'). This resulted in a large

proportion of the pupils with whom I was involved being taught exclusively by male teachers, especially the male pupils, but including those few girls who were taking two science subjects at O-level or CSE.

Consideration of the suitability and legitimacy of school as a location for research which was not 'educational research'; describing the borough and local context of Torville; information about its internal structure and organization became one chapter of the thesis. The best part of two others is given over to an analysis of Torville School as a gendered institution and to a limited comparison of Torville with the national picture in this respect, using DES statistics (DES, 1975 and 1977). At this point in the writing up it became obvious that I had to decide whether to further change the emphasis of the final account from that initially envisaged, and if so to consider what were the possibilities given the material I had. By September 1977 I had made sufficient headway working on the thesis part-time to realize that I wanted to give greater priority to the more ethnographic aspects of the study than to the 'hard' data. Trained in the positivistic tradition (though sceptical of it), and with only this short experience of working in a different tradition, I did not feel safe in relying solely on the qualitative material. Additionally, in changing the focus after the event from pupils' perceptions of gender to their careers as gendered people, I saw that I needed rather more information about the pupils than I had obtained during my time at Torville.

Before making any more decisions, I discussed the issues with Philip Gammage in the School of Education at Bristol, and embarked on a concentrated course of reading about classroom interaction, ethnographic work in schools and the sociology of education, thus for the first time encountering the work of Lacey (1970 and 1976), and the 'new' sociology of education (Young, 1971) and began the work of tracing back studies of classroom interaction from Delamont's (1976) review. It was both exciting and alarming to discover that I had designed a research strategy which had precursors in the field of education. In many ways it was a relief to find that my work was not an oddity, but could be seen as part of the new tradition in the sociology of education. Equally, though, I remember nasty moments like the occasion in the LSE bookshop when I glanced for the first time at the chapter headings in Sharp, Green and Lewis (1975) and thought they had 'got there first' and that any claims to originality in my thesis would be untenable.

I decided that if I concentrated on the qualitative material to hand I would be able to say something about their careers as gendered *pupils* and how, in this particular school, there were structures and processes which countervailed or supported certain norms about gender. This emphasis would allow me to tackle the relationships between gender and race in a more extensive way than I would have done if I had relied on the BSRI test results, but it also pointed up that there was additional information about their careers as pupils which I would still need to obtain. Consequently in December 1977 I sent each young person (now aged 17+) a questionnaire addressed to their parents' home. The questionnaire aimed to discover their CSE/ O-level results and their subsequent school, further education and employment histories. It was eighteen months since I had seen them, but the response rate to this questionnaire (without any follow-up reminders) was 61 per cent: there was no response bias attributable to ethnic group or sex, although 'good' pupils were slightly more likely to return a completed questionnaire than others. (The typology of pupils into good, conspicuous, bad and unobtrusive was derived from a content analysis of teachers' comments on pupils' reports written about fifth year pupils in the school year 1975/76.) This response rate was sufficiently encouraging that I felt able to discuss some of the educational outcomes, thus giving more breadth to the picture of how race and gender mattered for this particular group of young people.

The thesis was submitted to the Sociology Department of the University of Bristol in September 1978. It bears the marks of my ambivalence about the different research traditions, and, I think, some of the positive aspects of a dialogue between the quantitative and qualitative material. Although the work has aroused considerable interest when I have talked about it to groups of teachers and at academic gatherings of various kinds (such as BSA study groups), I have not yet completed the book length manuscript which would make it available to a wider readership. Between submitting the thesis and taking up a new job in September 1979 I wrote two articles, both commissioned and subsequently published (in 1980 and 1982). The new job marked something of a career change in that I moved from full-time research into full-time lecturing and involvement in teacher education particularly. Since that time I have written other articles (also published), developed my research interests along somewhat different lines from those in the thesis and indeed look back with some amazement to a time when research budgets were sufficiently generous and my personal and other commitments so relatively few that I could consider participant observation as a method to be decided upon solely in terms of its appropriateness for my research focus.

Acknowledgements

I should like to record my thanks to Ann Caro, Bob Platt and Clem Adelman with whom I have had fruitful discussions while writing this chapter.

Appendix. Data Sheet for Recording Classroom Notes

Week_____ Date_____ XYZ   Target SS

wib _____	wig _____	Sub _____
eb _____	eg _____	Tname _____
ab _____	ag _____	Pno _____
ob _____	og _____	Rmno _____
Tb _____	Tg _____	

x   x   x   x   x   x   x   x

Special observations_____

Explanatory Notes:

Week   Each full or part week in the autumn and spring terms was numbered consecutively, ignoring the Christmas holiday.

XYZ   There were two forms in which pupils were taking one modern language, one science subject and both history and geography at CSE/O-level; their forms were labelled X_1 and X_2. Pupils taking two science subjects were in form Y_1 or Y_2. Pupils taking two foreign languages were in form Z. Each letter, as appropriate, was circled if there were pupils from the form in the particular lesson being observed.

Target SS   Pupils whom I especially wished to observe were listed in this column.

Left-hand column   Used to record the number of boys present and the number who should have been present. *wib* = West Indian boys, *eb* = White British boys, *ab* = Asian boys, *ob* = other boys, and *Tb* = total number of boys.

Middle column   Used to record similar information about girls, as detailed above.

Mary Fuller

Right-hand column
Sub = subject (for example, maths, French)
Tname = abbreviation for the name of the teacher taking the class or set.
Pno = Period number; indicates the time of day.
Rmno = Room number in which the lesson was taking place.

Special observations   Used to record any information which might affect the observations recorded. Examples include change of room, change of teacher, my state as an observer, reasons for pupils' absence (such as field trips).

References

BEM, S. (1974) 'The measurement of psychological androgyny', *Journal of Consulting and Clinical Psychology*, 42, pp. 155–62.

BEM, S. and WATSON C. (1976) 'Scoring Packet: Bem Sex Role Inventory, mimeo, Stanford University.

BERNARD, J. (1973) 'My four revolutions: An autobiographical history of the ASA', *American Journal of Sociology*, 78, pp. 773–91.

CARLSON, R. (1972) 'Understanding women: Implications for personality theory and research', *Journal of Social Issues*, 28, 2, pp. 17–32.

DELAMONT, S. (1976) *Interaction in the Classroom*, London, Methuen.

DEPARTMENT OF EDUCATION AND SCIENCE (1975) *Curricular Differences for Boys and Girls*, London, HMSO.

DEPARTMENT OF EDUCATION AND SCIENCE (1977) *Statistics of Education, 1975: Volume 4: Teachers*, London, HMSO.

FULLER, M. (1978) Dimensions of Gender in a School, unpublished PhD thesis, University of Bristol.

FULLER, M. (1980a) 'Black girls in a London comprehensive', in DEEM, R. (Ed.) *Schooling for Women's Work*, London, Routledge and Kegan Paul.

FULLER, M. (1980b) 'Growing up black', *New Society*, 18/25 December.

FULLER, M. (1982) 'Young, female and black', in CASHMORE, E. and TROYNA, B. (Eds) *Black Youth in Crisis*, London, Allen and Unwin.

FULLER, M. (1983) 'Qualified criticism, critical qualifications', in BARTON, L. and WALKER, S. (Eds) *Race, Class and Education*, London, Croom Helm.

HARGREAVES, D. (1967) *Social Relations in a Secondary School*, London, Routledge and Kegan Paul.

LACEY, C. (1970) *Hightown Grammar*, Manchester, Manchester University Press.

LACEY, C. (1976) 'Problems of sociological fieldwork: A review of the methodology of "Hightown Grammar"', in HAMMERSELEY, M. and WOODS, P. (Eds) *The Process of Schooling*, London, Routledge and Kegan Paul.

LUPTON, T. (1963) *On the Shop Floor*, Oxford, Pergamon.

ROBERTS, H. (Ed.) (1981) *Doing Feminist Research*, London, Routledge and Kegan Paul.

SHARP, R., GREEN, A. and LEWIS, J. (1975) *Education and Social Control*, London, Routledge and Kegan Paul.

WOLCOTT, H. (1975) 'Criteria for an ethnographic approach to research in schools', *Human Organization*, 34, pp. 111–27.

YOUNG, M.F.D. (Ed.) (1971) *Knowledge and Control: New Directions for the Sociology of Education*, London, Collier-Macmillan.

5 The Man in the Wendy House: Researching Infants' Schools

Ronald King

Editor's Commentary. Ronald King has been a key contributor to the sociology of schools and schooling. His work has predominantly focused on secondary education using a range of research methodologies among which large-scale survey research with a research team has loomed large. While the study that is discussed in this chapter continues to demonstrate King's interest in the process of schooling, it finds him in new territory in infant school classrooms. Here, King used a different range of methods: non-participant observation, interviews and documentary evidence to focus on the work of teachers and pupils in his study, *All Things Bright and Beautiful?*

Ronald King's account demonstrates the way in which an experienced researcher designed, conducted, analyzed and wrote up an observational study over a period of five years. In this respect, King's account has the virtue of covering many key features of the research process. As well as dealing with such practical issues as limiting a field of study, the role of non-participant observer, observing in classrooms and the problem of interviewing pupils aged 5 and 6, Ronald King also examines the relationships between theory and research. He provides a discussion of Weberian action theory and the use of grounded theory. Finally, he turns to the question of how research evidence is received by examining some responses that reviewers have made to his study. In this sense, the chapter takes a broad view of the research process.

Among the questions that Ronald King addresses are: how can a researcher handle a non-participant observer role in a school classroom? In what way can the constant comparative method advocated by grounded theorists be used in the collection and analysis of data? By a detailed discussion of these questions Ronald King shows how the methodological and theoretical skills of the researcher interact with each other throughout the research process.

My research in infants' schools is, in the ordinary sense, completed. The fieldwork, including some 600 hours of observations in the classrooms of thirty-eight teachers in three schools serving different social areas of the same local authority, was spread over the three years 1972–75. The analysis, of about half a million words of the observation notes, school records, children's writing, drawings and reading books, occupied a further year. The writing of the book (King, 1978), which forms the main account, took another year, and, like the fieldwork and analysis, was fitted into my teaching, reading, other writing, and administration. Here, I have taken the opportunity to write about some of the things I did and that happened which were not dealt with, or only briefly so, in the book. These particularly concern my relationships with my research subjects, the interpretation and analysis of the data, the writing of the account and its reception. As here, I continue to draw upon the whole experience, both personally and professionally, not only out of affectionate regard for what was for the most part a rewarding and satisfying time, but also in reflecting on my previous and subsequent research, and on the nature of the sociology of education.

The Origins of the Research

In 1970 the Social Science Research Council gave me a two-year grant to study forms of post-16 education (reported in King, 1976). This included a tertiary college being set up in the pseudonymous Newbridge. Its creation was part of the reorganization of the whole school provision, including the creation of first schools for 5–8-year-olds from the infants' schools. Some unexpected research capacity enabled us to survey these eighteen schools (including infants' departments of primary schools) before reorganization, with the vague plan, not yet fulfilled, to return to them after the changes.

Following some periods of observation in primary schools outside the area, we (that is, my assistants, Joan Fry and Bonnie Lucas, and I) made our Newbridge survey in the summer of 1972. Each headteacher completed a questionnaire, mainly about basic organization, and was later interviewed. Every teacher was also interviewed about their teaching practices and the prospect of reorganization, using a loosely structured schedule. Joan Fry prepared an outline of some of the basic results which was sent to each teacher, but a detailed analysis of the data was not attempted, and much of it remained uninspected until after I had completed the three-year period of lone observations already mentioned.

The setting up of the survey had stimulated my interest in

primary schools and so I applied for a grant from the SSRC to extend the work to other areas using Newbridge as a pilot. I was not disappointed when the application was turned down on the grounds of my not asking for enough time or money, because by that time the experience of going into the schools had persuaded me that I would prefer to carry out a detailed study in a small number of schools. Two other factors were important in this. The first was that I had spent six years directing fairly large-scale research projects, including research assistants and computerized data, and wanted the refreshment of doing something on my own, in my own time. The critical event was when both assistants obtained new jobs and I no longer felt obliged to try to provide for them.

The second factor was the coming of the 'new' sociology of education. Having studied the subject since 1959 and taught it since 1966, I was perhaps, by definition, 'orthodox' (see Gorbutt, 1972). I can still remember my mixed feelings at that time. The arrogant and often ignorant dismissal of previous work, including that of one of my teachers, Jean Floud, was irritating and even hurtful. The promise of new theoretical perspectives, particularly phenomenological, was fascinating and intellectually exciting. But what I responded to most was the attention that was drawn to the neglect of classroom studies. At that time there were very few studies of any kind into infants' education, and so infants' classrooms seemed a good prospect.

The Schools' Sample

I chose to start my observations in the Burnley Road School. Even without detailed analysis the survey had shown it to be conspicuously the most working-class in pupil composition of all Newbridge infants' schools. At my first meeting with Mrs Brown, the head-teacher, without my prompting in any way, referred to Burnley Road as the 'EPA school of Newbridge', a definition subsequently official-ly confirmed by the designation of social priority status by the local authority. Towards the end of my year at Burnley Road I asked the headteacher, Mrs Baker, if I could begin visiting her school, Seaton Park, after the summer holidays. In Seaton Park I hoped to have a school of similar size with a predominantly middle-class composi-tion. After a short time in the school I discovered this was not the case. Due to recent changes in the catchment area the children came from both council and owner occupied houses. However, I decided to continue, a decision I do not regret, but I knew I would have to extend my research to a third school with a more middle-class social composition. As I wanted the schools to be of similar size, I had little choice in asking the help of Miss Fox, the headteacher of the Langley School, the following year.

Access and Sponsorship

Colin Bell (1969) has provided excellent value in his two-page note sketching the dimensions of participant observation. Schools are not, in his terms, open systems, like street corners or discos, with relatively easy access for research purposes, but closed systems requiring 'sponsorship' for entry. In approaching the headteachers I was seeking such sponsorship. However, I was not a complete stranger to them, having been allowed to be an observer at meetings they had attended concerned with primary reorganization. They, and their staff, had all received copies of Joan Fry's outline of the survey results, and had been interviewed either by Joan or Bonnie Lucas.

The research purpose I outlined was vague but honest. There had been little sociological research about infant education and I had a general interest in filling the gap. I stressed my status as a non-expert in infant-school practice, and my professional undertaking to be confidential about anything I heard or saw. This was accepted in that they, and the observed teachers, never asked direct questions about colleagues. Even the oblique enquiries could be dealt with without betraying confidences or causing offence. My assurances were trusted enough for me to be allowed to make notes from the schools' records, and for me to become a confidant of each of the three headteachers in matters concerning staff, plans for the future and even personal matters.

The Teacher Sample and Research Relationships

After our first two-hour meeting Mrs Brown introduced me to Mrs Pink, in her classroom, where I stayed for half an hour. This began my apprenticeship in observation, returning for an hour the next day, the whole morning the day after, and then for four whole days spread over a number of weeks. I originally intended to observe in Mrs Pink's class over the school year to study changing relationships. However, it was clear by half-term that Mrs Pink was pregnant and so I changed my plan so that I observed all the classes. This was accomplished at Burnley Road, but at the two other schools the headteachers asked that I should not include probationer teachers.

Although I was clearly 'sponsored' by each of the headteachers, I took care to ask each teacher privately if she would allow me to observe in her classroom. Their ready acceptance was not, I think, much influenced by my being passed down the hierarchy, but more an indication of the professional assurance of a group of teachers who generally felt themselves to be doing an important job as best they could. No doubt my visits were talked about in my absence, so after a time most teachers I approached had some idea of what to expect in giving me access. They were in any case used to other adults sometimes being in their classrooms, including students and tutors on teaching practice. Most adults who enter classrooms, make value-judgements about what they see. The teacher may not know what these are, but she knows they are being made. By my demeanour and talk I tried to make it clear that my interest was in seeing what happened and trying to understand why it happened. Some found it a little puzzling that a grown man should spend his time in the way I did; I explained it was part of my job. After a few weeks in each school I felt I was considered by most to be fairly benign and certainly no threat. The basis of the research relationship was that the teacher and I were the only adults to have witnessed particular events in her classroom. This was a unique shared experience and some said they found it rewarding and useful to them.

Unlike Stephen Ball, in this volume, I could not have offered to do some teaching in gaining access and approval for the research enterprise since I lacked the professional competences. I was too old to fit either the student-teacher category, as did Sara Delamont, or become an 'honorary pupil', as did Mary Fuller (both in this collection). In my relationships with teachers I drew upon the social qualities of polite acquaintance between middle-class men and women. A few, I felt, would have preferred a closer relationship. My manner was partly a reflection of what I think is my personal style — polite but private — but I was also mindful of the problems of Elizabeth Bott (1957) that followed the forming of friendships with her subjects. As it was, I found it fairly easy to give acceptably brief replies to personal questions, mainly about my own children.

The term 'ethnography' had little currency in the sociology of education when I started the research. Since then it has become an academic cachet applied to many studies using observations, and in some cases those based mainly on interviews. Although I felt I was drawing on the anthropological tradition, I was not concerned with the whole way of life of my subjects, which ethnography usually implies. My interest in the teachers was as teachers. Whilst it was clear that their age, marital status, motherhood and previous teaching did have consequences for their subjective experience of teaching, there was little evidence to relate these clearly to their practices. For example, several with grown-up children, said that their pupils had, in a sense, taken their children's place, but they were not, say, obviously more professionally affectionate than their colleagues. In addition, as in all research, I was in Devon's and Gluckman's (1964) terms 'delimiting the field'. 'Within a field thus delimited and isolated the social scientist assumes that there is a system of interrelations which can be considered separately from the rest of society' (p. 17). My field was 'the school', so that although I spent most time in classrooms, I also attended school assemblies, sports days, carol concerts, parents' meetings, went with teachers on playground and dinner duties, and spent time in the staffroom and with teacher helpers, speech therapist, education welfare officer, and longer periods with the headteachers.

My research interest in the children was similarly delimited to their being pupils at school. My knowledge of their home lives as brothers, sisters, sons, daughters, and so on was similar to that available to their teachers. This included their dress and state of cleanliness, their reports of home made at 'news time', their explanations of some of their drawings, their responses to teachers' direct questions, observations of parents bringing them to school and talking to teachers, sometimes at special meetings, notes written by parents about illness or absence, notes made by speech therapists, education welfare officers and educational psychologists, and even reports of crime and divorce in the local newspapers. Thus I had access to much the same kind of information that the teachers used in defining the home backgrounds of individual children and 'children in this school'.

Non-Participant Observation and Recording

Colin Bell points out that 'participant observation' varies from total participation with no observation, to observation with no participation. I learnt to use something close to the latter, which is why I described my method as non-participant observation, although this is usually applied to covert observing. I did allow myself to be approached by children to begin with, but I soon found that they treated me as a teacher-surrogate as they did other non-teacher adults, showing pictures, asking me spellings, which I sensed Mrs Pink was not happy with and which prevented my observing clearly and researching effectively. My routine became to spend a short first visit to a new classroom, making no notes, to be observed by the children rather than to observe. This was to allow the teacher and the children to get over any unease or curiosity. I politely refused requests for help, referring the child to the teacher, and met requests for approval only with smiles. To begin with I kept standing so that physical height maintained social distance. Most importantly, I avoided eye contact; if you do not look, you will not be seen. These measures led to my being, for the most part, ignored by the children in my later visits (although I did sometimes talk to individual children). I tested this by moving from one observation spot to another, and then noting some children looking at where I had been, before finding me in the new position. I found it helped to sit down at this later stage, often using furniture or even the unoccupied Wendy House as a convenient 'hide'. This was not deliberate concealment, but an attempt to be unobtrusive. Other adults entering the classroom would usually not see me.

Overt observations of social relationships involve a relationship between observer and observed. I found it easier to present my observations as being of the children, but every teacher knew she was also being observed. I usually asked if my presence had changed things, and, sometimes without my asking, they usually said, by a second visit, that they had forgotten I was there. It seemed to me that a few times I was given a special performance, and it was not unusual for a private remark explaining an activity to be made to me in the classroom. My intended relationship with the teacher was that of an interested, non-judgemental observer.

Many observational studies of classrooms concentrate on the ways teachers control pupils' behaviour. This may sometimes be an end in itself, part of Durkheim's (1961) moral education or the absurdly named 'hidden' curriculum (see Dale, 1977), but the overt curriculum tends to be neglected. After a few weeks of observations I felt I had a fairly clear idea of the pattern of teacher control, and began to take an interest in their purposes in so doing, other than the desire for order. These were principally the teaching and learning of reading, writing, number and craft skills. To this end, I borrowed copies of reading and mathematics texts, and obtained samples of children's writing and pictures. With the help of my elder daughter, I took an inventory of all the contents of one classroom. It took half a day to note everything in this emporium.

My main method of recording was to make direct notes whenever possible in a pocket sized notebook. I concentrated on recording what seemed to be significant incidents including talk. (Politeness forebade my writing notes in the staffroom, and like Whyte (1955) I found new uses for the lavatory.) I acknowledge that it is impossible to record everything, but I am reasonably confident that records of speech events were fairly accurate. With the teachers' permission and knowledge I did tape record some classroom sessions, and comparisons of the transcripts with my written notes showed a fair correspondence. As soon as possible after each session I would read through my notes and then make notes on them.

The observations and notes were the first steps in the establishment of the social structure of infants' classrooms. Here, following Collins (1975), I am using a non-reified definition of structure as the repeated patterns of purposeful behaviour of the participants in a defined social situation. It took a number of hours before I saw any pattern to Mrs Pink's and her pupils' behaviour, a diurnal pattern only appreciated by whole day observations, usually two, non-consecutively, with each teacher. To be in a classroom before school started, and to observe the familiar patterns of social relationships as the teacher and children arrived, was to see the creation of a social structure. Also, as the day continued, to see how this structure was not static but a process — the continued interactions of the participants. None of them was 'inside' the classroom structure; what they repetitively did *was* the structure.

The observed structure of relationships in Mrs Pink's classroom became a first stage ideal type, in that my observations in the second class I visited were, almost in the act of observation, compared with incidents in Mrs Pink's class. Effectively Mrs Pink was my ideal typical infants' teacher. Observations of successive teachers led to the creation of my social type infants' teacher, and therefore social type infants' classroom. This is Popper's (1957) methodological individualism; the study of the actions of individuals in order to explain social 'wholes', in my case the social structure of infants' classrooms. It was not my purpose to explain why individuals per se behaved as they did. That would be psychology not sociology, and as Devons and Gluckman (1964) advise, 'the cobbler should stick to his last'. Each teacher (and child) was, of course, an individual, and the slight differences in their actions may be accounted for in these terms. But they had far more in common with one another, and this was social, that is, they shared the acquired characteristics of infants' teachers.

The more I observed, the more familiar and predictable events became, so much so that towards the end of the research what was at first interesting was sometimes rather boring, and I made my notes shorter. I regret this in retrospect because it meant I could not attempt any simple quantifications. For example, if I had recorded every occasion a teacher publicly reproved children's behaviour I might have been able to show different incidences in the three schools.

Interviews and Understanding

My use of an action approach in research predates the new sociology of education, and, despite the attraction of the Schutzian phenomenological element, my basic source was Weber, particularly through the treatments of Collins (1975) and Rex (1973). Weberian action theory presents the opportunity to make explanations of human social behaviour which acknowledge that social structure is inseparable from the subjective meanings of the individuals whose repeated behaviour constitutes the structure (King, 1980). For the most part the social structure of a classroom was arranged or allowed by the teacher, my efforts were therefore concentrated on the understanding of her meanings in so doing.

My method in doing this was often no method at all. Knowing I had observed a particular incident, the teacher would often comment upon it, sometimes in the classroom, but more commonly outside during the break, or at the end of morning or afternoon school. Whilst observing I would keep a written aide memoire of questions to ask about why specific things happened, which I would use if the points were not covered in the interview conversation. With time and familiarity I would sometimes suggest why a teacher had done something; usually with an 'of course' kind of confirmation. These loosely structured interviews gave not only retrospective accounts of actions, 'because' motives in Schutz's (1972) terms, but also his 'in order to' kind, in that she often explained something that she planned to happen next. This distinction of Schutz is one of his criticisms of Weber's action approach, but in real social action, rather than talking about it in prospect or retrospect, the exigencies of doing, particularly of habituated behaviour, leave meanings in a largely unexamined, taken for granted state. When 'in order to' motives are fulfilled then they are the same as 'because' motives.

I am aware of my neglect of the meanings of the most numerous participants — the children. It is possible to make imputations of meanings through direct observations, and the affective elements of young children's actions seem clear and unfeigned, through their facial, bodily and oral expressions. I assumed that a 5- or 6-year-old who cried was probably upset and one that laughed was happy; assumptions not always justified with adults. Interviewing individual 5- or 6-year-olds was difficult. When I tried it, I got down to their physical level and usually asked 'why' questions about specific incidences. Any accidentally leading questions were always affirmed. 'Yes' is easier to say than 'no'. I did not get very near to the typical child's meanings of classroom activities. The power of the teacher in deciding and controlling these is usually legitimized at a taken for granted level, although I have described situations where this was not so.

Mackay (1970) has been critical of what might be called the deficit model of children as lacking basic social competences, claiming the existence of a culture of childhood, on the slender evidence of the Opies' (1958) study of playground activities. The studies directed by Cicourel (1974), of which Mackay's is a part, have dealt only with investigations of the meanings of individual young children, where, with typical ethnomethodological solipsism, each child's reality is judged to be paramount, and the imposition of the teacher's definition an affront to the investigators' romantic individualism. There are considerable methodological problems in investigating the social (that is, shared) subjectivities of small children. Questionnaires are impossible and interviews difficult, although David Hartley (1977) has had some success with infants' school children. Whatever their competencies in relation to other children and to adults, such as parents and teachers, they seem to lack those for being interviewed. It could be that they have not become sufficiently reflexive about their experiences to recount their motives. As Brian Davies (1976) points out, Mackay's interpretation of the child Tom's meaning of the story of Chicken Little is based upon what Tom said, and not on his account of what he said, so that we learn more about the subjectivity of Mackay than of Tom.

Before I started the research I was rather impressed by the grounded theory of Glaser and Strauss (1968), and took seriously their idea of the investigator putting his or her theories to the subjects of investigation.[1] I never considered doing this with the children, but in each school at the end of the period of investigation I did so with the whole staff, where I invited them to comment on my explanation of what I had seen. (At Seaton Park and Langley I structured the occasions by the use of a list of topics given out at the meeting; a copy of one is appended.) Their general assent may have been partly due to politeness (but this did not prevent a few objections being made), or the presence of the headteacher. With certain reservations I will come to later, these meetings seemed an acceptable way of testing one kind of validity. They were an important contribution to my attempts to make my explanations, in Weber's (1947) terms, adequate at the level of meaning. This is the process of *Verstehen* which requires 'that the sociologist go through a process of re-socialisation into his subjects' social world, that is their commonsense constructs and experience' (Leat, 1972); the attempt to realize the course of the typical teachers' purposeful behaviour in the classroom. I felt I had succeeded when, after one meeting, a teacher said, 'You've really got us taped'.

The teachers had given me their time and access to their classrooms, and I felt, if only on the grounds of politeness, I should give something back. The opportunity to talk about their work with what I hope was a sympathetic non-judgemental, interested person, with no authority over them, seemed welcomed by many. The group meetings were a way in which I as a guest for a year in each school explained what I had been doing. For some of them, particularly in working-class Burnley Road, these meetings were also occasions where they realized how much they had in common with one another (they never stepped beyond the threshold of a colleague's classroom without tacit permission), and that many of what they as individuals defined as problems were problems for others too.

The Comparative Method

Glaser and Strauss, and Weber long before them, advocated the comparative method. I used it within schools and between schools. Mrs Pink at Burnley Road was my ideal type infants' teacher and her class my ideal type social structure. Each new class I observed was compared with the combined common features of all the previous ones to arrive at the typical Burnley Road teacher and classroom. The move to the second school, Seaton Park (serving a more mixed social area), was an attempt to find out which features of the social structure of Burnley Road classrooms were particular and which were common. This process was extended at Langley (serving a mainly middle-class area), so that not only the typical features of each school became clearer, but also the typical features of all three.

The discovery of the small number of what I called 'deviant' teachers was very important in confirming what I had supposed to be typical features, a diagnosis confirmed by the headteachers independently defining them as not being 'proper' infants' teachers, and by their own awareness and acknowledgement of their atypicality, explained by both parties as being due to their not being 'infant trained'. The career of an observer proceeds from being an outsider, where what the participants regard as unremarkable is seen as strange, to being an insider, where the observer shares their taken for grantedness of events. In my experience this measure of 'going native' did not lead to only the expected being observed. Each of my encounters with the few 'deviant' teachers was a mild jolt to my expectations. The relative absence of the professional affection, pleasantness and equanimity, and use of oblique control typical of their colleagues, was apparent within minutes.

The extent to which I could include the teachers' validations of my interpretations was limited by the ethics of confidentiality. When I asked Mrs Baker of Seaton Park for help I told her I had spent time at Burnley Road, and later told Miss Fox at Langley I had been to the two previous schools. They may have had some idea of this and would certainly have found out since I told each where I was leaving for, and they saw one another at occasional meetings of headteachers in the area. However, I was careful to say nothing about the schools previously visited, and, although sometimes curious, the headteachers asked few questions. This behaviour was an assurance that *their* confidences would also be respected.

I did not tell the teachers in the second and third schools where I had been before, although a few indicated that they knew, possibly through the headteachers. The respecting of confidences within schools was not a problem in that I presented to the group of teachers my interpretation of the typical teacher in that school. But this meant that my between-school comparisons could not be presented, and so the explanations I was able to make to them of their school were lacking some of the evidence used. This was particularly so at the third school, and was partly the reason why the teachers at the two meetings held there did not agree with some of the points of my presentation. Unlike teachers at Burnley Road and Seaton Park, those at Langley did not define 'the children in this school' as being discrepant with how they 'ought' to be. My suggestion that this may be explained in terms of the children's background was refuted by some who claimed it was due to their good teaching, but my assurances of confidentiality prevented me from referring to the other schools to illustrate my view. That Glaser and Strauss do not consider this limitation on the researcher/researched relationship may be an indication of the relative importance of privacy in British and American culture.

Data Analysis

The process of analysis was a continuous one. In the act of observing I would often be effectively analyzing the course of action as it occurred, so that my notes not only recorded what happened but also my preliminary interpretation of what happened. Effectively this was a process of my typifying typical actions. I invented names for these, some quite quickly. For example, having observed for only two and a half hours I detected what I subsequently named the 'product/effort dilemma' concerned with children's craft work and paintings. The teachers valued these efforts as an expression of the children's natural development, but when these were on public display recognized that some parents judged the product. Reluctantly and sometimes covertly, some teachers strengthened the outlines of children's pictures and even added details. I had created enough of these named typical actions to make them the basis of the presentation of my observations to the teachers at Burnley Road at the end of my year there. Some were modified but most survived to be presented, with others, to the teachers at Seaton Park and Langley (see Appendix).

When I had finished my observations in all three schools I read through all my field notes annotating them as I went, marking up typical actions such as 'politeness', 'reading', 'parents', and so on. I then collated all of these separately, but under subheadings for each school. I will illustrate this process of abstracting and collating with one example.

Mrs Gold was the second teacher I observed at work at Burnley Road. My first visit was for forty minutes, making no notes on the spot, but writing up some soon after. My second visit, two days later, was for the whole day starting at 8.50 a.m. By 3.20 p.m. I had made some 2500 words of notes. My actual notes until 3.30 p.m. were as follows. (The quotations are of the teacher — T.)

3.20 'Stop painting'
New girl using dustpan and brush. T. 'I'm glad to see you're sweeping.'

> Three boys struggle over puzzle — it drops. Scolded
> by T. made to do it.
> 3.25 'It's just about time to clear up.'
> 3.30 Big clear up. 'Stop what you are doing.' End of
> afternoon. 'Boys like aeroplanes.' To girl trying to take
> over aeroplane puzzle from boy.

Three years later, the 'boys like aeroplanes' section was annotated 'sex differences' and collated with forty-one other examples.

I next began to analyze documentary evidence. (A preliminary analysis had been made of some from the second school, Seaton Park, and, at the headteacher's request, made available to the teachers). Data from registers, records and confidential files were collated for simple quantification where possible. Teachers' written comments on children were classified on the same basis as the observations. For example, 'quiet' and 'noisy' were used by teachers in the classroom in controlling children, when talking about children to me and others, and in making written reports on the children. Examples of children's writing and drawing were all read and inspected, and then classified using the teachers' criteria of content. For example, children's written stories were classified into those where there was a domestic setting and those with reference to fighting and violence. The independent variables in their analysis were based upon differences expressed by the teachers: age and sex of pupils, and, in one school, housing class.

The analysis of children's reading books involved reading all thirty-seven of them, writing a synopsis of each story and a description of the accompanying drawings. The emergent categories were 'real life' (Peter and Jane), 'animal-humanoid' (lost kittens) and 'traditional story world' (princesses and magic). In addition to the analysis of these 'found' data, I carried out an analysis of the enumeration district census figures for Newbridge to characterize the school catchment areas, in terms of social composition, housing, and so on.

The analysis of a course of action illuminates its elements but loses some of its integrity. In delineating the process of teachers' typifying individual children, the different elements were quite clear — peer-group relations, learning progress, compliance with rules, pathological state, home/family conditions — but the relation between them was not. I examined all of my sources of these elements, teachers' accounts of individual children, teachers' public reference to individual children and written records, and collated all the examples of two or more elements occurring together. After several attempts all the relationships among separate elements were summarized verbally and expressed in a figure which was in good fit with the few examples of typifications where all the elements were present.

> Each child possesses a unique, developing personality, which is expressed in his or her compliance with classroom rules, relationships with other children, and learning progress, each of which may influence the others. Children change naturally as they develop, but changes may also be due to changes in home or family circumstances, or illness (King, 1978, p. 60).

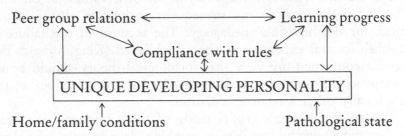

My theoretical touchstone whilst observing and analyzing was W.I. Thomas's (1928) definition of the situation, 'If men define situations as real, they are real in their consequences.' I had seen its potential, having read about it in Silverman's (1970) advocacy of an action approach to organizations. In several ways this is a neat summary of Weber's view of social action (see Mennell, 1974). Observations of social behaviour form the basis of an investigator's imputation of the subject's definition of real consequences, and, therefore, if the behaviour is repeated, of 'real' situations. I introduced the Thomas theorum to the teachers at the group meetings, and used it in my explanations of their practices, starting with their taken for granted definitions of young children and their concomitant child-centred recipe ideology of practice. Bearing in mind the relativist element in this, I was careful not to appear critical or to undermine the basis of their professional activities, confining myself to pointing out, for example, that not everybody defines young children as basically innocent in the intentions of their behaviour (a distinctive element of the infant teacher's ideology).

Writing the Account and its Reception

When I started the research there was little on the sociology of infants' classrooms, but before I had finished two other studies had been published which influenced my own writing. In 1974 the book by Brandis and Bernstein reported an analysis of teachers' extra-classroom, investigator-structured assessments of infant pupils. I sent a copy of the preliminary analysis of the Seaton Park records of teachers' assessments of children to Professor Bernstein, pointing out some similarities and differences. In reply he sent me a pre-publication copy of his article 'Class and Pedagogies: Visible and Invisible', which is not based upon original or any other empirical research (see Bernstein, 1975). Having read this complicated paper several times, I tried to incorporate in my observations at the third school, Langley, and in my subsequent analysis of all the data, a search for the 'invisible' pedagogy. The account of my failure to establish its real existence has been published (King, 1979).[2] This exercise confirmed my view that sociological theory should be the attempt to explain the empirically realized social behaviour of real people; any other kind is speculation.

Sharp and Green's (1975) study of three teachers, one head-teacher and a few children in one, working-class, infants' school was published after my fieldwork was completed. Their reliance on 'probing' interviews posing abstract questions was in contrast to my extensive observations. Their apparently retrospective Marxist ana-lysis (see Hargreaves, 1978) assumed a massive false consciousness on the part of the teachers, and confirmed my adherence to a Weberian perspective taking into account the meanings of those whose be-haviour we attempt to explain. Their analysis of Mapledene school traduces infant education in a way that still affronts me on behalf of teachers, including those they studied.

I had both of these studies in mind in my writing of the book, although my brief comments on them are confined to one chapter. Sociologists of education have a dilemma when they write books (as distinct from journal articles and theses). Who are we writing for: a readership of sociologists or a non-specialist one of teachers and students? There is the necessity to present theories, methods and results for academic scrutiny, and the desire to reach as many readers as possible. I attempted to orientate my writing more towards the non-sociological reader. In doing so I tried to imagine what one of 'my' teachers would have made of Bernstein's article, or what one of Sharp and Green's subjects would have felt about the explanations offered in their book. I want my account to be accessible, and free from gratuitous 'theorizing'. I wanted it to respect the integrity of those who helped me, and to confirm my own.

The main problem in writing an account of observational

research is what to leave out. I had to choose one or two examples from sometimes dozens to illustrate a particular activity. The reader must accept that the selection is fair and representative. In an account of a questionnaire survey almost all the data are literally on, or rather in, the table(s). (No-one expects the completed questionnaires to be appended). Most of my data remain private.

Bell points out that my kind of investigation, overt observations in a 'closed' system, means that the subjects may anticipate publication and may react to reading it. There is another variable in this — the degree of confidentiality. Some studies name the institution and even the individuals involved. Under these conditions it is common for a draft of a report of the investigation to be shown to those named, which may pre-empt any adverse reaction. However, published accounts of research are not written for the subjects' sake, and are not necessarily validated by their approval. As Rex points out, the sociologist has 'the capacity to make observations of social reality distinct from those of participant actors.' I had seen more teachers at work, for longer periods of time, in different schools, than any of the teachers or headteachers, individually or collectively. I made these observations on the understanding that confidences would be respected, which meant that pseudonyms were used. In these circumstances it would not have been easy to show pre-publication drafts without revealing identities. I sent copies of the book to the headteachers without comments, other than unspecified thanks. In meeting two of them separately, both commented on the book using the pseudonyms I invented.

The more detailed a study is, the more likely it is that some readers may make imputations of the origins of the reported observations. This is an obvious possibility with headteachers, there being only one per school. Many of the things I observed were not socially significant in the classroom context, for example, the physical appearance of individual teachers, and were not reported. I did preserve the distinction between Miss and Mrs although this was not significant in this sense.

An after-publication experience of mine was not a happy one, and in referring to it I am being carefully circumspect, for ethical and legal reasons. If the author of a report about research, carried out with assurances of confidentiality and written using pseudonyms, is accused by an individual of having falsely reported that individual's behaviour, the author is faced with a set of dilemmas, particularly under the threat of legal action. If the author knows that the complainant is correct in identifying him or herself in the report, then the author could either lie and deny this to the complainant, or confirm it. The honest latter course would immediately renege on the assurances of confidentiality given not only to the complainant, but also to many others who would be easily identifiable by association. If this were followed, then there would also be the problem of showing that the offending observations were accurate. Unless such revelations were kept scrupulously private, they would be likely to exacerbate the situation. But showing that the observations were accurately reported would be the only way to avoid the impugning of the researcher's integrity. There seem to be two ways of avoiding this possible unpleasantness. One is, be careful in writing to make individual identification difficult. This may mean leaving out important material, or the use of a safe but unsatisfactory vagueness, or even as Ball did, deliberately mislead sometimes. An alternative was used by Patrick (1973). Keep away from the area where the research was done and publish your account after some years' interval (not a help in an academic career).

Once a book (or article) is published it leaves the author's control, and readers can make what they can or want of it. There are two possible sources of readers' reactions; letters and reviews. Some publishers collate reviews of their authors' books, but not Wiley, so I can only comment briefly on a few that I have seen. The earliest, by Joan Tamburrini (*The Times Educational Supplement*, 24 November 1978) accepted the validity of my account, but used it to be critical of some of the reported infants' school practices. However, another expert, Joan Tough (*Journal of Educational Administration and History*, 23, 1, 1981), dismissed it as stereotypical expectations confirming those stereotypes. Nell Keddie (*British Journal of Sociology*, 31, 3, 1980) picked out sections to make her familiar point about the primacy of children's presenting culture. Her comment on the lightness of the sociological theory was one I expected, which may explain why no review has appeared in *Sociological Review* or *Sociology*. (Or is it because of what might be regarded as the book's frivolous title?) This was seen as a virtue in an embarrassingly good, but not uncritical, review by Rex Gibson, whom I've never met (*Higher Education Review*, 3, 2, 1979). Unfortunately, no-one else seems to regard it as 'probably one of the most important texts in the sociology of schooling to appear in the last decade; it is certainly one of the best.' It is not false modesty to say that I do not expect this view to be widely shared, for at least two reasons. Firstly, books or articles that gain quick and wide recognition are usually the author's first. My news was delivered by an old messenger. Secondly, my theoretical stance was, and is, at variance with the social phenomenology and the neo-Marxism that predominate in British sociology of education. However, I've always sought and found private and professional satisfaction in doing research and in writing about it, irrespective of its reception.

As may be expected most correspondents were complimentary about the book, if only out of politeness. I was particularly pleased with two letters. A colleague in another institution sent me some of his teaching material in which he referred to my research as 'sociology with a human face'. An infants' headteacher wrote that she had been laughing with recognition of the familiarity of some of what I had described. A Japanese translation is to be published soon; I enjoy the thought that it may amuse as well as inform those who read it.

The Lessons Learnt

Any account of research is a fragment of indirect autobiography, especially when the writer has been the sole researcher. Despite the occasional longueurs of familiarity towards the end of my three-year spread of observations and the unpleasant episode obliquely referred to, my experience of the research was a rewarding one, both professionally and personally. Doing it helped me to sort out my own views about the nature of the sociology of education, making sense of, perhaps justifying, what I had done before, and guiding what I have done since (for example, King, 1982). If, as I believe, our purpose is to explain the patterns of social behaviour of real people, then we should be empirical and not speculative, analytical rather than critical, and we should attempt to avoid value-judgements rather than make them. None of this is easy, but it is what I tried to do, and it is enough, for me, to have tried.

Notes

1 This corresponds to Schutz's (1954) 'postulate of adequacy'. Curiously, Glaser and Strauss make no reference to Schutz.
2 It was an editorial condition of publication that Bernstein be allowed to reply to the article. Disappointingly, he did not.

Appendix. Notes Used at Two Meetings with Seaton Park Teachers

Classroom Observations

1 The research.
2 How it was done.
3 *The basic sociological proposition* 'If men define situations as real, they are real in their consequences' (W.I. Thomas).
4 *The basic definition of the pupils.*
5 How it comes to be made.
6 The 'theory' used to explain it.
7 The 'evidence' used to support the theory.
8 Why this theory?
9 *The consequences of holding this definition* (a) economy of praise; (b) emphasis on politeness, tidiness, respect for property; (c) emphasis on 'work' over 'play'; (d) increasing range of experiences.
10 *Subgroups of children* (a) 'nice' children from 'good' homes; (b) children from one-parent families.
11 *Social control in the classroom* Essentially mysterious. Successful techniques: (a) Public voice/private voice (b) Eye-scanning and contact. (c) Explicit expectations, approval/disapproval. Other techniques: shaming, blaming and naming (act/individual). Telltales, feigned ignorance, threats, irony, sarcasm, jokes, smacking, games, question and answer, parent reference, headteacher reference. Also: silly question, no-need-to-answer question, thinking and wishing aloud.
    Teacher voices: 'now we are going to do something exciting' voice; 'I am being very patient with you' voice; slightly aggrieved sad voice; 'do as I say' no-nonsense voice; 'Oh never mind let's not have a fuss' voice.
12 *Value-orientations in the classroom*

Sensible/silly	Clean/dirty
Tidy/untidy	Nice/nasty
Helpful/unhelpful	Thrift/wasteful
New/old	Quiet/noisy
Busy/lazy	Work/play
Hard/easy	Outcome (product)/effort
Big/little	Polite/rude
Unhappy/happy	Good/naughty

13 *The nature of school 'work'* Who is it done for? Relationship to 'play'. Sequences of learning — transmission of meanings — order/disorder. Conventional reality.
    Latent learning. Polyphasic learning/teaching.
14 *Being the teacher* Professional equanimity and pleasantness, posture, voice, dress. Ownership of classroom.
    Preservation of self.
    The 'good' teacher: busy hum, pupil's behaviour in public places, performance in prayers, early arrival, late departure, appearance of room, quality of craft work, methods, disposition and demeanour.

15 *Playtime* Cathartic theory.
16 The idea of the sacred and concepts of authority.
17 *Being the sociologist* Taken for granted. What everyone knows. Exchange.

References

BELL, C. (1969) 'A note on participant observation', *Sociology*, 3, 3, pp. 417–18.
BERNSTEIN, B.B. (1975) *Class, Codes and Control, Vol. 3*, London, Routledge and Kegan Paul.
BOTT, E. (1957) *Family and Social Network*, London, Tavistock.
BRANDIS, W. and BERNSTEIN, B.B. (1974) *Selection and Control*, London, Routledge and Kegan Paul.
CICOUREL, A.V. *et al.* (1974) *Language and School Performance*, New York, Academic Press.
COLLINS, R. (1975) *Conflict Sociology*, New York, Academic Press.
DALE, R. (1977) 'The hidden curriculum of teaching', in GLEESON, D. (Ed.) *Identity and Structure*, Driffield, Nafferton.
DAVIES, B. (1976) *Social Control and Education*, London, Methuen.
DEVONS, E. and GLUCKMAN, M. (1964) 'Introduction' to GLUCKMAN, M. (Ed.) *Closed Systems and Open Minds*, Edinburgh, Oliver and Boyd.
DURKHEIM, E. (1961) *Moral Education*, New York, Free Press.
GLASER, B.G. and STRAUSS, A.L. (1968) *The Discovery of Grounded Theory*, London, Weidenfeld and Nicholson.
GORBUTT, D. (1972) 'The new sociology of education', *Education for Teaching*, 49, pp. 3–11.
HARGREAVES, D.H. (1978) 'Whatever happened to symbolic interactionism?' in BARTON, L. and MEIGHAN, R. (Eds) *Sociological Interpretations of Schooling and Classrooms*, Driffield, Nafferton.
HARTLEY, J.D. (1977) 'Some consequences of teachers' definitions of boys and girls in two infants' schools', unpublished PhD University of Exeter.
KING, R.A. (1976) *School and College: Studies of Post-Sixteen Education*, London, Routledge and Kegan Paul.
KING, R.A. (1978) *All Things Bright and Beautiful? A Sociological Study of Infants' Classrooms*, Chichester, Wiley.
KING, R.A. (1979) 'The search for the "invisible" pedagogy', *Sociology*, 13, 3, pp. 445–58.
KING, R.A. (1980) 'Weberian perspectives and the study of education', *British Journal of Sociology of Education*, 1, 1, pp. 7–23.
KING, R.A. (1982) 'Organizational change in secondary schools: An action approach', *British Journal of Sociology of Education*, 3, 1, pp. 3–18.
LEAT, D. (1972) 'Misunderstanding Verstehen', *Sociological Review*, 20, 1, pp. 19–38.
MACKAY, R. (1970) 'Conceptions of childhood and models of socialization', in DREITZEL, H.P. (Ed.) *Recent Sociology*, Vol. 2, London, Macmillan.

Ronald King

MENNELL, S.J. (1974) *Sociological Theory: Uses and Unities*, London, Nelson.

OPIE, I. and OPIE, P. (1958) *The Lore and Language of Children*, Oxford, Oxford University Press.

PATRICK, J. (1973) *A Glasgow Gang Observed*, London, Methuen.

POPPER, K.R. (1957) *The Poverty of Historicism*, London, Routledge and Kegan Paul.

REX, J. (1973) *Discovering Sociology*, London, Routledge and Kegan Paul.

SCHUTZ, A. (1954) 'Concept and theory formation in the social sciences', *Journal of Philosophy*, 51, 9, pp. 257–73.

SCHUTZ, A. (1972) *The Phenomenology of the Social World*, London, Heinemann.

SHARP, R. and GREEN, A. (1975) *Education and Social Control*, London, Routledge and Kegan Paul.

SILVERMAN, D. (1970) *The Theory of Organizations*, London, Heinemann.

THOMAS, W.I. (1928) *The Child in America*, New York, Knopf.

WEBER, M. (1947) *The Theory of Social and Economic Organization*, translated by A.M. Henderson and T. Parsons, New York, Free Press.

WHYTE, W.F. (1955) *Street Corner Society*, 2nd ed., Chicago, University of Chicago Press.

6 The Modification of Method in Researching Postgraduate Education

Mary A. Porter

Editor's Commentary. Traditionally, most ethnographic studies have been designed and conducted by a lone researcher. Furthermore, those ethnographies that have been conducted in educational settings have focused upon schools and classrooms. It is, therefore, in several senses, that the project discussed in this chapter raises new issues, for it was designed by John Wakeford (the project director) and principally conducted by Mary Porter and her fellow researcher, Sue Scott. The substantive focus was upon higher education and in particular postgraduate students who were engaged in part-time study in departments of sociology in different parts of the United Kingdom.

　　As there was relatively little previous research in this field of study and few requirements made by the project director, Mary Porter and Sue Scott found themselves in an area where they had space to develop methodological as well as substantive contributions. As Porter demonstrates, the problem that she had to resolve in these circumstances was how to handle project relations which had a direct influence on the research process. Her chapter directly addresses the question: how does a researcher modify 'methods' throughout a research project? On the basis of her experiences she is able to move from the project's origin and design to the modification of that design and the process of redesign that occurred while she was in the field.

　　In common with many other contributors she discusses key phases and key methods involved in the research process: gaining access, sampling and in-depth interviewing. However, she demonstrates how she was continually involved in modifying the director's research design as well as modifying established research procedures associated with interviewing. Her chapter, therefore, contributes to our knowledge of the design and redesign of social research as well as to a growing body of literature on project relations, collaborative research and team-based work.

The norms of professional sociology militate against self criticism: any expression of 'doubts' about the conduct of a project tends to raise doubts about the validity of the findings through a kind of 'guilt by association'. The ideology of scientism is responsible for this narrow view of research, by which, in the absence of any *reported* difficulties, each report confers on itself the badge of respectability.

(Payne *et al.*, 1981, p. 182)

I am acutely aware of the truth of the above statement as I embark on an account of the Postgraduate Research Project at Lancaster University on which I worked as a research associate for three years.[1] It is important, however, to emphasize that the production of ethnographic data and ideas is the result of social processes which should be documented in order that ethnography as a mode of research can develop and future researchers can learn from our lessons. Unless we are willing to document these ups and downs of the research process, and the particular social contexts in which they occur, our chosen field will stagnate.

It will be shown in this chapter that there are specific issues raised when ethnographic work is carried out by someone other than the individual who made the original research design. An ethnographic approach to the sociology of postgraduate education constantly generates new data which influence the course of research and cause modifications to be made.

Setting Up the Project

The Lancaster project was affiliated to the department of sociology at that university and was under the directorship of Dr John Wakeford, a senior lecturer in the department. He appointed Sue Scott and myself as research officers on the project and we all appointed Jackie Covill as secretary. Prior to this I had been working on a study of vandalism in Oldham, having recently graduated from Manchester University with a degree in social anthropology. Sue Scott was a part-time postgraduate at Lancaster doing various teaching jobs as well as her research, and Jackie Covill had recently moved to Lancaster from London where she had been a bilingual secretary.

My first knowledge that there was to be a study of part-time postgraduates was at the end of October 1978 when I saw an advertisement in *The Guardian* for two research associates. They were to 'work on a longitudinal study of the process and context of postgraduate research in sociology and social administration'. The advertisement went on, 'They should be prepared to spend a considerable proportion of their time carrying out interviews in various parts of the country'. Having to submit five copies of the application almost put me off before I started. However, I applied and the following January I was called for an interview.

At that time my understanding of the background to the project was that there had been discussions between the British Sociological Association (BSA) and the Social Science Research Council (SSRC) about the position of part-time postgraduates in sociology and social administration, including their lack of funding and their low completion rates. John Wakeford was one of the people representing the BSA when these discussions took place although I am not familiar with the details of the meetings. Following these discussions Wakeford applied to the SSRC for funding to conduct a longitudinal study of the context and process of part-time postgraduate research, and it was originally proposed that a cohort of part-time and full-time students first registered in 1978, plus their supervisors, would be interviewed three times each about their experiences of the research process. The interviews were to be semi-structured and recorded on a tape recorder for transcription, and the cohort would consist of about eighty people. Wakeford proposed too that he would distribute a report to universities and professional associations recommending actions to improve the position of part-time postgraduates. The Education Committee of the SSRC proposed that in addition a postal questionnaire should be sent out to a larger number of part-time postgraduates. He was awarded enough money to employ the three of us, full-time for three years. Apparently there was some ill feeling in the Lancaster department about Wakeford getting money for such a large research project, and there were accusations of empire building; a familiar theme in most academic departments.

When I went to Lancaster for the interview I did not expect to be appointed, even though I had the required anthropological background and current experience of in-depth interviewing which Wakeford hoped to use on the project. It was, as now, a period of fierce competition for social science research jobs and I was not particularly confident. After an evening of meeting members of the department, and then formal interviews the following morning, I returned home to Manchester assuming that in due course I would receive a polite rejection through the mail. To my surprise John Wakeford phoned me the same day to offer me a job, but on the 1B scale in the first instance rather than the advertized 1A because university regulations would not allow me on 1A until I had had one year's postgraduate research experience. I had to accept less money than anticipated, but I did not mind in the least; I was what can only be described as pathetically grateful, a condition not uncommon in young women researchers.[2]

At that time he also told me that he had appointed Sue Scott to the other position, and suggested that I come to Lancaster in a few days to interview potential secretaries with him and Sue. What he did not tell me, for obvious reasons, is that some members of the department had strongly favoured other candidates for my job. There was speculation as to why Wakeford had appointed two women, and there was some consideration given to the age and experience of the appointees. The sociology department did not have any rooms to spare for the project, and the university allocated us two rooms at the far end of campus away from the department. While there was indeed no room for us in the department, there was no expression of regret or attempt by the department to remedy the situation. Apparently there was no seen need for researchers to be near other sociologists. Sue Scott and I eventually got a room in the department by occupying a room vacated by students; the argument that we would need a base there while doing our undergraduate teaching seemed acceptable. This illustrates a commonly held view that researchers can be housed anywhere, but staff having contact with students need to be close to the department. Thus I began my time at Lancaster unaware of the specific disputes, but feeling rather surprised to be there and definitely marginal. It took most of the three years to be rid of those feelings.

Structural Constraints on Project Relations

As has been demonstrated by Jennifer Platt (Platt, 1976) and Colin Bell (Bell, 1977), the relationships between co-workers on a research project can have a profound effect on the quantity and quality of data and written material produced. Platt talks about the difficulties encountered in projects which are ostensibly egalitarian, but only for as long and in as much as the project director allows (Platt, 1976, pp. 76–7). At our first project meeting John Wakeford said to us that as far as he was concerned anything that we wrote in the project would bear all our names in alphabetical order (I don't think that included the secretary), and that it would be for us to make what we could of the project because it would be Scott and myself who would be doing the work; he had one term of sabbatical leave to help us begin. He said that this was an opportunity for us to develop further skills and gain valuable experience ready to apply for research jobs in the future. Wakeford's feeling that we should all have an equal voice in the project was genuine and we did not experience the domination described by Platt. What I did not appreciate at the time, however, was that the research would, by its nature, be moulded increasingly by Sue Scott and me as time passed. I assumed that Wakeford had some particular and substantial interest in the topic and that he had concrete ideas about what he wanted to be done. As time passed I realized that John Wakeford did not feel particularly possessive about the project and that he had far more realistic expectations than I did in terms of the influence a director can have over the field research when he or she is not there. Payne and his colleagues in *Sociology and Social Research* say of working with qualitative material, 'collecting and analyzing qualitative data demands substantial input of scarce academic time and cannot satisfactorily be delegated' (Payne, *et al.*, 1981, p. 182). While in an ideal research world it might be more satisfactory for the person planning the qualitative work to do it as well, it is not uncommon for these tasks to be divided between two people or sets of people. This situation occurs because grant giving bodies are particularly willing to give funds for qualitative fieldwork to tenured university and polytechnic teachers who are unlikely to have enough time to do it themselves, while people who have the time to do the work are not yet considered sufficiently well qualified or well connected institutionally to be awarded funding in their own right. Given these circumstances, the only logical thing for Wakeford to do was to delegate the project to Scott and myself. Had I been more experienced I would have realized the implications of this, and have made more confident decisions in the field, knowing that it really was up to me to decide what to do based on information available to me at the time. The attitudes and expectations of others outside the project both in our department and elsewhere also led me to expect John Wakeford to take more of a lead. It was assumed that he was responsible for all the decision-making, and it was to him that our departmental head would go to discuss any project related matter, and it was from him that the SSRC expected progress reports. People to whom we mentioned that John was leaving much of the planning to us assured us that like all male project directors Wakeford would step back in at the end of the project, take over the data, and claim most of the credit for himself. That did not happen, but such remarks reinforced the idea in my mind that ultimately the decision-making was Wakeford's.

Sue Scott, Jackie Covill and I developed close friendships with each other; Sue and I became particularly close, partly because we spent so much time together in our work. I do not know for sure but I think that Wakeford wanted to employ a research team for the fieldwork; two people who could work well together particularly as he planned that the first round of visits to departments should be done jointly, and a high degree of cooperation and coordination was required. At the time of the interviews for our jobs John took Sue and me off for a cup of coffee and a chat together. We always wondered whether he did this to see whether, at some superficial level at least, we appeared to be compatible. While at one level it is desirable for co-workers in our kind of situation to be friends, this does lead to ambiguities; as far as I can remember we never disagreed over the way we should do a particular piece of work, but we did get personally irritable with one another as do any two people who spend a great deal of time together. Our strategy for dealing with this seemed to be for one of us to go and work in another part of the university for a few days, rather than to give voice to the irritations. This seemed consistent with the idea of maintaining good project relations, but I'm not sure that it was very good for our mental health.

When Scott and I were appointed on different scales we agreed that we would ignore this imposed hierarchy and that I would do the same job as originally planned. The difference between us as far as university regulations were concerned was that Scott was expected to make 'original contributions' to the design and theory of the research, and I was not. After a year I was promoted which made no difference at all to what I was actually doing. Although we had agreed to work equally, I felt very aware of the fact that Scott was a little older and had more teaching and research experience than me. I felt too that she had a better idea of what we were supposed to be doing because she had been at Lancaster when Wakeford was planning the project. I thought that certain things had already been decided before I arrived; these included the decision to use the tape recorders, that the first round of interviews should be done together, and that there was already some notion of which departments should be included.

I had never had a secretary before, and found it difficult to delegate work to Jackie Covill apart from the tape transcribing and some letters. Our relationship as friends overrode any more formal kind of working relationship, and I was very conscious of the fact that her job was boring and badly paid; it made me feel uncomfortable.

Getting Started

For me the most aimless part of the project was the first few weeks. We had frequent, as least weekly meetings which I think all four of us attended. John Wakeford gave me a lot of books to read on methodology and education. As I recall I found the methodology books far more interesting. The books included Bell and Newby (1977), Platt (1976), Rudd and Hatch (1968), Kelsall *et al.* (1972) and Welsh (1979). This coincided with a period when I was living in digs in Lancaster during the week and going back to Manchester at weekends, and so I had lots of time to read. Although much further into the project I was glad that I was familiar with that literature, at the time I felt I was reading in a vacuum; I did not have anything material to which I could relate what I was reading. At that time we wanted to set students' accounts of their lives in the contexts of the departments and places of work in which they found themselves. The only major study of postgraduates was that of Rudd, from which the main publication came in 1975. That was a survey and so it was not of direct use as a point of departure for our study. I think Wakeford may have envisaged a period of about three months before we began interviewing, but we did not believe that we could make any concrete plans until we had done some interviewing. Within weeks we began interviewing each other and people around the department, and at the same time began negotiating access to other departments.

Locating the Cohort

There is in all ethnographic work a time lapse between making the first moves to gain access to the target population and being granted or denied permission; this project was no exception. We decided from which departments we wanted to draw students onto the cohort by considering such characteristics as the departments' claims to aid part-timers and the number of each category of student they were supposed to have registered. We considered also the sociological community's notion of 'centres of excellence', for although those categories were denied by the SSRC for a long time they were certainly embodied in the reputations of particular departments. We considered the location of departments and we tried to draw from most regions of the British Isles. Having decided which departments we would like to draw from, we then drew up a list of people whom we knew in those departments. In my case I knew almost no-one in sociology or social administration; Scott knew some people, and Wakeford knew someone almost everywhere. John Wakeford wrote letters to these contacts asking if we could visit them and have access to the names and locations of their students. The responses came back in a matter of weeks, most of them positive, one of them asking for more guarantees of confidentiality, if, for example, one of their graduates ever applied for a job at Lancaster. We were able to assure them that the geographical separation of the project from the department was an added guarantee that the transcripts of the students' interviews would be available to no-one but ourselves. Most of Wakeford's letters went to professors and heads of departments, and this had some disadvantages for us when we got in the field. Although some departments had discussed our request in meetings of staff and/or students, some heads had said yes without consulting anybody, and so although we had formal access the access on the ground had to be negotiated as we went along. Even in places where students had been consulted, the part-timers were still unaware of us because they had so little to do with the departments in which they were registered. Through the very process of attempting to locate the part-timers we began to get some idea of just how marginal they were.

Wakeford's original idea was that we would be sent the lists of students' names and addresses, and that contacts would be made and appointments for interviews arranged from Lancaster; he envisaged that the project secretary would make the appointments. It did not work out like that; some departments sent lists of addresses but no 'phone numbers and so we were unable to do follow up 'phone calls. One large collegiate university said that we would have to wait until the new registrations had been collated before we could have the names and addresses. Some places said simply that we should see the secretary when we arrived. One of the more unpleasant aspects of being in the field was having just been given a student's name and 'phone number and having to 'phone them to ask for an interview 'cold'. Even after years of practice I still hate having to explain to someone over the 'phone who I am and what my credentials are. When it actually comes to requesting an interview in that situation it does not help at all that Professor Bloggs and Dr Wakeford have exchanged a friendly correspondence agreeing that this person can be contacted; I have to convince them in the first few seconds that my request is legitimate. It was far easier 'phoning people who had already received a letter; they had time to think about what we wanted and we did not have to explain the whole project over the 'phone. As we learned, where we only had an address we sent the person a stamped addressed postcard with the letter and asked them to suggest a time and date for interview and/or to give us a 'phone number where they could be reached; this helped enormously but the majority of arrangements for meetings were still made on site and so Jackie could not help with these.

Scott and I kept a personal journal when we travelled; it was not always up to date, and there are events which I wish now I had recorded in greater detail, but it is a useful record. We also made notes about every interview after it had happened and attached the notes to the summary or transcript of the tape. The notes and journal are clear reminders of the muddles and frustrations which we experienced at times, and one of the problems we had was getting the names of people who had originally registered part-time as opposed to those who were full-time writing up. We had one particularly frustrating day very early on, which I recorded in the journal, at the end of which we had it very clear in our minds just how important it was to define exactly what we wanted:

> An awful day! I rushed off to Town to interview Jane Smith, had trouble finding the house, was some minutes into the interview when I discovered she had never been part-time. I continued the interview and when we'd finished we chatted for about two and a half hours — a very pleasant and interesting woman who has been at the university for six years altogether so she knows a lot about it. Rushed to Suburbia to give Sue the front door key and then rushed up to Watchtown. That woman had also never been part-time, and she has submitted. She gave me a cup of coffee and I gave her a lift back into Town to buy new brake shoes for her car. Sue also had a highly frustrating day. Fred is not SSRC funded and he is really a geographer.

The accuracy of record-keeping varied from place to place; in one department the secretary pulled out a drawer and said, 'Oh, these are all people who have completed' and the first name we saw was an acquaintance of ours whom we knew had not completed. In another place the secretary just handed us all her index cards which were up to date and allowed us to look through and decide which people were of interest to us.

Wakeford seemed to have some idea of how many part-time students there were registered in the departments in which we were interested when we began. The research proposal had suggested that in order to get eighty people on the cohort we would have to go to about six departments. Inevitably some of the students on the lists were not available for interview; more significantly, the numbers of actual names on the lists were not the same as the numbers Wakeford had originally been led to believe were registered; the most extreme example of this is where an estimate of thirty-six part-time students was followed by a list bearing just four names. We had, therefore, to draw students from more than the original six departments. It had been proposed originally that the cohort would consist of students registered initially in 1978, but there were not enough people who fitted that category and so we included students registered both more recently than, and before, 1978 and this turned out to be very useful. We were able to get data on the process of thesis examination and on the students' decisions to abandon research; these would not have occurred so frequently in an all 1978 cohort.

We interviewed supervisors of students on the cohort, and tried to find two full-time SSRC funded students in each department in order to compare their experiences with those of the part-timers. Owing to declining numbers of awards there were some places where it was almost impossible. We assumed that supervisors and full-time students could be found easily when we visited the departments, and while they were easier to locate than the part-timers we did spend a fair amount of time waiting around for people to appear back from seminars and coffee breaks.

The statistics produced by Rudd on the completion rates of different disciplines in his study (Rudd, 1975) held chemistry students to be an example to us all. It therefore seemed appropriate to interview a handful of these students to give some perspective to the main focus of our research. We interviewed two chemistry students and a supervisor at each institution we visited. Our access to the students was controlled directly by the graduate convenor whom we had contacted by letter. In each case we interviewed the supervisor and then he (it was always he) went out to the laboratory and summoned students to be interviewed.

Fieldwork

Almost all the fieldwork was carried out by Sue Scott and myself. John Wakeford did a handful of interviews at our suggestion when we were very busy and he happened to be going to a particular town for something else. As well as our journal of encounters, and background notes to the interviews, we attended departmental seminars and meetings which gave additional information about where, if anywhere, part-time students fitted in, and what the view of 'normal' research was.

Once Scott and I started going away interviewing together we worked far more closely than any other combination of people on the project. The decision to do the first round together was a wise one; we were able to establish a joint piece of work which might otherwise have become two separate ethnographies. We travelled to the different universities and polytechnics together, and made the initial contact with departmental secretary and postgraduate convenor. This means that we both visited all the towns on our cohort and we were familiar with all the departments right from the beginning, which facilitated later discussion about the research. It should also have meant that we had both established ourselves with each department ready for the next visit, but it did not work like that in some places; secretaries and convenors changed and sometimes the same people just did not recognize us. The second time we had to re-establish the purpose of our visit.

Going away together for the first round meant that we spent a great deal of time talking on trains. It was in this relationship for me that the boundary between work and non-work became completely blurred. We were both very curious about people's actions and motives and we talked about our department and related it to others with which we were familiar. While talking about our own department can be classed as gossip, talking about other departments can be classed as work; the boundary however is arbitrary. While we were away we discussed interviews we had just done, observations we had made, and the implications for the research as a whole. During the terms when we were in a different town every week we lived project. In the second round of interviews, which we did separately, I enjoyed having some time to myself, but the daily events were not discussed as they happened, and the notes I made did not allow ideas to develop as fully as they had when we had had conversations. We had made assurances of confidentiality, so I did not talk to anyone else about it; if I had it probably would have been a very one-sided conversation.

We both became tired and run down during long periods of travelling. There was generally some anxiety over whether or not we would track down all the people that we wanted to see by the end of the week. They usually did materialize but there were often doubts, and problems like having to plan transport late at night; this was made worse for us interviewing in parts of the country where 'Ripper' murders had occurred.

Developing Members' Categories

As mentioned above, we soon began to interview students in our own department and one other for a pilot study. In an attempt to get at the themes of being a postgraduate student from the students' perspectives we wanted them in the first instance to tell us as much as possible with little prompting, and see how they responded to the tape recorder. My first interviewee responded to the tape much better than I did, for I found myself overcome with awkwardness as the transcription of the first few moments shows:

> Mary: Can you first of all tell me about — like a sort of case history — tell me about your educational career from when you left school — what institutions you have been in, and those sorts of things.
> Interviewee: What institutions have I attended, not been in.
> [Laughter]
> Mary: Attended, sorry.

On the Oldham study I had not used tape recorders but had become skilled at taking notes and remembering a lot afterwards. There were clearly disadvantages in that I had to try to write notes as well as follow the meanderings of the interviewees. On the other hand, I had manageable amounts of data, while as Scott (1984) mentions we had too much data for the time that was available for analysis on this study. When I first came to Lancaster I was doubtful about whether we could successfully get in-depth interviews on the tape recorder. I think now that those doubts were more a reflection of my own discomfort around them as after about half a dozen interviews I felt more at ease. The students and supervisors interviewed at this stage knew that they were our 'guinea pigs' and were most helpful. We spent hours with them both with the tape on and off discussing whether our questions made sense and what they thought we had omitted or needed to clarify. These pilot interviews allowed us to be better prepared in a way recommended by Dexter (1970). He emphasizes that anyone about to embark on interviews must be well prepared; the interviewer must know a lot about the interviewee's social world in order to be able to ask intelligent questions and to understand complex answers (Dexter, 1970, p. 14). This is precisely what we were trying to do, and it contrasts with the classic idea of interviewing embodied in the work of researchers like Moser and Kalton (1971) where a female interviewer employed by a male sociologist goes out and establishes rapport, but not too much, with the interviewee who is socially her inferior and is available to pour out information as required. The interviewer records this information in a manner which ensures that it is a 'true' representation of what the interviewee said. While this may seem to be putting it a little crudely, there were interviewees, particularly professional sociologists, with quantitative backgrounds who complained that what we did was not a 'proper' interview, and one person suggested that I would do far better to ask fewer, more structured questions of many more people so that it could be run through a computer for analysis.

Several times at the beginning Scott and I did joint interviews, not in a systematic way, but when we were both free and had the time. Providing that it did not intimidate the interviewee it had definite methodological advantages in that we could each see how the other interviewed. Sometimes one of us would do more of the questioning than the other, other times we would do about half each; that did not matter because we both knew what we wanted to cover. It allowed us to see how the other worked and afterwards we could discuss the interview. We had a small Sony tape recorder each which did not bother interviewees, apart from one exception where notes were taken. It had rechargeable batteries which were useful except that they made the tape recorder heavy to carry round and I usually had a stiff shoulder by the end of the week. Interviewing together allowed us to develop a common approach. We were not attempting to standardize the interviews in any positivistic way; we were not attempting to reproduce the same circumstances and order of questioning. Interviews such as ours require the interviewer to embark on a series of mental acrobatics; although we may have some schedule of the topics that should be covered we have to trace the interviewee's meanderings, bring out the significant points and prompt the informant to return to points half made and then abandoned for more pressing issues earlier on. Inevitably the success of this venture depends in part on the experience and physical and mental state of the interviewer. I improved with practice.

Soon after the pilot interviews the summer holidays began and we suspended interviewing because many of the people that we wanted on the cohort were unavailable. Scott and I spent the entire summer working through the transcripts. We filled in sections that Jackie (our secretary) had found inaudible and did some of the transcribing too. This allowed us fully to refine the categories that were emerging, and to arrange them in a schedule for future interviews. In this we were doing theoretical sampling as described by Glaser and Strauss:

> Theoretical sampling is the process of data collection for generating theory whereby the analyst jointly collects, codes and analyzes his [sic] data and decides what data to collect next, and where to find them, in order to develop his [sic] theory as it emerges. This process of data collection is *controlled* by the emerging theory, whether substantive or formal (Glaser and Strauss, 1967, p. 45).

While this aspect of Glaser and Strauss' method is useful there are problems with their work; they do not state *how* they begin the sampling, and how they decide what is theoretically relevant data. They make an interesting distinction between the ethnographer and the sociologist, who, they say, 'must remember that he [sic] is an active sampler of theoretically relevant data, not an ethnographer trying to get the fullest data on a group, with or without a preplanned research design (Glaser and Strauss, 1967, p. 58.)

This seems a very naive view of what ethnographers do; they *are* selective in their choice of material, they cannot present a whole social world. The distinction made between sociologists and ethnographers must seem particularly crude to many ethnographers. Both Scott and I felt when doing the research that the grounded theory approach was useful as a method, but that it does not constitute theory. Scott (1984) mentions her uneasy feelings at the lack of theory production that was done on the project, and I too was aware of this. The brief of our research proposal was a practical one, and focused on collecting information in the field; there was not sufficient time remaining to work through the material to refine it to the level of theory. Unlike ethnographies of schools we were hampered by a shortage of other research findings in our area from which to draw and make comparisons. When Scott and I were preparing a paper for the BSA conference (Porter and Scott, 1980) we were examining structures affecting the process of postgraduate research; in particular the workings of the SSRC. We soon realized that to give a good theoretical explanation would have required us to look at government decision-making and ultimately at theories of the State; this was clearly unmanageable.

The categories that seemed to us to be the most important in the summer of 1979 were as follows:

Biography
Negotiating entry: Decision to apply
                            Qualifications
                            Topic

> Supervision
> Expectations
> How the work is going and how the time is organized
> Evolution of thesis — content
> Practical problems of research
> How they perceive their research — within sociology and as an activity — usefulness, ethics and so on
> Relationship with supervisor
> Networks/conferences — contacts, other sources of criticism
> Academic aspects of the department
> Position in the department
> Facilities in the department and library, what they are entitled to
> Submission and assessment
> Future plans/career
> Political activities
> Finances, fees and so on
> Other commitments
> Particular features of being part-time
> Publications.

These categories were current at the time we decided we had better do something with the transcripts. We realized that although they were full of fascinating detail they would be overwhelming when we wanted to go through a lot of them at once. Scott and I decided that from then on we would transcribe the tapes into the current categories so that all the material would still be there, but it would be arranged according to topics. We took the questions out and they were inferred by the subject heading in which that section was put. The speech was changed from first person to third person reported speech, but the vocabulary was retained and this helped to keep some of the character of the interview. At first it is hard to make any changes to raw data; I felt that it became depersonalized, but I realized too that as social scientists our job is to select material which we deem to be of use and interest and to present our ideas and findings to others. The logical conclusion to excessive sentimentality about our data would be publish the transcripts!

We had a pile of separate pieces of paper, on each was one of the headings listed above. We listened to a tape and decided into which category particular sections would fit. Using the digital counter on the tape recorder we made a note of the number of the section as we wrote it down in the appropriate category; this was so that we could easily find the relevant section of the tape if we wanted subsequently to go back and listen to it. The resulting summary looked like this:

> Biography
>
> ooo State grammar school in Portsmouth, 3 A-levels — English, History and Economics. BA in History. Applied immediately for research here. Did theoretical history of ideas/philosophical history so that's why he could come to a sociology department.
>
> 019 He has always been interested in academic work. Messed around until his O-levels. From A-levels always envisaged some kind of academic career.

Some of the interviews contained repeated material and we did not keep repeating it in the summary. If a tape was of particular interest we still had it transcribed completely. The categories that were developed, expanded and contracted over time as our ideas about what was happening to the students changed and developed.

Jackie Covill who had been typing up the summaries that we did eventually decided that she was sufficiently familiar with the material that she could do the summaries too, as it would be less boring. She did a very good job and we tried to have her job changed, but the SSRC had given us money for a secretary and that is what they expected us to have.

The Social Relations of the Interview

The interviewees can be divided into several categories in terms of my social relationships with them, and they have significance in that in this type of interviewing our social relations affect the type of information that is given. The categories are: the chemists, with some differences between students and supervisors; high status occupations, and my peers.

As mentioned above we gained access to the chemistry students directly through their supervisors who often just told the student that they were going to be interviewed. The following journal entry is representative of what happened when interviewing in chemistry departments:

> Arrived very late last night, after getting lost and didn't go to
> bed until 1 a.m.
> Went to the chemistry department this morning and inter-
> viewed one chemistry lecturer and two students all in a
> row —
> The usual problem of the students not knowing what the
> hell's going on, the supervisor having nominated them to be
> in a specific place at a specific time.

And this is another illustration:

> Went to interview James Brown the chemist. He was very
> smarmy, didn't like him at all. He took me to the tea room
> where all the students were having their afternoon tea break at
> the same time. He introduced me to some of the students and
> he tried to persuade them to be interviewed but they weren't
> playing. I think he put them off by being so pushy. After that
> I interviewed him, at the end of which he dashed off and came
> back to tell me the names of two students who were 'willing'
> to be interviewed the next day.

This coercive way of persuading students to be interviewed raises the
issue of informed consent; while sociology interviewees had an idea
of what to expect, the chemistry students seemed puzzled by the
situation. I had to take some time to explain to them what we were
attempting to do. I found myself constructing explanations of the
research to the students in a simpler way using more 'scientific' terms
in an attempt to be understood. The students were up to four years
my junior and (the men particularly) were less articulate than their
peers in sociology. Their answers to questions were brief and to the
point, and problems were not highlighted in the same way as in the
social sciences. Scott and I both got the impression that we were
hearing what should happen rather than what necessarily did happen.
Those interviews were all conducted within the chemistry departments, often in supervisors' cramped offices which were the only
place of refuge from the laboratories. There was a sense that the
students were wary of being overheard (which was not the case), but
the location of the interview did inhibit their responses. When the
interview ended, that is, when I thanked them and turned off the tape
recorder, they rarely asked any questions but left at once to get back
to their work which also structured the interview; they were frequently in the middle of doing some experiments and would have to
end the interview accordingly.

The chemistry supervisors, rather like their students, talked about what happened as though it was unproblematic; the interviews stayed close to their original schedules because tangential points were rarely raised. The comment of one interviewee, that he was glad to see that we did not claim that sociology is a science, was a representative one; however, when he became concerned about confidentiality if he got any of the information wrong, the interviewer was able to point out to him that one of the advantages of not seeing sociology as a science is that we do not expect people to tell the truth. The point of loosely structured interviews is to allow the interviewee to dictate the most relevant points of the research question, but the natural scientists seemed confused if they could not detect any structure to the interview, and there was a contradiction for me trying simultaneously to create a dialogue in which research arrangements were discussed, and to maintain the feeling that it was an interview as a natural scientist would expect it.

Platt, in discussing interviewing other sociologists, talks about interviewing her peers (Platt, 1976). As a young female researcher some of the sociologists would generally be considered to be my superiors rather than my peers, in terms of age and professional achievement, and the attitudes of some of them towards me reflected this. The people who fall into this category are some of the supervisors, mainly heads of department and other senior positions. Also falling into this category are part-time postgraduates with high status occupations outside academic social science; these occupations included clergy, civil servants, and the medical profession. The people in this category were interviewed at their place of work, not because that had been deliberately planned but because that was most convenient to them. The interviews in the work place, especially those in non-educational settings were quite formal even though we saw the part-time students more than once. The combination of unequal status between interviewer and interviewee, and the constant reminder to the interviewee of their work as manifested by interruptions from secretaries and colleagues, made it more difficult for a detailed dialogue to develop. Platt talks about sociologists knowing how to adopt the appropriate interviewee role (Platt, 1976). The high status interviewees behaved appropriately during the period that the tape recorder was turned on, but felt free once it was turned off to make critical comments about how the interview had progressed; one senior academic insisted that I should wait while he decided whether or not I had asked him everything that he considered appropriate. After a few moments I was dismissed with, 'well, yes, you do seem to have remembered everything.' It is interesting to note that several part-time students in high status occupations believed that they had the professor or head of department for a supervisor because of their own high status occupations outside sociology; this seemed peculiar when their sociological interests and orientation did not coincide.

The members of the cohort whom I felt to be my peers were the full-time postgraduate students, and part-time postgraduates close to me in age, occupation and often gender. Relationships with these students were the most complex and the most interesting. Because of the longitudinal nature of the research, the relationships developed and there were exchanges of information and news between us at the second meeting.

Peers did not act out the role of interviewee very well at all; they would often stop in the middle of the interview and ask such awkward questions as: 'who else have you interviewed?' Ann Oakley writes about her informants asking questions about her knowledge of childbirth (Oakley, 1981). She does not believe that it is ethically or methodologically sound to deny the questions by claiming ignorance, as a more traditional, positivistic model would demand. I concur in this view, and gave information to students providing that it did not break the confidences of others.

The nature of the questions asked and the information required became more complex by the second interview; for example, during the first round of interviews, one of the questions that students were asked was to what facilities they were entitled in the department. Many of them gave their reply and then asked whether there were facilities of which they were unaware. It was quite simple to suggest that we wait until the end of the interview, after which I told them what I knew. This was not problematic; the information was obtainable from graduate convenors and the SSRC and it was appropriate that they should receive something in return for the time that they had given. Scott and I discovered that in one sociology department, following our visit the students organized and demanded certain facilities to which they decided they were entitled after having talked to us.

In the second round of interviews, we were asking for an updating and elaboration of information given earlier, and there were often in-depth discussions on one topic such as supervision or work. During the course of discussion the interviewees asked for opinions, or specific advice about what they should do. This was more difficult to defer until the end and consideration had to be given to the fact that they sometimes had no other source of advice; that, in itself, is a reason for giving it freely, but it also raises the issue of altering the course of events in the area being studied, a traditionally forbidden action for a researcher. It was impossible to confine these requests for advice until after the interview where they would have been more appropriate. I interviewed a part-time student who talked about problems with supervision; he had had several different supervisors culminating in having one with a completely different theoretical orientation to his own. He was due to submit his thesis and believed it to be a fair piece of work but the supervisor was very cautious about it because it was not of the theoretical orientation he considered to be most appropriate. As the supervisor was to be an examiner, the student was naturally concerned that he might fail. On reaching this stage in his account, he asked me what I thought he should do, and I decided that I should respond; I gave him a verbal outline of what usually happened in his department with regard to student participation in choice of external examiner. This was information gleaned from other interviews, not from any declared departmental policy. I suggested that the student should attempt to insist on choosing his external examiner, and given the experience of other students, this looked like a possibly successful course of action. I was perhaps altering the course of events but there was a commitment to the students which would not allow total detachment from their interests.

A number of the interviewees who I considered to be my peers were interviewed in their homes. In contrast to the interviews conducted in the work place, the ones in the home were more relaxed and generated large quantities of secondary data. Sometimes the interview was disrupted by other people and animals in the home, and at times it was hard to get it started at all; one informant said during an evening interview at home that he worked on his thesis at home every evening. However, given that there was nowhere quiet in the house to do the interview, and that the first hour after I arrived had been spent putting small children to bed, I found his statement hard to believe. This kind of secondary data is very useful in trying to build a picture of the experiences of the students in the context of the structural constraints on their actions; it makes one speculate too on all the things which we did not find out about some of the high status informants who presented such a coherent and unproblematic view of their part in the research endeavour.

Conclusion

By the end of the Lancaster project we had filing cabinets full of neatly labelled transcripts and summaries. Both Scott and I were saturated with information about the research process, and in the final six months we each began to write papers; we should have started sooner. Scott and I had rather a unique experience in doing so much of the work together and sharing so many ideas; however, we would have accomplished more in terms of detailed analysis and production of papers had we divided the tasks between us earlier and then had regular meetings to discuss our work. As Scott subsequently pointed out, we should have anticipated our separation sooner and allocated tasks accordingly.

I left Lancaster as soon as my contract ended in February 1982; I moved to the USA taking copies of all the data with me. Sue Scott stayed in Lancaster for most of that year, and then she too moved away. I have done project work since then, but with difficulty as the focus of my life shifted to other activities. I am remote from the contacts made through the project and the resources that were available at Lancaster, making further contributions problematic. From abroad I quickly became out of touch with the latest news on the cuts in public spending, but even before I left, it seemed quite clear there would be no new financial aid to part-time students. While departments are fighting for their very existence, providing better facilities for part-timers is bound to be at the bottom of their list of priorities.

This set of circumstances has led me to the conclusion that although we have been able to make substantial contributions to the body of knowledge on postgraduate training, and to the development of qualitative methods in education, our desire to improve substantially the quality and efficiency of the part-time research process remains unfulfilled.

Notes

1 This chapter is my personal view of the project rather than an official one.
2 For an illuminating discussion on this see Hanmer and Leonard (1980).

References

BELL, C. (1977) 'Reflections on the Banbury Restudy', in BELL, C. and NEWBY, H. (Eds) *Doing Sociological Research*, London, George Allen and Unwin.

BELL, C. and NEWBY, H. (Eds) (1977) *Doing Sociological Research*, London, George Allen and Unwin.

DEXTER, L.A. (1970) *Elite and Specialized Interviewing*, Evanston, Northwestern University Press.

GLASER, B. and STRAUSS, A. (1967) *The Discovery of Grounded Theory: Strategies for Qualitative Research*, Chicago, Aldine.

HANMER, J. and LEONARD, D. (1980) 'Men and culture: The sociological intelligensia and the maintenance of male domination; or superman meets the invisible woman', in *Transactions of the British Sociological Association*, London, British Sociological Association.

KELSALL, R.K. *et al.* (1972) *Graduates, the Sociology of an Elite*, London, Methuen.

MOSER, C.A. and KALTON, G. (1971) *Survey Methods in Social Investigation*, 2nd ed., London, Heinemann.

OAKLEY, A. (1981) 'Interviewing women: A contradiction in terms', in ROBERTS, H. (Ed.) *Doing Feminist Research*, London, Routledge and Kegan Paul.

PAYNE, G. *et al.* (1981) *Sociology and Social Research*, London, Routledge and Kegan Paul.

PLATT, J. (1976) *The Realities of Social Research*, Sussex, Chatto and Windus for Sussex University Press.

PORTER, M. and SCOTT, S. (1980) 'Postgraduate students, sociology and the cuts', in *Transactions of the British Sociological Association*, London, British Sociological Association.

RUDD, E. (1975) *The Highest Education: A Study of Graduate Education in Britain*, London, Routledge and Kegan Paul.

RUDD, E. and HATCH, S. (1968) *Graduate Study and After*, London, Weidenfeld and Nicolson.

SCOTT, S. (1984) 'Working through the contradictions', in BURGESS, R.G. (Ed.) *Field Methods in the Study of Education*, Lewes, Falmer Press.

WELSH, J.M. (1979) *The First Year of Postgraduate Education*, Society for Research in Higher Education Monograph.

For other useful material on ethnographic work see:

ACKROYD, S. and HUGHES, J. (1981) *Data Collection in Context*, New York, Longman.

BARNES, J.A. (1979) *Who Should Know What? Social Science, Privacy and Ethics*, Harmondsworth, Penguin.

BECKER, H. and GEER, B. (1957) 'Participant observation and interviewing: A comparison', *Human Organization*, 16, 3, pp. 28–32.

BRENNER, M., MARSH, P. and MARSH, M. (Eds) (1978) *The Social Contexts of Method*, London, Croom Helm.

DENZIN, N.K. (1970) *The Research Act: A Theoretical Introduction to Sociological Methods*, Chicago, Aldine.

DEUTSCHER, I. (1973) *What We Say, What We Do*, Glenview, Scott Foresman and Company.

DITTON, J. and WILLIAMS, R. (1981) *The Fundable vs the Doable: Sweet Gripes, Sour Grapes and the SSRC*, Background Papers 1, Department of Sociology, University of Glasgow.

FARADAY, A. and PLUMMER, K. (1979) 'Doing life histories', in *Sociological Review*, 27, 4, pp. 773–98.

FILSTEAD, W. (Ed.) (1970) *Qualitative Methodology: First Hand Involvement with the Social World*, Chicago, Markham.

FLETCHER, C. (1974) *Beneath the Surface: An Account of Three Styles of Sociological Research*, London, Routledge and Kegan Paul.

HALFPENNY, P. (1979) 'The analysis of qualitative data', in *Sociological Review*, 27, 4, pp. 799–825.

PORTER, M. and SCOTT, S. (1981) 'Women postgraduates and liberal academics: A new dimension to disadvantage', presented to Society for Research in Higher Education Conference.

SCHWARTZ, H. and JACOBS, J. (1979) *Qualitative Sociology: A Method to the Madness*, London, Macmillan.

SCOTT, S. (1983) 'The personable and the powerful: Gender and status in sociological research, in BELL, C. and ROBERTS, H. (Eds) *Social Researching: Policies, Problems and Practice*, London, Routledge and Kegan Paul.

WAKEFORD, J. (1984) 'The director's dilemma', in BURGESS, R.G. (Ed.) *Field Methods in the Study of Education*, Lewes, Falmer Press.

WOODWARD, D. and CHISHOLM, L. (1981) 'The expert's view? The sociological analysis of graduates' occupational and domestic roles', in ROBERTS, H. (Ed.) *Doing Feminist Research*, London, Routledge and Kegan Paul.

7   Wards and Deeds: Taking Knowledge and Control Seriously

Paul Atkinson

Editor's Commentary. Although sociologists of education have raised questions about what counts as 'education' and what counts as 'knowledge', it is relatively rare to find these crucial issues examined in empirical studies that go beyond the school and classroom. Yet there are numerous educational settings in churches, trade unions and hospitals where these questions could be addressed. It is in this sense that Paul Atkinson's study, *The Clinical Experience*, provides a different perspective by focusing upon the clinical teaching which is given to trainee doctors during their first year of medicine and surgery. He is, therefore, able not only to contribute to substantive concerns in the sociology of medicine but also to shed further light on central issues in the sociology of education.

In this chapter Paul Atkinson discusses the origins of his work which was conducted from the Centre for Research in the Educational Sciences in the University of Edinburgh where Sara Delamont was doing research on school classrooms. Accordingly, his study was part of a range of ethnographic work that was housed in the Centre at the beginning of the 1970s. Paul Atkinson examines particular aspects of the research process: the beginning of his project, the character of early field experiences, the acquisition of knowledge and the transmission and reception of data; all of which complements his reflections on the research that are contained in an appendix to his study.

A central section of this chapter considers how researchers can handle the familiar and the strange while conducting studies in their own society. Atkinson also discusses the way in which researchers can study those situations that are considered deviant for what they reveal about routine events and everyday occurrences. In turn, he provides a number of useful insights on the ways in which a researcher learns a language and acquires technical knowledge. Accordingly, his chapter addresses such questions as: how can researchers question the taken-for-granted? How can researchers conduct studies in situations with which they are familiar? By focusing on his research experience Atkinson simultaneously addresses these questions while pointing out the relevance of his study for broadening our understanding of education and educational settings.

Confessions of a Justified Ethnographer

The ethnography described in this paper was a study of bedside teaching in the Edinburgh medical school. The conduct of that study has always given me a foot in at least two sociological camps — the sociology of medicine and the sociology of education. I have published and taught in both areas, as well as contributing to the literature on occupations and 'the professions'. Educationally speaking, my research, which was conducted in the early 1970s, addressed a number of themes which were to be central to the 'new' sociology of education: knowledge and power, curriculum and pedagogy, the social construction of specialized knowledge. Likewise, it was undertaken at a time and in an academic context where the ethnography of educational settings was rapidly achieving significance. My fellow research students at Edinburgh and I made some contribution to that emergent research tradition (see Delamont in this volume).

On the other hand, my own dual citizenship has rarely been recognized by colleagues in the sociology of education. As I have indicated, one could see my work as part of that development of educational ethnography in the 1970s. Yet recent textbooks (Robinson, 1982; Meighan, 1981; Shaw, 1982; Cohen and Manion, 1980) make no reference to the work at all, although articles on it have appeared in explicitly 'educational' publications (for example, Atkinson, 1975; Atkinson and Delamont, 1976) as well as more obviously 'medical' literature (for example, Atkinson, 1977; 1981a).

It is not only the case that my research has suffered neglect in educational contexts. Its educational relevance has been explicitly denied. Some years ago, for instance, I took part in an SSRC sponsored seminar, organized by Clem Adelman, on the analysis of 'talk' in educational settings. At that seminar I presented a paper on how medical students attempt to arrive at appropriate responses to their clinical teachers' questions. In that paper I was explicitly addressing a topic in the sociology of education on which Hammersley (1977) had already published, and which others were to comment on subsequently (for example, French and Maclure, 1979).

The original, privately circulated, version of the proceedings of that seminar contains my paper on bedside interaction in the medical school. But when Clem Adelman found a publisher for a selection of papers from the SSRC seminar series, it was a condition that my paper on bedside teaching be dropped. The publishers insisted that 'education' must refer to schools, teachers and pupils. The published version, therefore, was based upon some transcripts of school lessons

I happened to have available (see Atkinson, 1981b): the original paper remains unpublished.

There have been other contexts — including the conference on which this collection of papers is based — in which the 'educational' relevance of my work has escaped some colleagues. For all too many social scientists 'education' is treated as synonymous with 'schools': anything else is all but ignored. The scope of the sociology of education is, for the most part, extraordinarily restricted. Delamont (1981) has pointed out the blinkered vision of most of what passes for the sociology of education, while herself indicating the value of investigating a wide range of different institutions and settings. But studies of teaching, socialization and training in other educational sectors are rare, and tend to be ignored. Anyone who wishes to make a mark in educational research should avoid working in further or higher education, adult education, occupational training, industrial training or any other non-school setting. Incidentally, it is worth noting that even in studies of schools the 'mainstream' is confined to pupils in state schools, aged 7 to 16, who are neither exceptionally gifted nor slow, educationally subnormal or maladjusted. For the most part, the pupils are to be observed working at English, maths, science, history or geography. Any other focus of study is likely to be consigned to its own academic ghetto in the literature.

Of course, the important point is not whether or not my own work has been neglected in certain quarters. Rather, I wish to emphasize the fact that ethnographers — above all other researchers — should be able to transcend the taken-for-granted conceptualization of what counts as 'education'. Moreover, they should be committed to the *formal*, comparative analysis of different substantive issues and social settings. The very methodology enjoins a broader vision. Sara Delamont and I did attempt such a formal, comparative exercise. We suggested that there were some very fundamental similarities between the pedagogy of bedside clinical medicine on the one hand, and guided-discovery approaches to the natural sciences in schools (Atkinson and Delamont, 1976). But it is noticeable that exercises comparing substantively different educational settings are rare. Literatures are for the most part treated as hermetically sealed. Indeed, there is a marked tendency even for ethnographers of similar educational settings not to develop formal comparative frameworks. Many such ethnographers are — for instance — quite remarkably ethnocentric (Delamont and Atkinson, 1980).

The relative neglect of my work in educational circles was

slightly galling, as it seemed to me that I was being particularly successful in documenting some of the main themes of the so-called 'new sociology of education'. This movement in the sociology of education was emerging into public discourse at about the same time as I was beginning my research into medical education. The new paradigm placed at the heart of the sociological programme the investigation of the social construction and reproduction of knowledge (Young, 1971). The 'new' sociology was noticeably long on theoretical and programmatic statements, while its advocates were equally short on empirical research. My own work on bedside medicine was centrally preoccupied with the social construction of medical knowledge and medical discourse. I attempted to show how much knowledge production was embedded in the three-party encounter of doctor, patient and student(s). My work has rarely, if ever, been treated as a contribution to such developments in the study of educational knowledge.

One of the first papers I published was primarily methodological. I contributed to a seminar, and its published proceedings, on 'classroom observation' (Atkinson, 1975). That paper was intended to be part of that general debate between the 'ethnographers' of educational settings, and the advocates of pre-coded 'interaction analysis'. It has rarely been referred to in subsequent references to that debate.

The point of this introduction is not simply to voice personal pique or regrets: personal grudges are of little or no interest to anyone but their bearer. Rather, I have tried to indicate a general methodological point about the conduct and interpretation of ethnographic research in educational settings. The scope of such work has tended to be remarkably narrow. Researchers have failed to generate analytic insight by the systematic and comparative inspection of diverse contexts. The failures consequent upon such tunnel vision have been indicated by Delamont (1981).

Background to the Research

As is congruent with the foregoing remarks, the research was conducted in an institutional and intellectual climate of educational research. Some of my fellow research students were working on schools, others on institutions of higher education. The initial impetus to study the Edinburgh medical school arose out of a mixture of biography and circumstance. I had gone to Edinburgh with the intention of working on language and phenomenology, an interest which derived from my reading of Alfred Schutz, and an optional course in general linguistics during my first degree in Social Anthropology at Cambridge. While casting about for a specific focus, I expressed an interest in the topic of typifications. It happened that Liam Hudson, the Head of the Centre for Research in the Educational Sciences (CRES) had some unanalyzed semantic differential data on medical students' stereotypes of occupational categories, including a number of medical specialties. Those semantic differentials had been collected at a London medical school some years previously. The same students were then in their final year, and I administered the same research instrument to them again.

I spent some time analyzing and writing up those semantic differential data. Interest in this material was sustained by Hudson's own work on stereotypes of Arts and Science specialists (for example, Hudson, 1968), and sociological work on occupational titles by Tony Coxon, who was then in the Sociology Department at Edinburgh (for example, Coxon, 1971). In retrospect that work was something of a blind alley, and the methodology crude. It really had little to do with my main theoretical preoccupations. I only ever published one *New Society* article related to those data, and much remained unanalyzed. It was, however, valuable experience in getting research started, in data processing and the use of computing packages. It also introduced me to the literature on medical education. That literature included two classics in the field: *The Student Physician* (Merton *et al.*, 1957), and *Boys in White* (Becker *et al.*, 1961). My reading of these indicated that my research topic was an important one, and whetted my appetite for a much more thorough investigation of medical education: there appeared to be no research in Britain comparable with the American studies.

By the end of my first year at Edinburgh, then, I had completed a report on the London medical students' occupational stereotypes, and had decided to try a study in Edinburgh akin to *Boys in White*. The foreshadowed problem of that ethnography was still the medical students' stereotypes or typifications of different medical specialities. In the event, the focus of the ethnography shifted. In common with many ethnographers I found that my foreshadowed problem became transformed as I concentrated progressively on the conduct of clinical teaching in the students' first clinical year, in the specialties of Medicine and Surgery. My initial interest was not lost to sight entirely, however, since the students' reactions to Medicine and

Surgery were intimately related to their images of the two specialities (cf. Atkinson, 1976).

I do not intend to comment in any more detail on the atmosphere and organization of CRES. But I should like to make two remarks on the methods and origins of my medical school ethnography. In retrospect, it is tempting to account for the choice of method and topic in terms of 'movements' or 'developments' in sociology. The beginning of my own research activities in 1969 almost exactly coincided with the establishment of medical sociology in Britain and the establishment of the study group of the British Sociological Association. Since about that time the subdiscipline has developed enormously, and most of my own activities have been in 'medical' sociology. But I had no sense at the time of getting into a 'coming' area: my choice of a medical setting was largely accidental.

Likewise, the choice of ethnographic field methods was in no sense part of a self-conscious development or movement in the study of educational settings. The development of ethnography in schools may have been something of an innovative trend in the late 1960s and early 1970s, but for many of us in CRES it was unremarkable. For those of us with an undergraduate background in social anthropology participant observation hardly seemed innovatory. Indeed, what is noticeable in retrospect is the fact that what was novel for us was the use of pencil-and-paper research instruments. Partly under the influence of Liam Hudson's social psychology, many of the research students at CRES began their work with techniques like the semantic differential, repertory grid, study habits' inventories and the like.

Finally, retrospective accounts of the early days of our ethnographic work tend to link it with the emergence of the 'new' sociology of education, as proposed by M.F.D. Young and his collaborators. I have already referred to parallels between that tendency and my own interests. But that was a matter of later interpretations and theoretical convergence. The similarities derived from a common stock of theoretical assumptions, in symbolic interactionism and phenomenology. But they were largely independent in their origins. Histories of the area which conflate the two strands of development (for example, Karabel and Halsey, 1977) are quite misinformed. In large measure, I suspect that this sort of inaccuracy confounds many retrospective accounts of 'schools', 'trends' and 'movements' in academic work. The experience and motivation of individual workers is often much less purposeful, and less consciously guided by the research community than appearance suggests. In this, as in all things, we should beware of whiggish history and the anachronistic attribution of motive.

As for my own project in the Edinburgh medical school, I have already published a brief autobiographical account as a methodological appendix to the published monograph (Atkinson, 1981a). Those observations are not recapitulated in detail here. Rather, I want to select a restricted number of themes from that study and use them as the basis for some more general methodological remarks.

Familiarity, Learning and Becoming an Expert

Ethnographers are recurrently confronted by problems of 'familiarity' and 'strangeness'. We seek to render the familiar strange, and the strange familiar. These efforts of imagination and understanding are not straightforward, however, and they created problems in my study of medical education.

Medicine is an important and intensive element in contemporary culture. A broad picture of what goes on in a hospital ward is part of the stock of knowledge possessed by every adult member of one culture; it is often part of children's play as well. As Blanche Geer writes in her discussion of generating research problems in the field:

> The concept of working hypothesis is not difficult, but field workers often have trouble explaining it to others and sometimes to themselves. The concept is clear, but its mechanics, the doing smacks of magic. *Untrained observers, for instance, can spend a day in a hospital and come back with one page of notes and no hypotheses. It was a hospital, they say: everyone knows what hospitals are like.* (Geer, 1964, my emphasis)

When I began my research I was in no sense a 'trained observer', and although my first field notes were not as sparse as Geer suggests, I was certainly in some difficulty with much of the action that I observed. Although I was able to get some useful preliminary material from the various introductory lectures I attended with the students, when it came to my own observations of 'where the action was', I was much more at a loss. The problem resided in part in the obviousness and familiarity of the action scenes that I observed.

This problem is generic, and is particularly noticeable in studies of educational settings. Almost by definition, academics have a particularly long and thorough personal acquaintance with education

— as learners and, sometimes, as instructors as well. The problem of familiarity can therefore be massive. George Spindler, for instance, writes that he came near to giving up his first attempt at school ethnography for just this sort of reason:

> I sat in classes for days wondering what there was to 'observe'. Teachers taught, reprimanded, rewarded, while pupils sat at desks, squirming, whispering, reading, writing, staring into space, as they had in my own grade-school experience, in my practice teaching in a teacher training program, and in the two years of public school teaching I had done.... (Spindler and Spindler, 1982, p. 24)

Becker has also commented in this vein:

> We may have understated a little the difficulty of observing contemporary classrooms. It is not just the survey method of educational testing or any of those things that keeps people from seeing what is going on. I think, instead, that it is first and foremost a matter of it being so familiar that it becomes impossible to single out events that occur in the classroom as things that have occurred, even when they happen right in front of you. I have not had the experience of observing in elementary and high school classrooms myself, but I have in college classrooms and it takes a tremendous effort of will and imagination to stop seeing only the things that are conventionally 'there' to be seen. I have talked to a couple of teams of research people who have sat around in classrooms trying to observe and it is like pulling teeth to get them to see or write anything beyond what 'everyone' knows.
> (Becker, 1971, p. 10)

The general features of clinical medicine or surgery, and of clinical teaching, are generally familiar. As a reasonably well read and well informed layman, what I observed in the teaching hospitals came as no great surprise. In Britain, such portrayals as those in Richard Gordon's fictionalized accounts of medical life (such as *Doctor in the House*) feed such familiarity. Although it is explicitly humorous in style and intent, *Doctor in the House* rings many bells with qualified doctors. As Cramond points out, for instance:

> One of the fascinating things about Dr Richard Gordon's book *Doctor in the House* was its universality. It did not

matter at what Medical School one was trained, one could unerringly identify the broad characteristics of the better remembered, somewhat eccentric Medical School teachers. (Cramond, 1973, pp. 13–14)

Time after time, I was struck in the course of my own research by the fidelity of Gordon's accounts.

Faced with such familiarity, there is a danger that must be faced by many researchers. One looks hopefully for the exotic, the bizarre, the deviant or the problematic — anything to fracture the surface of familiar, routine doings. It is not hard to see why writers on educational settings have sometimes seemed obsessed by deviant and disruptive pupils. As Delamont (1976) points out, at a commonsense level, it is easier to create 'news' and 'interest' out of such colourful deviation, rather than by documenting the accomplishment of ordinary, routine — even 'boring' — events: 'Conflict between pupils and school is easier to dramatize' (Delamont, 1976, p. 70).

If one were to look only for such exotica, then in many settings one's notebook would remain all but empty. Certainly that would have been the case for my observations in the medical school. If one were only to look for the bizarre or the shocking, then little would be accomplished. It is undeniable that there were and are events which the lay observer might find startling or shocking: the very nature of medicine and surgery can lead to such reactions quite commonly, and I shall return to the significance of that later. On the other hand, as in most social settings, what went on in the hospital wards seemed, even to an outsider, quite unremarkable. For the most part, bedside teaching consisted of more or less unproblematic encounters between doctors, patients and students. These occasions looked pretty much like any other educational undertakings: teachers taught, demonstrated and asked questions, while students attempted with various degrees of success to respond appropriately. Likewise, the social action appeared to be unremarkably similar to other varieties of medical activity, such as wardrounds: patients' histories were taken, physical examinations were conducted, test results and X-ray films were discussed, differential diagnoses canvassed, and the like.

While I dutifully recorded as much of the interaction as I could, my first days — indeed, my first weeks — in the field were formless. I recall a conversation I had at a medical sociology conference some weeks after I had begun fieldwork in the hospitals. Betraying myself as a green tyro I confessed over breakfast one morning that as yet I could discern no neat patterns in the data. My companions displayed their seniority and experience by smiling, tolerantly, and pointing out that it was 'early days yet' and I really couldn't expect things to emerge during these initial stages.

My fellow conference-goers were being perfectly reasonable, of course. What is striking is the extent to which we embark on research of this sort as an act of faith. We persuade ourselves and our students that provided we plug away with the fieldwork, and we maintain the right sort of mental attitudes or methodological procedures, then things will start to fall into place. The fact that we can so often bring it off with some degree of success seems to be no small tribute to our collective sociological imagination, and the robust good sense of ethnographic methods. But it is hard to keep going during the first days and weeks. It is so often frustrating: the notes accumulate, and information is undoubtedly acquired, and to that extent we can always persuade ourselves, our students, or our supervisors that we are 'getting somewhere'. But the translation of observation and information into a systematic understanding of a given social setting or sociological problem — that is a different matter. Getting somewhere in that sense is usually much more arduous an adventure.

In continuing to take steps in the dark I had many sources of motivation. Other students with whom I was working had completed or were in the course of school ethnographies, and it was clear that they were producing innovatory and interesting work. I would not have been satisfied with anything other than a full-blown 'proper' ethnography of my own. Moreover, I had invested a great deal of time towards gaining access to the teaching hospitals. I have documented some of the features of these access negotiations elsewhere (Atkinson, 1981a), and I will not repeat them here. Suffice it to say that a substantial proportion of my second year as a research student was occupied with seeking, and ultimately gaining, access. Had the Social Science Research Council been more stringent in those days about awarding money for a third year, then my own research in the medical school might have been still-born. But having got that far, I was thoroughly determined to see it through. Not least of my motivations, however, was the feeling that whether or not I was making first-rate sociological sense of it all, it was extraordinarily interesting.

I suspect that many ethnographers have similar feelings. I was gripped by the sort of fascination medicine holds for many lay people. The success of numerous series about health and medical practice in the mass media — from the early days of *Your Life in their*

Hands onwards — testifies to such interest. Simultaneously, I was pleased and a little flattered to be able to go behind the scenes, to work in otherwise private settings, among a professional elite.

To some extent, these two sources of motivation and satisfaction corresponded to two varieties of knowledge and expertise I sought access to in the field. Ultimately, my understanding of them helped me to unpack and make strange the sort of familiarity I referred to above. My own interests here also paralleled those of the medical students I was studying. Broadly speaking, in the course of my fieldwork I found myself needing to gain knowledge of two sorts. Both were varieties of 'inside' knowledge in the medical school, and both constituted areas of learning for the students themselves. They may be referred to as 'organizational knowledge' and 'technical knowledge'. In practice, the two areas intersect in many ways: ultimately it is the relationships between them which prove important. At this stage they may be distinguished for analytic purposes, however.

The first type of knowledge — 'organizational' — has been widely researched and commented on in ethnographies of educational and equivalent institutions. It would include, for instance, the 'folk taxonomy' of persons and occasions employed by groups. They are the everyday, practical ways in which workers classify their clients (and vice versa), routine tasks and troubles, strategies of coping and survival, the operation of informal systems, rules, maxims and precedents, and so on.

I and the medical students found ourselves needing to accumulate a good deal of such organizational expertise. There were good practical reasons for this. As I have described elsewhere in some detail (Atkinson, 1981a), the students — like students and pupils in all educational settings — had to act as informal data-gatherers about the medical school: the various clinical specialties, the different teaching hospitals, the clinical 'firms' and the consultants who taught them.

The 'student culture' of the medical school therefore included quite complex typifications, taxonomies and situated vocabularies (cf. Mills, 1940) whereby the students generated and shared their perspectives on their collective experiences and expectations of clinical work. The understanding of such categories and their use is of fundamental importance. Manning (1971), for instance, suggests that the collection of such situated vocabularies constitutes a fundamental approach to socialization in organizational settings. As novices are inducted, they acquire their sense of social structure, and of their position in it, through the medium of such typifications. The acquisition of competent membership is equivalent to the competent use of such cultural resources (cf. also Stoddart, 1974; Wieder, 1974).

My interest in such topics thus paralleled the everyday, practical concerns of the medical students themselves. While I was not interested in evaluating the various clinical firms myself, a good deal of my data collection and analysis was directed to understanding how such evaluations were arrived at by student members. I became an 'expert' in the students' views of the medical school. I probably had a much more detailed and extensive repertoire of folk wisdom and anecdotes concerning hospitals, firms and teachers, than any one student could ever have had access to.

As I have indicated, these elements of student culture were not special to the Edinburgh medical school. Parallel themes have been documented from studies of school pupils as data-gatherers about their schools and teachers (cf. Beynon and Atkinson, forthcoming). Likewise, earlier studies of medical education had highlighted very similar themes. The classic neo-Chicago-school study of Kansas medical school (Becker *et al.*, 1961), for example, had been preoccupied with the documentation of student culture and shared 'perspectives'. Although by no means identical with my Edinburgh material, the Kansas data revealed comparable student preoccupations. In this respect the two studies had very similar characteristics: they both drew on the same tradition of interactionist studies of organizations, within which 'socialization' has always been a major theme.

Indeed, there were some colleagues who — at the outset of my research — believed that any work on medical education was an ill-conceived undertaking. They pointed out that it had 'been done', in the Kansas study, and the parallel functionalist classic of the genre (Merton *et al.*, 1957). I must confess that there were times during the research when I myself had similar misgivings. My research was undoubtedly 'original' in a purely formal sense: nobody had even replicated the American research in a British medical school. But something more was clearly required if that empty sort of originality were to be transcended. In the event these self-doubts were not long-lasting. A detailed comparison of my own rapidly accumulating fieldnotes and the published accounts of previous research showed a very fundamental difference. (Or so I thought, and still think.) That difference brings one to the second type of knowledge that I acquired some familiarity with, and which complemented the organizational perspectives I have just referred to. It is to this second type of 'inside', technical knowledge that I now turn.

Learning Medicine

There was, I discovered, an absence at the heart of the Kansas medical school ethnography. This was captured for me by a remark made by a fellow British sociologist: 'Oh yes, *Boys in White*, it tells you everything except what's really going on!' Now at first sight, that might appear to be an odd remark. *Boys in White* is a long and detailed monograph, which reports a substantial piece of ethnographic team-work. But what is missing is the detailed treatment of how students learn medicine and how students engage in medical work. Likewise, there is a lack of documentation of what students *do* as medical students. In a purely personal sense, therefore, I sought to ensure an 'original' contribution to the literature by concentrating my efforts on the processes of social interaction on the wards and in the teaching rooms, in operating theatres and clinical conferences, while medical knowledge was being formulated, reproduced and transmitted.

I suspect that the lack of such discussion in comparable studies reflects a fairly general methodological issue. Many ethnographics are, or claim to be, based upon participant observation of social action in naturally occurring settings. Participant observation is, of course, often 'triangulated' with other research methods, such as those of the survey and interviews (cf. Zelditch, 1962; Denzin, 1970). But an attentive reading of many published monographs reveals that the observation of action is strangely missing. While the researcher's first-hand involvement and immersion in the field no doubt informs understanding and analysis, it is often the case that the account rests largely on data gathered from interviews and conversations. In some studies, the illustrative data extracts which are included in the text are disproportionately drawn from such sources. This is particularly odd, given the methodological commitments which most ethnographers would probably endorse — not least, the fundamental difference between 'words' and 'deeds' (cf. Deutscher, 1973). It is the case, however, that *Boys in White* relied heavily on students' accounts as evidence of 'perspectives' and was disappointingly thin on their everyday activities. Some of these activities, including the most vital aspects of clinical work, are glossed over in just one paragraph (p. 315). The clinical encounter remained invisible, and the sociological commentators silent on it.

Now it never occurred to me not to pay attention to the processes of interaction in bedside teaching encounters. It was not an entirely conscious decision: given my chosen setting and cohort of students, there was relatively little else for me to observe. I should have gathered previous little data had I concentrated only on students' conversations during coffee breaks and the like. Nevertheless, it was taken for granted that the processes of bedside instruction should be a topic of my research. This led directly to a consideration of the management of medical knowledge itself.

Specialist knowledge of various sorts is the stock-in-trade of most occupational groups, and it is self-evidently the case for medicine. It is significant that one of the major texts in the sociology of medicine, Eliot Freidson's *Profession of Medicine* (1970), is sub-titled 'A Study of the Sociology of Applied Knowledge'. In studying such occupational groups, or equivalents, such as academic communities, the problem arises as to the extent to which the ethnographer needs to master such esoteric knowledge in order to conduct research on that epistemic collectivity. This problem has, it seems to me, been inadequately discussed by writers on fieldwork methods. It is, perhaps, taken for granted that such knowledge is not the proper concern for sociological understanding. Yet it is an extremely important topic and resource for the community members themselves: it may be the subject of discussion, debate and difference of opinion; its ownership or otherwise may be used to define the boundaries between one group and another (cf. Sharrock, 1974); competent grasp and use of the knowledge may be constitutive of memberships; censure and negative sanctions will accompany recognized failure in the use of specialist knowledge; membership may rest on the formal accreditation of knowledge and skills. The list of potential issues is all but endless, for the acquisition and deployment of specialist knowledge is of such fundamental and pervasive significance.

Therefore, it may be of great importance that the ethnographer gain some acquaintance with the esoteric knowledge of the group or occupation under scrutiny. Much previous research on professional socialization had suffered on this score, I wrote in my thesis in 1976, and it has continued to be a characteristic failing in the field. I have recently had occasion to publish a paper drawing attention to this continued neglect of knowledge in studies of professional education (Atkinson, 1983). In medical sociology generally it is the case that the social construction of medical knowledge has tended to receive more systematic treatment from historical studies than from the ethnographic (cf. Wright and Treacher, 1982; Armstrong, 1983).

It is, in passing, worth noting that despite the *succès d'estime* of the 'new' sociology of education, in directing attention to the *content* of educational processes, the sociology of education is not well-endowed with empirical studies of knowledge at classroom level. The original programme outlined by M.F.D. Young and his colleagues (Young, 1971) was not systematically carried through with detailed investigations, although Young himself did work on school science (Young, 1976). I do not wish to imply a total absence of relevant work in this context, but it is remarkably sparse. It is even the case that, paradoxically, curriculum evaluators adopting an 'illuminative', 'case study' or ethnographic approach have said little that is systematic about the content, transmission and evaluation of knowledge per se. Like the authors of *Boys in White*, they tell us everything except what's really going on. A case in point is the fact that a number of the 'evaluations' of American school science conducted under the guidance of Stake (1978) barely make mention of science at all, so busy are they discussing the personalities and the politics of the school setting.

There is so much attention, still, to the 'hidden curriculum' that the specialized knowledge of educational and occupational settings gets short measure. Likewise, there is a tendency among educational ethnographers to concentrate on and celebrate the academically less able — the 'lads' (Willis, 1977), the 'dossers' (Turner, 1983) and the deviant. There is therefore little sense that knowledge and educational work might matter to students, and the ethnographer may implicitly be absolved from troubling with specialized knowledge.

In the context of my own research it was not at all difficult to gain some acquaintance with medical knowledge. The events which I was witnessing and participating in were explicitly defined as *teaching* episodes: the students themselves were being taught the knowledge which formed much of the content of the interaction. In treating this material I probably had a methodological advantage over some researchers in school classrooms. Although it was not totally alien to me, the medical knowledge probably came rather fresher than would, say, 'the Vikings', 'decimals', 'how to use a Bunsen burner' or 'doing' *The Mayor of Casterbridge* for the umpteenth time. (This is not an excuse: we should at least *try* to make the Bunsen burner anthropologically strange.)

Although I did not possess any special grounding in the medical sciences, I found that I too was being 'taught' medicine — vicariously, as it were, through my participation with the medical students. Bedside teaching is an extremely vivid form of teahcing: 'real' patients provide very memorable 'audio-visual aids' in teaching, and at times the ceremony of the clinic approximates to a sort of ritual drama.

Willy-nilly I picked up a good deal of ad hoc medical information, and some rudimentary understanding of diagnosis and management in medicine and surgery. I also made some attempt (albeit spasmodically) to refer to medical textbooks (such as Davidson's *Principles and Practice of Medicine*, contributed to by members of the Edinburgh staff) and read up on conditions to which the students had been introduced. Needless to say, I did not assume that the textbooks gave me the 'right' answer in clarifying what was said and done at the bedside. The contrast between book-knowledge and practical experience is a major theme in the transmission of clinical knowledge.

The students themselves often found it hard to believe that I was genuinely capable of following what was going on. On occasion they would commiserate with me on my 'obvious' inability to understand what I was observing. They sometimes seemed unable or unwilling to believe that I was indeed able to keep up with the greater part, if not all, of what was going on. Some students even appeared to resent my professed ability to make sense of things without the background training in the basic and medical sciences.

I do not want to overstate the case. There was clearly an enormous amount of fundamental knowledge in anatomy, physiology, biochemistry, pathology, bacteriology and so on that the students had assimilated, and that I was totally ignorant of. On the other hand — and this was heuristically significant — it was remarkable how little of that scientific preparation was absolutely essential to an understanding of the students' clinical work. Moreover, much of that work was translated into everyday terminology, although it was invested with special connotations. In addition, much of what was taught and practised was based directly on mundane powers of observation and reasoning: as such, it was in principle accessible to anybody with the privileged access to the teaching encounters. Whilst diagnostic inferences are informed by knowledge of medical sciences, the observation of a patient's complexion and general physical appearance, gait and other behaviour, such as gestures, does not in itself depend on such esoteric knowledge. Their particular clinical significance is a matter of special understanding, but is open to the ethnographer's gaze. The medically unqualified, for instance, has no difficulty in understanding that valuable diagnostic clues as to the location and character of pain are furnished by movements and gestures of the hand while the patient tells his or her history.

To some extent, then, the management of such clinical knowledge and my understanding of it created minor problems of self-presentation on my part. While I made no explicit attempts to claim any such expertise, the maintenance of credibility in the field sometimes meant that I could not admit to or claim complete incompetence either. My concern here goes beyond that issue, however. Rather, I am addressing the general theme of the social distribution of knowledge in the field, and the role of the ethnographer in coming to grips with it.

In developing this point further I shall begin by outlining Schutz's characterization of ideal-types of knowledge, and their associated roles. Schutz (1964) distinguishes in people's repertoires of knowledge about the world, three types of knowledge. In the first place, there are areas where we have 'explicit knowledge of *what* is aimed at'. Secondly, there are areas where we have 'knowledge *about* what seems to be sufficient'. Thirdly, there 'comes a region in which it will do merely "to put one's trust"'. These varieties will be related to the degrees of relevance to the actor in his or her daily life — there will be ranges of topics in which a close and detailed knowledge is needed, and ranges where a 'nodding acquaintance' is sufficient for all normal practical interests. Schutz uses this notion to develop an ideal-typical formulation of three social types associated with such 'attitudes': the 'expert', the 'well-informed citizen' and the 'man in the street'.

On entry to the field, whilst I was familiar with the general nature of hospital life, I was certainly a 'man in the street' when it came to the technical vocabulary and knowledge of clinical medicine. However, in the course of doing the research I found myself becoming a 'well-informed citizen' on such matters. To some extent I cultivated some basic medical knowledge as a resource in doing the research. I did try to make a point of noting and, if necessary, looking up technical terms in medicine and surgery. This was a personal reward for the conduct of the research — a personal satisfaction gained in the acquisition of such knowledge. I also found it necessary to note some of the technical detail. For example, it might happen that there was disagreement over the diagnosis of a patient between the doctors who taught the students; or, in the course of time, the diagnosis would be changed. In following such developments, some attention to the technical detail of the doctors' and students' talk provided me with benchmarks in charting these shifts of definition and in the comparison of the divergent opinions. More generally, it is always difficult to follow prolonged discussions on topics which are mostly alien and poorly understood. Not only do the nuances and details of such talk get overlooked, but also major topics of discussion may otherwise pass over the observer's head.

The topic of pharmacology was an area in which I found it particularly expedient to develop some acquaintance with specialist medical knowledge — primarily a grasp of the range of generic and proprietary names of drugs that were most commonly referred to. This did not mean that I was tempted to become an expert in the various specialist subjects. In recording my notes, I was not concerned with evaluating whether the students were 'right' or 'wrong' in their replies to doctors' questions. Nor was I worried about whether what the doctors told their students was in accord with contemporary scientific orthodoxy. Thus I did not need to learn the precise metabolic action of the drugs and so attempt to become an expert on pharmacology and biochemistry (even if I had been capable of such a task). However, the ability to recognize and make some clinical sense of the topics of teaching sessions did enable me to produce much more detailed and faithful field notes than would otherwise have been possible.

What I am suggesting is that while there is no necessity for a fieldworker to become an 'expert' in medicine (or whatever), it may be advantageous to become something of a 'well-informed citizen' in performing the research. In the context of my own research, the fact that I was observing educational occasions made the acquisition of such knowledge fairly straightforward. There were many areas of clinical work which were novel to the students themselves, and had to be explained to them by the clinicians. In the course of such educational talk, things were made more explicit to the students, and spelled out in some detail; hence I often found that by following the content of tutorials or bedside teaching sessions I also picked up the same basic clinical knowledge. In this respect, educational situations may be more easy to follow than those involving only qualified and competent members of a group or occupation, when more things might be taken for granted and passed over without explanation.

Although it occasionally created troubles, I also used the ignorance of the lay observer as a research resource. The fact that I was not medically trained meant that I could (often genuinely) plead ignorance and lack of understanding. Such appeals permitted me to ask for clarification of particular activities or accounts which could have come oddly from an 'expert'. As Lofland points out, it is often expedient to act in such a way as to portray oneself as an 'ignorant-student-who-has-to-be-taught', and to make a virtue of ignorance. One may thus legitimately ask those questions whereby 'what everyone knows' is rendered explicit by the members concerned. As Lofland (1971, pp. 100–1) puts it, 'there may . . . be a split between being an acceptable incompetent and needing to be an inside expert'.

My argument, based on my own 'clinical experience', is that the split Lofland refers to — between incompetent stranger, novice or lay person, and inside expert or well-informed citizen — needs explicit recognition and careful management. While the ethnographer should never become an 'expert' in the sense of 'going native' and taking on the distinctive knowledge of a given culture, that is not an adequate argument against an informed appraisal of specialized knowledge. If ethnographers set their faces against such activity, then they are in danger of reproducing extremely partial views of the social world. If we cling too strenuously to the most naive versions of 'incompetence', then we shall capture only the lowest common denominator of everyday life. We populate our social scenes with teachers who do not teach any particular subjects, doctors who do not practise medicine, lawyers who do no legal work, and so on. We reduce them all to a sort of Everyman and Everywoman, mirroring our chosen position of man or woman 'in the street'.

Finally, these remarks are not to be read as advocacy of an unduly reverential attitude towards professional or educational knowledge. The medical knowledge which is reproduced in teaching hospitals, learned journals, and daily practice is not to be taken on trust. Medical work is not necessarily informed by the 'science' it professes. It is shot through with 'everyday' assumptions, with elements of 'ritual' and 'magic' (for example, Comaroff, 1982; Posner, 1976; Hughes, 1976). Practitioners do not always act like Schutz's ideal-typical 'expert'. They rely upon their own versions of practical reasoning (Murcott, 1981; Strong, 1980). But our understanding of such features is ultimately to be informed by a willingness to 'get inside' the social construction of such forms of knowledge.

In retrospect I find that my own work on medical education did not go far enough in that respect. I hope that fellow sociologists today do not think that I have 'done' medical education in Britain, flattering though that might be. The study of occupational and professional socialization needs constantly to be invigorated and informed by dialogue with the sociology of other varieties of education. By the same token, the sociology of 'education' needs to be reminded of the potential breadth of its subject matter.

Conclusion

As will have been apparent, I have not attempted in this paper to present a complete autobiographical-cum-methodological account of my work in the Edinburgh medical school. In the first place, I have already published one such account as the appendix to the published monograph (Atkinson, 1981a, pp. 123–38). Secondly, in contemplating this exercise I have been struck by the sheer complexity of documenting even a modest — and fairly straightforward — ethnographic project. A much fuller account, based on the relevant section of my PhD thesis, runs to some 20,000 words, and that is far from complete. Whole aspects of the research process remain unreported: my files contain draft sections on the conduct of the research which never found their way into the thesis or any subsequent publications. Other topics — of equal if not greater importance — did not even reach that stage.

Here I have addressed myself to a very restricted range of themes in an attempt to illuminate some problems of more general interest. For while we can often learn much from autobiographical confessionals, they should be used to develop more systematic perspectives on the conduct of ethnographic research.

In developing my argument I have tried to indicate the relevance of my own work to that which is more familiarly designated as 'educational'. I regret that such heavy-handedness seems to be necessary. Ethnographers, above all other researchers, should not be bound by the culturally arbitrary divisions, such as the different substantive 'sociologies of. . .'; nor should they be blinkered by commonsense assumptions, such as what counts as 'education'. I know that we all are, and cannot absolve myself from these strictures. We make some things 'strange' against a background of unexamined assumptions. The value of autobiography and reflection may be in helping us to conjure up and confront these personal and methodological failings.

Acknowledgements

My research in the Edinburgh medical school was supported by an SSRC postgraduate studentship and by a grant from the Nuffield Foundation. It would not have been possible without the help and support of Professor A.S. Duncan and Professor H. Walton, as well as the clinical staff and students of the medical school. My doctoral work at Edinburgh was supervised by Liam Hudson and Peter Sheldrake, to whom I repeat my thanks. My understanding of the sociology of medicine, education and ethnographic methods has gained immeasurably from the colleagueship of Sara Delamont, Anne

Murcott and Martyn Hammersley: my misunderstandings are my own responsibility. I am also grateful to Robert Burgess for his editorial advice and support.

References

ARMSTRONG, D. (1983) *The Political Anatomy of the Body*, Cambridge, Cambridge University Press.

ATKINSON, P. (1975) 'In cold blood: Bedside teaching in a medical school', in CHANAN, G. and DELAMONT, S. (Eds) *Frontiers of Classroom Research*, Slough, NFER.

ATKINSON, P. (1976) *The Clinical Experience: An Ethnography of Medical Education*, unpublished PhD thesis, University of Edinburgh.

ATKINSON, P. (1977) 'The reproduction of medical knowledge', in DINGWALL, R., HEATH, C., REID, M. and STACEY, M. (Eds) *Health Care and Health Knowledge*, London, Croom Helm.

ATKINSON, P. (1981a) *The Clinical Experience: The Construction and Reconstruction of Medical Reality*, Aldershot, Gower.

ATKINSON, P. (1981b) 'Inspecting classroom talk', in ADELMAN, C. (Ed.) *Uttering, Muttering*, London, Grant Macintyre.

ATKINSON, P. (1983) 'The reproduction of the professional community', in DINGWALL, R. and LEWIS, P. (Eds) *The Sociology of the Professions: Lawyers, Doctors, and Others*, London, Macmillan.

ATKINSON, P. and DELAMONT, S. (1976) 'Mock-ups and cock-ups: The stage management of guided discovery instruction', in WOODS, P. and HAMMERSLEY, M. (Eds) *School Experience* London, Croom Helm.

BECKER, H.S. (1971) Footnote to WAX, M. and WAX, R. 'Great tradition, little tradition and formal education', in WAX, M., DIAMOND, S. and GEARING, F. (Eds) *Anthropological Perspectives on Education*, New York, Basic Books, p. 10.

BECKER, H.S., GEER, B. HUGHES, E.C., and STRAUSS, A. (1961) *Boys in White*, Chicago, University of Chicago Press.

BEYNON, J. and ATKINSON, P. (forthcoming) 'Pupils as data-gatherers: Mucking and sussing', in DELAMONT, S. (Ed.) *Readings on Interaction in the Classroom*, London, Methuen.

COHEN, L.C. and MANION, L. (1980) *Research Methods in Education*, London, Croom Helm.

COMAROFF, J. (1982) 'Medicine: Symbol and ideology', in WRIGHT, P. and TREACHER, A. (Eds) *The Problem of Medical Knowledge*, Edinburgh, Edinburgh University Press.

COXON, A.P.M. (1971) 'Occupational attributes: Constructs and structure', *Sociology*, 5, 3, pp. 335–54.

CRAMOND, W.A. (1973) *Prescription for a Doctor*, Inaugural Lecture, University of Leicester, Leicester University Press.

DELAMONT, S. (1976) *Interaction in the Classroom*, London, Methuen.

DELAMONT, S. (1981) 'All too familiar? A decade of classroom research', *Educational Analysis*, 3, 1, pp. 69–84.

DELAMONT, S. and ATKINSON, P. (1980) 'The two traditions in educational ethnography: Sociology and anthropology compared', *British Journal of Sociology of Education*, 1, 2, pp. 139–52.

DENZIN, N. (1970) *The Research Act*, Chicago, Aldine.

DEUTSCHER, I. (1973) 'Words and deeds: Social science and social policy', *Social Problems*, 13, pp. 253–4.

FREIDSON, E. (1970) *Profession of Medicine*, New York, Dodd Mead.

FRENCH, P. and MACLURE, M. (1979) 'Getting the right answer and getting the answer right', *Research in Education*, 22, pp. 1–23.

GEER, B. (1964) 'First days in the field', in HAMMOND, P. (Ed.) *Sociologists at Work*, New York, Basic Books.

HAMMERSLEY, M. (1977) 'School learning: The cultural resources required by pupils to answer a teacher's question', in WOODS, P. and HAMMERSLEY, M. (Eds) *School Experience*, London, Croom Helm.

HUDSON, L. (1968) *Frames of Mind*, London, Methuen.

HUGHES, D. (1976) 'Everyday and medical knowledge in categorising patients', in DINGWALL, R., HEATH, C., REID, M. and STACEY, M. (Eds) *Health Care and Health Knowledge*, London, Croom Helm.

KARABEL, J. and HALSEY, A.H. (Eds) (1977) *Power and Ideology in Education*, New York, Oxford University Press.

LOFLAND, J. (1971) *Analyzing Social Settings*, Belmont, Calif., Wadsworth.

MANNING, P.K. (1971) 'Talking and becoming: A view of organizational socialization', in DOUGLAS, J.D. (Ed.) *Understanding Everyday Life*, London, Routledge and Kegan Paul.

MEIGHAN, R. (1981) *A Sociology of Educating*, London, Holt, Rinehart and Winston.

MERTON, R.K., READER, G.G. and KENDALL, P.L. (Eds) (1957) *The Student Physician*, Cambridge, Mass., Harvard University Press.

MILLS, C.W. (1940) 'Situated actions and vocabularies of motive', *American Sociological Review*, 5, pp. 904–13.

MURCOTT, A. (1981) 'On the typification of "bad" patients', in ATKINSON, P. and HEATH, C. (Eds) *Medical Work: Realities and Routines*, Aldershot, Gower.

POSNER, T. (1976) 'Magical elements in orthodox medicine', in DINGWALL, R., HEATH, C., REID, M. and STACEY, M. (Eds) *Health Care and Health Knowledge*, London, Croom Helm.

ROBINSON, P. (1982) *Perspectives on the Sociology of Education: An Introduction*, London, Routledge and Kegan Paul.

SCHUTZ, A. (1964) 'The well informed citizen, an essay on the social distribution of knowledge', in *Collected Papers Volume 2*, The Hague, Nijhoff.

SHARROCK, W. (1974) 'The ownership of medical knowledge', in TURNER, R. (Ed.) *Ethnomethodology*, Harmondsworth, Penguin.

SHAW, B. (1982) *Educational Practice and Sociology*, Oxford, Martin Robertson.

SPINDLER, G. and SPINDLER, L. (1982) 'Roger Harker and Schönhausen: From the familiar to the strange and back again', in SPINDLER, G. (Ed.) *Doing the Ethnography of Schooling*, New York, Holt, Rinehart and Winston.

STAKE, R. (Ed.) (1978) *Case Studies in Science Education*, Champague-Urbana, CIRCE.

STODDART, K. (1974) 'Pinched: Notes on the ethnographer's location of argot', in TURNER, R. (Ed.) *Ethnomethodology*, Harmondsworth, Penguin.

STRONG, P.M. (1980) 'Doctors and dirty work — the case of alcoholism', *Sociology of Health and Illness*, 2, 1, pp. 24–47.

TURNER, G. (1983) *The Social World of the Comprehensive School*, London, Croom Helm.

WIEDER, D.L. (1974) 'Telling the code', in TURNER, R. (Ed.) *Ethnomethodology*, Harmondsworth, Penguin.

WILLIS, P. (1977) *Learning to Labour*, Farnborough, Saxon House.

WRIGHT, P. and TREACHER, A. (Eds) (1982) *The Problem of Medical Knowledge: Examining the Social Construction of Medicine*, Edinburgh, Edinburgh University Press.

YOUNG, M.F.D. (Ed.) (1971) *Knowledge and Control*, London, Collier-Macmillan.

YOUNG, M.F.D. (1976) 'School science — innovation or alienation?', in WOODS, P. and HAMMERSLEY, M. (Eds) *School Experience*, London, Croom Helm.

ZELDITCH, M. (1962) 'Some methodological problems of field studies', *American Journal of Sociology*, 67, pp. 566–76.

8   A Study in the Dissemination of Action Research

Jean Rudduck

Editor's Commentary. While it is now common to find that the process of dissemination is a crucial stage in curriculum research and development projects, it is still relatively rare to find studies of the dissemination process in action. In this chapter Jean Rudduck discusses her study of the dissemination of two projects: problems and effects of teaching about race relations and teaching about race relations through drama. Both these projects, together with Rudduck's study, were housed at the Centre for Applied Research in Education at the University of East Anglia. Jean Rudduck's study continues to broaden our notion of an educational setting with its focus on educational events: a series of conferences in which teachers acted as the disseminators of an action research programme. Rudduck begins by outlining the context of her study; she describes the curriculum projects and the dissemination activity before focusing on the study itself.

Her chapter highlights the interrelationship between projects in a research centre, and the use of fieldwork strategies as well as the development and use of case records. Jean Rudduck focuses on several crucial aspects of her research role as well as on styles of recording data, keeping field notes and making transcriptions. In particular, she begins to explore the nature of a case record, how case records can be constructed and the relationship between case records and case studies. Among the questions that her chapter addresses are: What is a case record? How are case records established? What is the relationship between data recording, case records and a case study? In short, Rudduck's account of her project deals with a series of methodological issues on which many researchers engaged in action research projects at the Centre for Applied Research in Education have worked, and which are also discussed by Lawrence Stenhouse in the next chapter.

This is study of the dissemination of an action research project is worth reviewing for two reasons. First, in terms of content, it documents a move to support teachers as disseminators of an action research approach to teaching about race relations; this is unusual for although many national curriculum research and development projects have invited practising teachers to contribute to dissemination, teachers have not usually taken major responsibility for the tasks of communication and induction into new methods. Secondly, in terms of methodology, the fieldworker, faced with the problem of storing evidence from related but discrete events taking place over time, developed the idea of the case record. A subsequent project (also housed at the Centre for Applied Research in Education) which is described in the next chapter of this book, used the case record as the methodological backbone of a multi-site school study programme.

This chapter falls into five parts: part 1 describes briefly the two related projects on teaching about race relations that fuelled the dissemination activity; part 2 describes the dissemination activity and discusses possible reasons for its limited success; part 3 describes the study of dissemination and the use of the case record; part 4 explains why case records were used in the study and what form they took; part 5 argues the case for case records.

The Two Projects That Lay Behind the Dissemination Study

The two projects were closely related and conducted, in different schools, at the same time; one, funded by the Social Science Research Council, was on the problems and effects of teaching about race relations; the other, funded by the Gulbenkian Foundation, was on teaching about race relations through drama. The projects (both directed by Lawrence Stenhouse) were designed to support teachers in experimenting with three different teaching strategies: strategy A: in which teachers acted as neutral chairpersons in classroom discussions of racial issues (an approach developed in the Humanities Curriculum Project); strategy B: in which teachers were free to express their social commitment in teaching about race relations; strategy C: in which teachers worked through drama.

In all, forty schools and over 100 teachers were involved, each school committing itself to one particular teaching strategy. The project was conceived as *action research* and teachers accepted responsibility for documenting, throughout one term of experimental work, their teaching about race relations. The fieldworker who was appointed to coordinate the research in schools, Bob Wild, refused on principle to enter classrooms to observe the teaching; instead he worked from data supplied by teachers which included audio tapes of classroom discussion, teachers' diaries, and examples of students' work; this material was supplemented by evidence from tape — recorded interviews with pupils and teachers, and documentary and other evidence of the school, its curriculum, and its social setting. A pre-test/post-test measurement programme, using experimental and control groups, was designed and carried out by Gajendra Verma and Lawrence Stenhouse (see Stenhouse, *et al.*, 1982; chapters 5 and 6). Stenhouse commented on the problems of experimental design in an action research context:

> Our job in the project was to design a research from which they (the teachers) and we learned as much as possible from their educational actions. This meant that we had to respond to educational actions in a spirit of systematic inquiry. Working in this way, with action that has to be justified in professional rather than primarily in research terms, is a characteristic of action research. We had to work alongside teachers, respecting their educational aims and professional judgment, but trying ourselves to learn as much as we could for a wider audience about the 'Problems and Effects of Teaching about Race Relations'. We wanted to ensure that the participating teachers had the best possible opportunity of learning too. Both their needs and our own meant that it was part of our job to support them as they developed a research role alongside their main role of teaching.
>
> How does one design a research to capture educational acts in a spirit of inquiry? One way is to attempt to cast them in the form of an experiment; another is to observe them carefully and record them. An experiment is shaped to sharpen the bearing of observations on certain questions and if possible to enable observation to be expressed as measurement. Naturalistic observation responds to the natural shape of events and attempts to portray them in a way that makes them open to people who did not have first-hand experience of them. We tackled our problem from both ends, using both experiment and descriptive case studies. In experiment we are fishing for generalizations; in case study we are portraying experiences that while they do not offer general laws, can be applied to the new situations we meet, as all thought-through experience can (Stenhouse in Stenhouse, *et al.*, 1982, p. 29).

The two projects were reported through case studies of the teaching in individual schools and through the generalized statements of the measurement data, the latter contributing a pattern of effects against which individual experiences could be set, and the former enabling readers to critique the blandness of the generalizations and perceive their inadequacy as a guide to action in particular settings. The project teams did not try to suggest a 'best strategy' for teaching about race relations in schools, but aimed instead to alert teachers to the potential and characteristic problems of each of the strategies studied; readers seeking specific guidance for action found no prescription but instead they were offered evidence which they had to weigh in relation to their understanding of the context in which they proposed to start teaching about race relations and the inclination of their own teaching style. The report has been criticized for its preoccupation with the *problems* of teaching about race relations — it is seen as pessimistic where its authors would claim that they had merely been realistic — but close scrutiny of the report justifies the authors' caution and their determination to appeal to teacher judgement through evidence, for there was a minority of settings in which teaching about race relations had, against the general trend, a deleterious effect on the attitudes of most pupils in the class. The case study data helped teachers to understand the conditions of action in these settings and to predict, by matching their own setting with the settings of the case studies, whether similar effects might obtain if they embarked on teaching about race relations with their own pupils. Too much was at stake to risk pleasing teachers who wanted recipes for action; teachers had to face the responsibility of professional judgement, and the project provided the grounds for judgement as well as a rationale of the need for teachers to make such judgements.

The Dissemination Activity

Although the final report was not published until 1982, some years after the research and development projects had ended, in the interim an active dissemination programme hd been undertaken. The Gulbenkian Foundation provided financial support for the dissemination; the SSRC provided financial support for the study of the dissemination.

The idea of moving into a dissemination phase was proposed by teachers from all three experimental teaching strategies who came together to a final conference (summer 1974) to review what had been learned and achieved. The conference report records the mood of the small group sessions on the morning of the final day:

> Through all the groups ran the sense of urgency, the need to *do* something — and the impotency of what might face the teacher on returning to his own situation. The loss of face to face contact established at the conference became a matter of increasing concern to many. Hence the fear of dissipating energy and ideals.

At the final plenary there was a direct appeal to the project's central team to take the initiative; to provide 'a driving force' in the shape of a report which might 'get teaching race relations on the road'. Then came a more impatient proposal that the teachers themselves should be the ones to take the initiative:

> It's time we stopped hiding our light under a bushel and instead of waiting for somebody at the top to say to us: "We believe you have been doing so and so. Would you like to talk about it?", we should start going to Teachers' Centres and to local education authorities saying: "I have got the expertise" — and we *have* got a certain amount of expertise — "Are you going to use me?" It's time we started to advertise what we have got ourselves.

The outcome was discussion between the project team and teachers that led to the setting up of a programme of dissemination activity — and a research proposal to study that activity. Stenhouse, who wrote the proposal, said this:

> I believe that difficulties will be encountered in disseminating the results of the project to practitioners in such a way that they can use them; and since those difficulties hinge on the induction of teachers into an understanding of the nature of action research, I believe that the process of dissemination will merit study. Such a study will be worthwhile, both for the light it throws on the presentation of research to teachers and because the report of the study will itself be a means of communicating an understanding of the relation of action research to teaching, which will generalise beyond the study.

It was called: A study in the dissemination of action research.

By the end of 1975 the ground had been prepared for dissemination and the proposal for its study had been approved. The central team in discussion with teachers decided that conferences were to be the main vehicle for communicating the experiences of the original projects and that teachers should accept the role of disseminators, with background support provided by Lawrence Stenhouse and his colleagues. Some teachers had already met to collect and edit teaching materials used in the original projects, and members of the central project team had produced case study material to illustrate the variety of experiences of the schools participating in the original projects (the data from the measurement programme had not at that stage been fully analyzed and were not, therefore, available at the start of the dissemination programme). A conference was organized in January 1976 for teachers who wished to continue their involvement into the dissemination phase (one or two interested newcomers also attended). This conference had two important functions: first, the central team had to induct potential teacher disseminators in techniques for communicating the experiences of the original projects in ways which kept faith with the principles of action research; secondly, the central team had formally to hand over responsibility for dissemination to the teachers and to define the nature and terms of their subsequent relationship to the teachers as they embarked on this new phase of activity.

Early in the conference Lawrence Stenhouse had a major heart attack. The conference proceeded but the teachers felt some uncertainty. Tensions reflecting a hitherto latent competitiveness among teachers representing the three different experimental teaching strategies now began to express themselves in distressing arguments. However, before the end of the conference the teachers rallied; they formed themselves into an association: National Association for Race Relations Teaching and Action Research (NARTAR), established a constitution, assigned roles on the executive committee, and outlined the beginnings of a programme of conference activity.

An initial grant from the Gulbenkian Foundation was intended to see the new association through the first year of its life by which time it expected to be financially self-sufficient — as a result of income from membership subscriptions and from royalties on the publication of the proposed teaching materials. But circumstances were not favourable; publishers, who had at first been eager to market the teaching materials, became cautious; one withdrew after a period of lengthy negotiation. A second asked for changes that were not acceptable to the teachers; a compromise was arrived at, but eventually this publisher also withdrew. The climate was changing, and by the time the teachers, now NARTAR, were ready to launch their dissemination programme, cut-backs in support for in-service were already taking effect:

> The Authority have had to reduce the financial provision for in-service education during the past year and I am afraid that owing to the present economic situation it is not possible to meet all demands that have been made, and we are obliged, therefore, regretfully to decline grant aid to a number of colleagues wishing to attend courses.... I must stress that this refusal in no way implies that the course would not be of value to you, nor that we are unappreciative of your keenness to attend. (Letter from an LEA to a teacher who sought support for attending a NARTAR course.)

NARTAR recognized that it was unrealistic in the circumstances to attempt to offer the five-day residential courses which were essential if participants were both to understand the principles of action research and to respond critically to the reported experiences of the two research projects. The teachers accepted that they had instead to work through small slots in established short courses run by other agencies; for instance, annual DES and subject association meetings. In three years, apart from small-scale local events, NARTAR members contributed to eight fairly major regional, national and local courses and conferences, as Table 8.1 shows.

The dissemination programme failed. The unfortunate and on the whole unpredictable turns of event mentioned above weakened its chances of succeeding. Gradually the programme of activities ground to a halt. The reasons for failure are complex:

1   The absence of teaching materials: it is a common experience in curriculum development work that teaching materials are perceived as an easy solution to classroom problems. Certainly, participants at short courses are inclined to feel that they have not had their money's worth if there is nothing to take away, and materials in the hand may be more reassuring than a set of ideas that participants have to carry away in their minds and translate later into action. The teacher disseminators were aware of this. They were worried about 'the way in which dissemination implies a concentration on product' and noticed that 'people want to come in and grab the stuff and put it under their arm'. They felt somewhat ambivalent towards teaching materials but would have preferred to have them available and to re-educate their audience than not to have them available and risk losing their audience.

Table 8.1. Summary of Major Dissemination Events

Date of event	Organizing agency and length of course/ conference	Size and nature of course/ conference	Pattern and time of NARTAR's contribution	Approx. number of people at NARTAR session(s)	Strategy 'A'			Strategy 'B'				Strategy 'C'		Newcomers		Central project team
					Alison	Dave	John	Jane	Peter	Don	Jimmy	Shelia	Jim	David	Jon	Lawrence Stenhouse
1 October 1975	Department of Education and Science regional 1 day	50 teachers approx.	1 hour 25 minutes	50		✓										✓
2 April 1976	National Association for Multi-Racial Education national 2 days	200 approx.	Group 1: 3½ hours Group 2: 3½ hours	25 25					✓			✓				
3 July 1976	Department of Education and Science national 8 days	60 teachers	Group 1: 15 hours Group 2: 4½ hours Group 3: 4½ hours	14 10 10	✓	✓	✓	✓			✓		✓			
4 September 1976	Association for the Teaching of the Social Sciences national 2 days	200 various	4 hours	7		✓		✓								
5 June 1977	Local Education Authority local 1 day	22 teachers	1 hour	22			✓									
6 October 1977	Local Education Authority local 2 days	40 sixth-form pupils	Assimilated in overall conference structure	40							✓		✓			
7 April 1978	Royal Society of Arts national 2½ hours	50 various	1½ hours	50							✓					
8 April 1978	Association for the Study of the Curriculum 1 day	100 various	3 hours	7										✓		✓
9 September 1978	British Educational Research Association 3 days	200 higher education	½ hour	80											✓	

2   NARTAR was an association which had no reputation:

> A new teacher organisation in the area of race relations, not
> yet weighed up and evaluated, and still to prove itself ... it's
> very difficult for people outside to see what we are doing
> because they can't see the teachers as part of the team.
> (Interview with Lawrence Stenhouse, 1977)

The publication of the teaching materials and of the report of the
original projects might have given status to NARTAR as a national
association.

3   The nucleus of active NARTAR members, who were also
members of the executive committee, all had fairly senior posts in
full-time teaching jobs and they were overstretched. Headteachers
were generous in allowing the teachers release, from time to time, to
lead sessions at national conferences, but teachers had to use their free
time for conference planning, for attending NARTAR committee
meetings and for editing the teaching materials. The difficulty of
coping with the planning of a major conference during term-time is
captured in this not untypical statement from an interview with the
then secretary of NARTAR:

> During the term I tried not to think about the conference at
> all under the pressure of more urgent but often more trivial
> problems — for example a visit by ten students to observe me
> teaching a class I can't control very well, attempts to get our
> sixth form executive committee to function, collecting re-
> sources for our mode C geography course, the school trip,
> preparing for a sixth form conference, a school fair, a school
> evening, extra lessons for my two S level pupils — and so on!
> By not thinking about the conference I managed not to panic.
> (Rudduck, 1982)

Over time there was some natural wastage among the nucleus of
staunch and reliable teacher disseminators — resignations related to a
new job, a new husband, illness and death in the family, and
increasing pressures in the old job.

4   There was little opportunity for the NARTAR committee
members, busy as they were with editing the abortive teaching
materials and planning and running conferences, to build up the
membership of NARTAR and to establish it as a credible organization. Many teachers from the original projects had joined NARTAR
when it was launched, probably on a tide of good intent that was
raised by the euphoria of the moment, but thereafter their direct

contact with NARTAR was slender and despite five newsletters in one and a half years, for them NARTAR must have had an insubstantial reality. New people joined but the total membership never exceeded sixty-four. Gradually, NARTAR was attenuated to the few members who were in the front line of action.

5 To communicate its complex message effectively, NARTAR disseminators needed a sustained period of contact with conference participants. Instead (as Table 8.1 shows) it was necessary drastically to compress what they had to say and there was no hope of the principles of action research being even partially comprehended by audiences to whom the concept was new; the teacher disseminators had to work in settings over which they had little or no control, and with groups who were sometimes conscript audiences, sometimes volunteers — but by no means all of whom had serious intentions of introducing teaching about race relations into their schools.

6 There was evidence that in some areas of the country race relations was not then a topic which had strong in-service appeal for teachers:

> I think the biggest problem is to get it [race relations] into people's consciousness in the first place. If I advertised a conference in my Centre ... the very title would put off 90% of the people, would stop them coming, because as far as they are concerned it's nothing to do with them. They are science teachers or maths teachers ... and this is the big problem — trying to get it into other people's consciousness. (Interview with a teacher disseminator)

In 1983 the treasurer of NARTAR, Dave, carried on virtually alone — handling income from royalties of the recently published report of the original projects (Stenhouse, *et al.*, 1982) and answering letters: 'I suppose what has kept me going is the expectation that something would happen ... because it's always been about to take off' (Interview). With the publication of the report in 1982 it was just possible that it could take off — but the cost of the hardback book meant that few teachers were likely to buy it. What we shall never know is what would have happened if Lawrence Stenhouse had compromised principles and instead of inviting the teacher researchers to act as teacher disseminators, had led the dissemination programme himself. As it was, the enterprise was a bold failure. In terms of teacher potential, the story is an encouraging one; in terms of teacher power within the system, the end is predictable. What matters is what can be learned from the failure.

The Study of Dissemination

When the proposal for the study of the dissemination was drafted, we already knew that conferences were to be the main vehicle for communication. We anticipated that there would be a number of intensive residential conferences run by the teacher disseminators devoted exclusively to the dissemination of the ideas and experiences of the two race relations projects that lay behind the dissemination study. We also anticipated that there would be occasions when the teachers would want to extend the range of people they were reaching by contributing to conferences run by other agencies. In fact, as we have seen, the in-service climate virtually eliminated the former as a realistic option.

My task was to study the conferences. A colleague, Bob Wild, who had worked with Lawrence Stenhouse on the original projects, was to study the impact of the conferences on participants' thinking and practice by post-conference interviews and observations — that is, when participants had returned to their schools. This half of the study was made difficult in two ways. First, as we have seen the circumstances in which the teacher disseminators had to present the work of the projects did not favour the exploration of complex messages: the possibility of informed action as an outcome of the conferences was slender. Nevertheless, some follow-up work was undertaken before the second problem occurred: my colleague, who was on 'soft money', accepted a job in Australia and left. I continued with my half of the study which was, if anything, enriched by the adverse circumstances in which the teacher disseminators were struggling for a foothold.

The issues that I was commissioned to illuminate through the study were these:

— the practicability of teachers taking major responsibility for the dissemination of a national curriculum project;
— whether teachers are perceived as credible disseminators by the different groups of people whom they encounter, including conference organizers (for example, HMI, advisers, teacher associations) and conference participants (for example, teachers, advisers, lecturers);
— the effectiveness of conferences as vehicles for the dissemination of the ideas and experiences of the two action research projects on race relations teaching;
— the persuasiveness, to teachers, of the logic of taking an action research stance in teaching about race relations.

I was in fact fairly well-known to the teacher disseminators through my peripheral involvement in the two original projects (I had planned and attended the final conference that brought teachers from all strategies together and I had acted as official reporter at two earlier conferences); my past relationship with them defined to a large extent the relationship that I took within the new study.

The task of documenting the conferences was recognized as important and the teacher disseminators readily collaborated with me in the accomplishment of the task. For instance, I was invited to attend all meetings of the NARTAR committee, meetings of the sub-committee set up to edit teaching materials, and planning meetings for the conferences. The action research approach which the teacher disseminators had pursued in the original projects, and which they were now proposing to others as an appropriate basis for teaching about race relations had, it seems, made them comfortable with the idea of self-study and with the notion that practice can be systematically improved through analysis of practice. It was therefore possible for them to see me as an extension of their teacher-as-researcher selves. I was present to gather data that in the more familiar setting of the classroom they might have gathered for themselves. The data that I gathered were the foundation of their self-knowledge as disseminators. Moreover, at the committee meetings and at the conference planning meetings I came to act as 'clerk'; the notes that I needed to take in my role of historian of dissemination allowed me to produce minutes for the teacher disseminators without much additional effort on my part and with a considerable saving of effort on theirs. In this way, I, as fieldworker, was able to support the people whose work was the subject of my study without unduly distorting the data that I was collecting.

My presence during the conferences was also seen as supportive. Lawrence Stenhouse's concern not to allow his authority and reputation to overshadow the authority and credibility of the teacher disseminators led him to remove himself from the action — although there were some occasions, a DES conference for instance, when his presence was the condition of the course organizers' acceptance of the teacher disseminators as a staff team (on this occasion he acted as a backstage consultant). But the teacher disseminators were in fact relieved to have a trusted outsider at the conference with them. Occasionally they would ask me for advice and when I saw that suggestions might help them consider alternative lines of action, I would respond. In addition, my readiness to tape record their feelings during and after the conferences was often cathartic, for the interchanges at conference sessions were sometimes heatedly aggressive or obstinately defensive and the teachers needed to talk out their anxieties and concerns. They were always strikingly open and non-self-protective in their accounts of their own moves, responses and emotions in difficult situations.

At all conferences or courses organized by agencies other than NARTAR I requested permission to attend in order to document the work of the teacher disseminators. Part of the agreement was that I would restrict my attention to them, that I would play as unobtrusive a role as possible, and that I would not interview conference members. At each event, at the start of the session or sequence of sessions that the teacher disseminators were responsible for, I would be introduced as someone who was present to help them study their performance. My social behaviour outside the sessions was controlled to help sustain such a relationship. I stayed close to the teacher disseminators, engaging in weather-type exchanges with conference members only when I had to, and avoiding using informal contacts at meals or at the bar as opportunities to elicit data from the conference members. During the formal sessions of the conference the teacher disseminators asked conference members' permission for me to record the discussion so that data would be available to help them analyze and improve their handling of the sessions. There were no uneasy questions and no refusals. The tape recorder was always clearly visible and placed close to the teacher disseminators — on two occasions conference members actually pointed out to me that the tape needed turning over! My field notes were accessible to the curious eyes of conference members who happened to sit next to me. I discussed the study freely with anyone who asked me about it. In this way, anxiety about my presence and purpose was, I think, allayed. I always sat within and not outside the formation of chairs set up by the teacher disseminators but spoke only if people present were asked by the teacher disseminators to introduce themselves in turn. Serious role dilemmas occurred on two occasions: first, some teacher disseminators chose to work through simulation and here I decided to participate, taking a non-differentiated one-of-the-crowd-type role, rather than to move into a full observer role; secondly, at a research conference which I normally attended as a member and where I knew many of the people present, I judged it more obtrusive for me to remain silent than to talk and so I allowed myself occasional non-controversial contributions; this strategy was of course discussed beforehand with the teacher disseminators responsible for the session.

I was always concerned to avoid participants gaining the impression that I was present at the conference as official historian or evaluator. I did not therefore attempt to document the event as a whole but tried instead to spotlight the activity of the teacher disseminators, leaving the rest in shadow. At plenary sessions not led by the teacher disseminators I was interested in recording whatever would help me to understand the complexity of the context in which the teacher disseminators were operating: for example, at the annual meeting of a subject association I noted the easy-going exchanges between the chairperson and individual members of the 200 strong audience, appreciating that the conference represented a meeting of in-group 'regulars' and that the teacher disseminators were, and knew they were, outsiders. On these occasions I did not use the tape recorder. The decision was political as well as ethical. In some plenary sessions which focused on broad multi-cultural issues the atmosphere could become highly charged and I was concerned lest the presence of the tape recorder might lead to questions which could prejudice conference members' attitudes to the work of the teacher disseminators. I relied instead on brief and unobstrusively made field notes.

During the sessions presided over by the teacher disseminators I used a tape recorder and took full notes (I wanted a running record of points made in the sessions to help me 'hear' the audio tape). Anxious to avoid the obtrusiveness of complicated technology I used an ordinary tape recorder with built-in microphone. This picked up most voices in the group. Since the conference members were often from different cultural groups, patterns of intonation and vocabulary were very varied and made transcribing by a secretary who had not been present at the conference very difficult. I therefore re-recorded the audio tapes onto dictaphone tapes using my notes as an aide-memoire. I was interested during these sessions in the following topics: the kinds of questions that were being asked about the two race relations projects; what lay behind apparent non-understanding or misunderstanding of what the teacher disseminators were trying to say; aspects of their work that held most appeal; whether conference members were concerned with process as well as product; what kind of attack was mounted and by whom; whether teachers, college lecturers, LEA advisers, white conference members, or black conference members made consistently different responses to the teacher disseminators (who were very conscious of themselves as an all white group). I had to find a way of coding participants as individuals (I did not want to, or need to, identify them as *named individuals* in my fieldnotes). This was difficult when the group was large, assembled for more than one session, and changed places from session to session! I used a caricature-like system of identification: 1: male; red-haired, white, adviser; 2: female; hoop earrings, black, secondary teacher; 3: female; heart-shaped glasses, white, college lecturer.

In addition to collecting data through field notes of conference sessions and tape recordings of sessions, I also gathered information about the setting and structure of each conference and its membership. I noted organizational details that seemed to me to hamper the teacher disseminators' work so that I could question them about their perception of such items. I made notes of any event I observed that was likely to throw light on the status of the teacher disseminators as perceived by the conference organizers as well as by the conference members. I also filed correspondence to do with the setting up of each conference; this was particularly valuable for it sometimes contained clear evidence of the reluctance of conference organizers to accept teachers as conference lecturers or conference staff. (For a full discussion of such evidence see Rudduck and Stenhouse, 1979.)

Why 'Case Records' Were Used in This Project and the Form They Took

There are two preliminary statements that I think are worth making in relation to this particular study. First, studying a conference is very different from studying a school. In a school case study, the fieldworker is permitted to enter, for a limited period, the world in which teachers and pupils act out their daily routines. The institution, and the processes it supports, have a continuity beyond the time of the fieldworker's contact, but in a study of an event — as opposed to an institution — the fieldworker's and the participants' experience of the event are coterminous with the event itself: that is, the event does not exist outside the period in which it is being studied, and the participants' acquaintanceship with it is no more extensive than the fieldworker's. Participants and fieldworker encounter the event together and the fieldworker is no more an outsider to the event under study than are the participants. There is no going back to the event for additional data. There is no span of time in which the fieldworker's view of the case being studied can develop and mature.

Secondly, I was involved in a series of cases that were spread out over time (not place, as in a multi-site programme). The cases were not a selection but the totality of major events that the teacher disseminators contributed to during the active life span of NARTAR. What I was interested in was the pattern of development of the teacher disseminators and the dissemination programme over time as well as the distinctive experiences of each individual event.

The writing up of the study did not begin until more than three years after the first conference took place. Clearly I could not have relied on memory: some record needed to be made. At the same time I was concerned lest I allowed interpretation en route to sift the data and move it into patterns that evidence from later events might have shown to be wrongly drawn. I needed to suspend judgement as far as was humanly possible in the early stages of the work. Producing case studies of each event and storing them did not seem appropriate, given my view of what a case study is. As I understand the term, a 'case study' is an interpretative presentation and discussion of the case, resting upon evidence gathered during fieldwork. It is constructed at the culmination of a period of fieldwork and is a public statement by the fieldworker about the case and a public presentation of the case. It is a subjective statement which its author is prepared to justify and defend. I was not ready to produce case studies of each dissemination event; I was more concerned to produce such a study of the dissemination programme overall. What I needed was a theoretically parsimonious condensation (Stenhouse, 1978) of the data I collected around each event — a case record (without some condensation, the accumulation of data over time could be overwhelming and physically unmanageable). The case record, then, was a cautiously edited selection of the full data available, the selection depending on the fieldworker's judgement as to what was likely to be of interest and value as evidence. For example, I cut out of the transcripts of planning meetings talk about coffee making and buying rounds of drinks; and from the recorded transcripts of the group discussions I cut passages where participants named themselves, and passages where the teacher disseminators repeated standard statements about the race relations projects or about their own biographies. Likewise I discarded items in conference handouts that gave travel instructions, details of shaving points and shops, and explained the local attractions.

Each case record included, as far as possible, the following:

    1   an account of the negotiations that led to the teacher disseminators presenting the project experiences and findings at the conference, including copies of important

letters and teachers' notes of important telephone calls or meetings;

2 extracts from transcripts of pre-conference and within-conference discussions among teacher disseminators;

3 information about the timing and content of the sessions or sequence of sessions that constituted the NARTAR presentation, and of numbers and backgrounds of people attending;

4 a selection of conference documents (such as advertizements and programmes which often revealed the conference organizers' perception of the status of the teacher disseminators and their work);

5 extracts from pre-conference and within-conference interviews with the teacher disseminators;

6 a description of the conference setting and any features of the conference management which might have affected the work of the teacher disseminators (for example, the absence of audio-visual equipment which had in fact been ordered in advance);

7 edited transcripts of all the sessions led by the teacher disseminators and accompanying fieldnotes;

8 field notes of sessions where the teacher disseminators were present but where they were not playing a leading part;

9 transcripts of any end-of-conference review meetings held by the teacher disseminators;

10 transcripts of any post-conference accounts of the conference (for instance, where the teacher disseminators present reported to the NARTAR executive committee;

11 fieldworker's reflections.

The preparation of the case records involved the following broad pattern of activity:

a collation of documents from various sources;

b transcriptions of tape recordings of relevant meetings, interviews, sessions and fieldwork notes (these were transferred from notebook to audio tape);

c anonymization of persons figuring in the case record (such as conference organizers) other than the teacher disseminators taking part;

d clearance by individual teacher disseminators of transcripts of interviews they had given, and of accounts of aspects of

the conference where the fieldworker was interpreting events
(for instance, the accounts of the negotiations that led up to
the teacher disseminators appearing at the conferences);

e modifications to the record in the light of justifiable requests
for changes or deletions, or for the inclusion of alternative
views of situations which I had interpreted or which teachers
had interpreted in their interviews;

f distribution of the case record to the active nucleus of teacher
disseminators and to the project director.

In the early case records I was finding my way: I overedited and
even restructured some material, ignoring the often untidy ebb and
flow of discussion and bringing together comments that were thema-
tically related even though on the tape recording they were distant in
time. I did this because of the dual purpose of the case records; not
only were they a basis for writing narrative and analytic reports of the
dissemination programme, but they had also to serve as a source of
formative feedback to the teacher disseminators. The two functions
were not entirely compatible. I was led to manipulate the data in
these ways because I was anxious lest the length of unedited and
discursive transcripts would prevent busy teachers from reading and
learning from the records. However, as time passed and the teacher
disseminators grew more confident and competent, and less reliant on
records as formative feedback, then I was able to respond to the need,
which I saw increasingly clearly, to stock the case records with as full
and as raw a set of relevant data as was feasible.

Another problem, given the situation I was working in, was the
nature of the fieldworker's reflections, which sometimes looked very
much like prescriptions! I had an easy going and mutually supportive
relationship with the teacher disseminators who knew that I had been
asked to act as fieldworker in this study because I had considerable
experience of planning and running conferences. There were occasions when I noticed that the techniques that they were using were
not wholly effective and could usefully be modified — and I noted
them, but added a comment. Here is an example of my field note
'advice':

Researcher's reflections:
1) non-participants who speak as the session ends or after it
has ended: does the chairperson need to find ways of helping
them to contribute during the session?
2) staff apologies — which are usually confessions of guilt

about their being unprepared or bids for sympathy: should they be avoided?

3) the difficulty of trying to be democratic and offering a group alternative ways of proceeding and yet not helping them with decision making structures. What usually happens is that one individual — the one who speaks first — determines what will happen. Or the chairperson decides;

4) the need to legitimise quiet reading in a group session, and to think why participants seem uncomfortable with it or even resistant to it. (Rudduck and Stenhouse, 1979)

Another dilemma was related to clearance: I was uncertain whether or not I should be allowing teacher disseminators the right to delete or modify any passages in the case record that they were unhappy about their colleagues seeing, or that they merely didn't want preserved in print. A passage from my notebook of fieldwork problems recalls the dimensions of my uncertainty. The passage was written after Don, one of the teacher disseminators, asked to change a statement that he made in interview during a conference:

The statement about his being 'no longer interested in talking about the project work' would be better replaced by a statement which suggests that his present distance from the work (he is no longer a teacher) undermines the credibility of his statement in talking about teaching about race relations. I feel very sympathetic to the teacher disseminator's complaint that comments — comments are *not* always measured — are committed to perpetuity through audio tape and print. Quite often what people *mean to say* comes across because it is helped by other signals and cues that print cannot represent. Moreover, there can be an emotional pressure in discussion or in interview which gives a more robust colour to the statements than the speaker may want to acknowledge after the event. I am also sympathetic to Don's comment that it is 'very difficult to recollect what my feelings were at the time'. So, another issue is whether in negotiating clearance we are, as report writers or record makers, concerned with the relative truth to experience at the time of the event or the truth to attitude at the time of reading about the event. Am I presenting, now, what Don wants it to be like or what it *was* like, and which is the more important since Don is clearly a key figure in the events I am studying? One way through is merely to add Don's comments to what I have assembled or written, but that means that there would remain in print passages that he felt were unacceptable, and I am inclined to remove them on request (spring 1976).

The case records, for all their limitations, were invaluable in enabling me to write a report of events that had spanned a three-year period. Had I produced instead of case records a succession of case studies — shorter, more elegantly fashioned, and highly interpretative, then I might have laid a series of snares for myself as author of the final report, trapping myself in premature judgements and preventing myself from being able to read the full history at the end of the fieldwork with a mind still capable of surprise.

Of course, in writing the final report, I had not only the nine case records to draw on but also minutes of the NARTAR committee meetings, copies of the NARTAR newsletters, details of membership numbers, and information showing NARTAR's contacts with members of the general public, with publishers, with project sponsors, and with the project director. I ordered and indexed all the supplementary data, and indexed the case records. Then I read and re-read the data, noting things that struck me on cards, building up some ideas into major lines of analysis, and discarding those that gained no weight from additional reading. Space does not permit a discussion of the many problems of writing up from such a mass of assorted material — including the temptation to give weight to highly articulate and arresting passages of transcription and to use them as the major building blocks of meaning (see Tripp, 1982; Hull, 1983). There was also the problem of writing about a group of people whom I had got to know fairly well so that at the time of writing up I detected in myself quite different attitudes towards different individuals in the group, some very positive and some slightly negative and reflecting a personal bias and not a professional judgement.

The Case for Case Records

First, I can claim the usefulness of case records as opposed to case studies to the person who, in a multi-site programme, has to write up a report across cases. The multi-site programme is best exemplified by the work of Bob Stake and Jack Easley in the United States (*Case Studies of Science Education*, reported in 1978) and by Lawrence Stenhouse in the United Kingdom (*Library Access and Sixth Form*

Study, reported in Rudduck, *et al.*, 1983). In both projects a team of fieldworkers conducted studies, roughly simultaneously, in a number of schools, but beyond that the approaches differed: the British team relied on condensed fieldwork (Walker, 1974), using the interview as the main source of evidence; the American team spent longer in schools and relied more heavily on observation; fieldworkers in the American team were commissioned to produce *case studies*; fieldworkers in the British team were commissioned to produce *case records*; Stake wrote his executive summary from the case studies supplied by the fieldworkers; Stenhouse planned to write the final report from the case records supplied by the field workers (after he died, in September 1982, I took responsibility for the report).

Stenhouse said of Stake's executive summary of the multi-site science education project that 'conclusions survive as evidence is progressively eroded'. Some richness of texture was inevitably lost when the fieldworker moved from case data to case study, arriving at an interpretation of the evidence, adducing a principle of relevance, and selectively presenting evidence in the case study. As Stake moved from case studies to executive summary there was another layer of erosion — or, as he puts it, 'multilation'. My concern, in both the multi-case programmes I have been involved with (the study of the dissemination of action research and the study of library access and sixth-form work) has been to delay the erosion, to minimize the mutilation, by working from the fuller and more theoretically open source, the case record, rather than from the explicitly coherent and personalized statement of the case study.

The case for case records has so far been made in terms of the writing up of a multi-case programme but there is another argument that relates both to the multi-case programme and to the single case study. It is to do with verification (Stenhouse, 1981). Stenhouse was uneasy with case studies that offer no evidence other than that cited by the writer in support of the interpretation: as a reader he had no means of judging the reasonableness of the interpretation except in terms of it resonating with his own experience. He grounds his argument in the discipline of historical method:

> At present most reporting . . . of case study seems to me both idiosyncratic and superficial. This is attributable less to the fault of the author of the reports than to the absence of a disciplined convention which could support scholarly work in this genre.
>
> I see the best promise for such a convention as lying in the

recommendation that case study workers produce case records from their field data which can serve as edited primary
sources accessible to other scholars. (1977, p. 2)

And again, elsewhere:

Given the accessibility criterion essential to history, I am
contending that field study should be seen as concerned with
the creation of sources and not, in the first instance at least,
with the creation of reports or portrayals. (1978, p. 25)

Stenhouse is suggesting that the existence of a public source (the case
record) makes it possible for the fieldworker's statement (expressed
in the case study) to be checked against evidence, even as historians,
provoked by possible anomalies in a published account, might
attempt a reinterpretation of events, drawing on the same pool of
primary sources.

The argument is beguiling, but I wonder if it holds for the kind
of educational case study with which we are familiar. Historical
events or situations may have sufficient intrinsic significance to
involve successions of scholars in reinterpreting the data, but I doubt
whether the events I studied in the dissemination project, for
instance, would merit such zealous enquiry among my professional
colleagues. If they consult my nine case records, it will probably be to
engage in an exercise in the interpretation of evidence as part of a
research training for their students rather than because they are
inspired to pursue fairness or truth in relation to my study of a group
of teacher disseminators.

Reid (1978, p. 29) sees something of the problem:

... caution is displayed by the reproduction of copious
recorded data, justified on the grounds that the reader may
interpret it if he disagrees with the author. Apart from
supporting the book and paper industry, it is a curious habit.
Not only is the possibility of reinterpretation not really on,
since the researcher always has more knowledge than can be
committed to paper, but it also begs the question as to why
the author should have bothered to present an interpretation
at all if it is not superior to another, or if the whole job can be
done by any reader from the limited data presented. In any
case, research has never been only about the collection of data
and it is always about interpretation, presentation and communication.

Reid is somewhat casual about the issue of appeal to public sources, assuming, it seems, that readers should trust researchers whose job it is to deal with data and who have presumably internalized a proper sense of standards during their training or research apprenticeship. Of course, researchers will offer the best interpretation in their view — but it may not be the only reasonable interpretation; and researchers *can* suffer from unconscious bias. More significant, I think, is the point Reid makes about the case record masquerading as a 'complete' or only lightly edited set of data: fieldworkers certainly carry recollections in their mind that go beyond the data given and that help them to interpret the data.

Stenhouse's interest in the case record was not confined to its contribution to the problem of verification. He had another claim up his sleeve. He suggests that case records of schools constitute a valuable historical resource in themselves:

> It is an exciting possibility that current interest in the careful study of cases might produce a national archive of ... case records. If we had such an archive now, we could understand in much greater intimacy and depth the recent history of our schools. (Stenhouse, 1980)

The nine case records produced for the dissemination project are publicly accessible and are anonymized, and offer a possible model for such an archive.

The case record is, then, alive and well and living in Norwich — if nowhere else!

References

BARTON, L. and MEIGHAN, R. (Eds) (1978) *Sociological Interpretations of Schooling and Classrooms*, Driffield, Nafferton.

HULL, C. (1983) 'Between the lines: The analysis of interview data as an exact art', unpublished paper, Norwich, Centre for Applied Research in Education (CARE), University of East Anglia.

REID, I. (1978) 'Past and present trends in the sociology of education', in BARTON, L. and MEIGHAN, R. (Eds) *Sociological Interpretations of Schooling and Classrooms*, Driffield, Nafferton.

RUDDUCK, J. (1982) 'Aftermath', in STENHOUSE, L. *et al.*, *Teaching about Race Relations: Problems and Effects*, London, Routledge and Kegan Paul.

RUDDUCK, J. and STENHOUSE, L. (1979) *A Study in the Dissemination of Action Research*, a report to the Social Science Research Council, HR 3483/1.

RUDDUCK, J., HOPKINS, D., GROUNDWATER SMITH, S. and LABBETT, B. (1983) *Library Access and Sixth Form Study*, a report to the British Library Research and Development Department.

STAKE, R.E. and EASLEY, J. (1978) *Case Studies in Science Education*, vol. XV, executive summary, Centre for Instructional Research and Curriculum Evaluation and Committee on Culture and Cognition, University of Illinois School of Education.

STENHOUSE, L. (1977) 'Exemplary case studies: Towards a descriptive educational research tradition grounded in evidence', a proposal for submission to the SSRC.

STENHOUSE, L. (1978) 'Case study and case records: Towards a contemporary history of education', *British Educational Research Journal*, 4, 2, pp. 21–39.

STENHOUSE, L. (1980) 'The study of samples and the study of cases', *British Educational Research Journal*, 6, 1, pp. 1–6.

STENHOUSE, L. (1981) 'The verification of descriptive case studies' in KEMMIS, S., BARTLETT, L. and GILLARD, G. (Eds) *Perspectives in Case Study 2: The Quasi-Historical Approach — Case Study Methods*, Deakin University Press.

STENHOUSE, L., VERMA, G., WILD, R.D. and NIXON, J. (1982) *Teaching about Race Relations: Problems and Effects*, London, Routledge and Kegan Paul.

TRIPP, D. (1982) 'The research interview: Validity, structure and record', draft paper, Murdoch University, Western Australia.

WALKER, R. (1974) 'The conduct of educational case study: Ethics, theory and procedures', in MACDONALD, B. and WALKER, R. (Eds) *Innovation, Evaluation, Research and the Problem of Control — Some Interim Papers*, Norwich, CARE, University of East Anglia, pp. 75–115; reprinted in DOCKERELL, W.B. and HAMILTON, D. (Eds) (1980) *Rethinking Educational Research*, London, Hodder and Stoughton, pp. 30–63.

9 Library Access, Library Use and User Education in Academic Sixth Forms: An Autobiographical Account[1]

Lawrence Stenhouse

Editor's Commentary. For many teachers and researchers the name of Lawrence Stenhouse is synonymous with the Humanities Curriculum Project. However, his contribution to educational research and development was much broader as he established the Centre for Applied Research in Education at the University of East Anglia which has housed a number of research projects on the curriculum that have influenced the shape and substance of debates in educational studies. In turn, many of these projects have not only dealt with substantive concerns but have also made contributions to key debates on the use of research methodology in the study of educational settings: on selection, on sampling, on condensed fieldwork, interviewing and case records. Lawrence Stenhouse made a number of important contributions to these debates on the basis of his own experience in educational research.

This chapter on the 'Library Access and Sixth-Form Studies' (LASS) Project, which was written six months before his death in September 1982, is particularly important as Stenhouse not only discusses his aim in this project but also demonstrates the way in which it relates to the main themes in his work over the last two decades. In this chapter he provides a discussion of research funding and research design as well as considering issues of selection and interviewing in case study research. He provides insights into theoretical issues as well as such practical matters as writing research proposals and conducting interviews.

A major theme that is covered in this chapter concerns the importance of case study methods, case records and data archives (also considered in Jean Rudduck's chapter); all of which were central issues on which he was still developing new thoughts. This chapter provides some examples of his work and of his thinking on these difficult issues in relation to a multi-site case study. Accordingly, he deals with such questions as: What social processes are involved in case study research? How can the researcher handle relationships with funding bodies, with informants and with fellow researchers? Stenhouse provides some clues on how he handled these relationships whilst doing research yet he is clear that he has not provided

the answer. His chapter will continue a number of debates in which he was
an active and distinguished contributor.

I take an autobiographical account to be simply a recollection, as
opposed to a 'retrospective analysis' in which recollection is verified
against documentary evidence and the recollections of others (Wise,
Singer, Altschuld and Berk, 1977). The project which is the subject of
this autobiographical account was funded under the title which stands
at the head of this paper, but we use the short title 'Library Access
and Sixth-Form Studies' (LASS). LASS is funded by the British
Library Research and Development Department as part of its programme of research in user studies. The proposal was written by me
and is dated June 1979. The project runs for two and a quarter years
from January 1980, and the budget is £47,850. Members of staff from
the following institutions are working on the project: Centre for
Applied Research in Education of the University of East Anglia;
Centre for Research in User Studies, University of Sheffield; Crewe
and Alsager College of Education; and Keswick Hall College of
Education (now the School of Education of the University of East
Anglia). Five freelance researchers are also involved. I am the 'Head
of Project' (BL's term) and the Coordinator of the Project is Beverley
Labbett, both of the Centre for Applied Research in Education.

Background to the Proposal

The proposal originated in the following way. I was unaware of the
existence of the British Library Research and Development Department until they sent me a proposal to referee. The proposal was
'illuminative' in style (cf. Stenhouse, 1979a; Parlett and Hamilton,
1972), and it cited my book as the source for its design (cf. Stenhouse,
1975). Another similar proposal followed, and then an invitation to
speak at a conference on library research, at which I was, to my
surprise, introduced as one whose work in curriculum was 'revolu-
tionizing' research on library user studies!

My previous research project on problems and effects of
teaching about race relations was coming to an end (cf. Stenhouse,
Verma, Wild and Nixon, 1982), and it seemed reasonable to try and
see if there were any coincidence between my research interests and
those of the British Library that would make for a profitable

partnership. Also I suppose I felt to some extent challenged to show that case study methods would pay off in this area of research.[2]

The primary substantive field in which I have been interested is the problem of emancipation through schooling in the face of the social control problem in the school. This was the theme of the Humanities Curriculum Project,[3] which I earlier directed, and this was followed by the project on race relations teaching, which focused on similar issues. I was attracted by the possibility of looking into the process of emancipation into individual study in the sixth form. And I had always been interested in libraries and in study.

Of course, you might ask why I should be writing proposals at all. The background to that lies in the history of our Centre, at the University of East Anglia, which carries a fair number of valued people on 'soft money', and is continuously concerned with proposal writing. When you finish one proposal, you start the next. So this seemed a good one to write. I submitted it to the British Library, and in due course it was funded.

The Research Proposal

When it comes to research aims, I think I have always worked with double sets of aims — one for the sponsor and one for myself! The proposal sets out the job I hope to do for the sponsor — in this case as follows:

1 to reconceptualize academic sixth-form education in respect to its relation to library access;
2 to draw implications for teaching in the presence of libraries and for user education;
3 to consider the significance of library access for educational opportunity at sixth-form level and draw conclusions for the organization of education and library provision at age 16–18;
4 to consider the concept and possible form of compensatory user education;
5 to document the styles of librarians and teachers as managers of knowledge;
6 to make recommendations for curriculum development in user education at sixth-form level.

The whole art of the business in funded research is to find scope for your own aims within and alongside the sponsor's aims — and without costing the sponsor anything. I saw in the project the possibility of building the theory of schooling on which I have been working for the last twenty years or so. The theme of emancipation, which I have already mentioned, is potentially a matter of conflict in the sixth form, and largely because of the growth of independent study and the student's capacity to appeal against the teacher to the library. As one of our students says in interview, teachers' encouragement of independent study places them in danger of a kind of redundancy. This is fascinating territory. So too is the possibility of making comparisons across the divide between private and state school systems. Finally, I was interested in undertaking the design and management problems of multi-site case study and hopeful of accumulating an archive through this research which would be a resource for other researches and researchers. I was confident both that I would get plenty out of the work for the British Library and that I would be able to follow my own intellectual quests, and so I was able to work in a style comfortable to my bent with comparatively little preordinate planning and plenty of responsive thinking.[4] Look for a rich seam and then dig!

What I suppose might be called the research design is treated in the proposal under the heading, 'Method':

> generalization across twenty-six descriptive case studies based upon condensed fieldwork involving tape recorded interviews, observations and collection of documents, including both qualitative and quantitative data. The fieldworkers will produce indexed case records to form an archive.

The use of the word 'generalization', here, is problematic and I must leave for later discussion: an explanation was clearly not of interest to the sponsors. The central design feature is multi-site case study based on condensed fieldwork.

The Context of the Proposal

Interestingly enough I had proposed a multi-site case study of Scottish comprehensive schools to the Scottish Education Department in about 1965, without of course using that terminology. It had been turned down. Later, as director of the Humanities Project, I had written a proposal for an evaluation which called for the appointment of a Schools Study Officer who was to study classrooms during the experiment as a basis for designing an evaluation of the Project in its dissemination phase. In practice, the evaluation, under Barry MacDonald, extended its study to schools. It could thus be called a multi-site case study, though again the term was in nobody's mind at the time. During that evaluation, two things became clear. In such an exercise you cannot employ traditional ethnographic methods because you must move at the pace of the events you are studying; hence the process which was later named by Rob Walker 'condensed fieldwork'.[5] Secondly, in case study work it is often difficult to get your data into shape for publication, and there is little or no access to that data until it is published.

My next experiences ran side by side. I directed a project on problems and effects of teaching about race relations in which there was a strong teacher-researcher element and in which Bob Wild contributed the case studies.[6] The case study element went alongside a fairly large testing programme with a conventional pre-test post-test design. Case studies were mainly of classrooms, and they were created from classroom tapes with supporting interviews with teachers. At the same time I was contributing a case study to Barry MacDonald's SAFARI Project (Success and Failure and Recent Innovation). This was my first fieldwork experience using condensed methods in schools. Out of all this came the conviction that qualitative case study was not being successfully integrated with the quantitative data based on sampling (cf. Sieber, 1973), that there were critical problems in organizing data in such a way that colleagues could discuss them together and that the problem of working across cases at the writing-up stage had not been satisfactorily tackled.

In a study of the dissemination of the Race Project, Jean Rudduck, who was responsible for executing the study, found herself case studying a series of events such as conferences and committee meetings.[7] Each might be regarded as complete in itself, and one approach would have been to produce case studies of each as she went along. In fact, however, she produced a lightly edited case record — that is, a collection of data — from each event, and used these as the basis of her final write-up. The case records were paper-bound volumes. It was easy for me to read them and to discuss her conclusions with her.

There followed a project funded by the SSRC on educational case records. In this, four or five colleagues undertook condensed case studies concentrating on the record of fieldwork. We produced various different records; I made an attempt to write up a very elementary case, citing records as an historian would. We held a conference on case study and case records in York in 1980.[8]

Meanwhile, over in the United States, Bob Stake and Jack Easley had conducted a multi-site case study, *Case Studies in Science Education* (1978), within the American responsive evaluation tradition. Rob Walker from CARE had contributed two of the case studies.[9] Bob Stake worked from case studies rather than case records, and I came to feel that this was a mistake, both because of what was lost from the good case studies and even more because I had the impression that some of the case studies were not too securely founded.

The message is that I have been interested in case study for a long time: in 1957 I wrote a proposal for a comparative study of Macclesfield Grammar School and Dunfermline High School; since 1968 I have supported and maintained active contact with school case study work, and since 1975 I have been directly involved in fieldwork for case studies. LASS is another course in the wall I have been some time building.

The LASS Project

In the LASS Project eighteen fieldworkers have, in the end, contributed twenty-four case records. The contract with each fieldworker is for an indexed case record of an institution agreed with the project. Because no case study is asked for, each participant researcher is free to do a case study negotiated with the institution concerned. We monitor lightly to make sure that nothing is going to blow up in our faces. There is a substantial area of freedom here, which I think is valuable. In addition, all participants have access to the archive on condition that they write no case studies of institutions or individuals where the fieldwork is not their own. There is an open invitation to contribute to the final report or to the book that we hope will follow it.[10]

The fieldworkers received support from the project in the form of travelling expenses and subsistence during fieldwork, and transcription of all their tape-record interviews. In addition they were invited to two conferences at which they had the opportunity of discussing together the problems and opportunities of fieldwork. Fieldwork was limited to twelve days for each school and on that basis it was possible for two experienced secretaries to handle the task of transcription. I should add that few fieldworkers used all twelve days. The shortest contact was three days — which was all the school would allow — but they were three days of undesirably intensive interviewing, brought off rather well, I thought, by one of our doctoral students. Beverley Labbett and I did four case studies,

Table 9.1. The Case Studies and the Fieldworkers

CR*	Present type	Sex	Formerly	Total number of students	Number of students in VI**	Number of books in library***	Fieldworker
1	comprehensive	m	amalgamation of 3	1400	165	4500?	Sue Stone CRUS
2	comprehensive	m	grammar	1050	170	?	Iain Smith C & A Bob Cooper C & A
3	comprehensive	m	sec.mod.	2050	350	?	Karl Openshaw USA
4	comprehensive	m	sec.mod.	1000	76	?	John Cockburn CARE
5	comprehensive	m	grammar	1150	220	10000	Lawrence Stenhouse CARE
6	comprehensive	m	sec.mod.	1100	40	?	Charles Hull CARE
7	comprehensive	m	grammar	1300	200		Bev Labbett CARE
8	comprehensive	m	middle	1050	150	5000?	Bev Labbett CARE
9	comprehensive	m	sec.mod.	650	30	?	Harry Torrance CARE
10	comprehensive	m	grammar	1000	120	5000?	Iain Smith C & A
11	grammar	m	tech.high	750	128	11000+	Jim Butler Australia
12	comprehensive	m	p.built	2200	235	19000	Cherry Harrop CRUS
13	comprehensive	m	p.built	1700	172	5000	Mike Hayhoe KH
14	comprehensive	m	p.built	1650	150	?	Iain Smith C & A Bob Cooper C & A
15	sixth-form college	m	grammar	500	500	12000	Pauline Heather CRUS
16	sixth-form college	m	grammar	700	700	12000	Christine Beal CRUS
17	public boarding	b	—	850	219	20000	Bev Labbett CARE
18	public boarding	m	—	370	149	27000	Lawrence Stenhouse, Beverley Labbett; Charles Hull CARE
19	public boarding	g	—	850	280	30000	Jean Rudduck CARE
20	independent day	b	—	550	160	8000	John Pound KH
21	independent day	g	—	700	160	12000+	Anne Murdoch UEA
23	college of FE	m	—	1700 f.t. 4500 pt.t.	—	35000	Ed Parr Australia
25	tertiary college	m	—	1000 f.t. 2500 pt.t.	—	32000	Lawrence Stenhouse CARE
26	independent day	b	—	1450	532	25000	Lawrence Stenhouse CARE

Notes:
* Numbers 22 and 24 were not completed.
** Number of students in VI include A-level and non-A-level students.
*** Several librarians did not know what the library holding was and would not hazard a guess. Some guessed. The figures listed are only a rough guide: it is not always clear exactly what is included in the figure given. (CRI: number is for upper school library only.)

Key:
CARE   Centre for Applied Research in Education, University of East Anglia
CRUS   Centre for Research in User Education, University of Sheffield
C & A   Crewe and Alsager College of Education
K.H.   Keswick Hall College of Education (now School of Education, University of East Anglia)
UEA   University of East Anglia.

and our two colleagues from Crewe and Alsager did three between them. Other fieldworkers did one case study each. The case studies that were done and the fieldworkers involved are shown in Table 9.1.

Of course, Beverley and (to a lesser extent) I were available for consultation and fieldworkers, especially those lacking experience, did seek our advice. I cannot speak for him, but though I did talk to the team about what I had in mind for the project, much more time was spent in explaining that what I had in mind was less than they suspected! I also explained that as all of them had some educational or library experience they could draw on this experience in interview and observation. In a way, it is a classic position on fieldwork: you learn by getting your hands dirty. And you have to remember never to submerge your own intelligence and sensitivity in the interest of some set of rules — certainly not on authority; it is not that there are no rules, but rather that you have to see the need for them in the context of experience of fieldwork and its problems.

Beverley, the project coordinator, has been much more closely in touch with the people on the project than I have, perhaps partly through my illness. But he, after all, is the manager. I imagine I'm a bit more remote, whereas he has travelled round more and consulted more and consoled more. Of course, it is crucial that people have a limited and clear contract and know what to do if they have any difficulties in keeping it. Two agreed case studies failed to arrive. One study is really very weak. But my general assessment is that the approach worked and that the risks with experienced professional people or selected doctoral students of the kind we were working with are containable. On the whole we are pleased with the case records and find them usable.

The biggest problem was getting people away from the notion that qualitative data had to be comparable in the sense that quantitative data do. With a background in history I am puzzled by this difficulty. If such comparability were necessary across sources, history could not exist; and I find history more rigorous than social science. It is certainly encouraging to my view to find in *Montaillou* that the records of the Inquisition allow the reconstruction of a vivid and largely convincing portrait of a mediaeval Pyrenean village (Le Roy Ladurie, 1978).

Gaining Access in a Multi-Site Project

So far as access to institutions is concerned, our procedures were variable. The CRUS people in Sheffield and the Crewe and Alsager staff were invited to negotiate access in their own way once we had agreed with them which institutions they would try to bring in. Most entries, however, were negotiated through the project either by Beverley or by myself. Where I accompanied a fieldworker on a first negotiating visit, it was my purpose to suggest that the worker and the institution could come to any agreements they liked within the framework of the minimum obligation to contribute an anonymized case record to the archive.

I can talk in greater detail only about the cases in which I was involved in some way. One case on which I worked with Beverley Labbett, but playing only a minor part, was an independent public boarding school. We started by writing to the head, and when we went to the school, Beverley found that one of the deputy heads had been at university with him: she acted to some extent as a key informant, but so did the librarian. Another case, an independent public day school, was also approached through the head. I saw him on my first and last visits but my interviews were arranged by the librarian, who acted as my host. In two other cases I negotiated access to schools through Chief Education Officers. In the county in which I worked myself, this led to a meeting with two advisers, a rather long discussion of several possible schools, and the final selection of three to our mutual satisfaction. Entrance was then requested by me in letters to the heads that took the following form:

> Centre for Applied Research in Education,
> University of East Anglia,
> Norwich NR4 7TJ
>
> 15 February 1980

Dear [head's name],

As you know, I came over to [place name] for a discussion with [name of LEA advisers] about the possibility of a limited number of schools participating in our British Library Project on Library Access and Sixth Form Studies. I have now heard from [adviser] that you are agreeable to our discussing the possibility of [your school] taking part.

Should you do so, the project would like to assign to the school one of its researchers. From the point of view of the project the researcher's task would be to produce a record or study of library access and sixth-form study in your school which would contribute to a descriptive national survey.

From the point of view of the school it is open to you to negotiate with the researcher whatever form of service in the way of report writing or consultancy seems best to repay you for granting us access for the study. All that has to be borne in mind is the background obligation to the project I have already outlined.

The project has only just started, and the study visits to the school will take place in the session 1980–81. It has been decided that I shall be the researcher working in [your] school if participation is agreeable to you, and I should very much like to make a visit on which I can explain the pattern of the project to you, so that you can make a final decision about participation. [There follows a passage about dates of possible meetings.] I am enclosing three copies of a short statement about the project and I can send you more if you should want more. We shall try to keep you in touch with developments as we set up the project, though, since we are assuming that our studies will keep schools anonymous, it is not possible for us to put the group of schools in touch with each other.

We look forward greatly to the possibility of our working with your school.[11]

Yours sincerely,

Lawrence Stenhouse
Professor of Education
Director of Centre

I visited each school to talk to the heads personally. The approach was different again in relation to a tertiary college: here, my first contact was with the Chief Education Officer, who approved my writing to the principal; the matter was then passed to the vice-principal with whom I negotiated. The librarian was my informant,[12] so far as I had one. I saw the principal in the corridors, but I never met him.

Issues of Selection

I should say something about sampling — I do not think we are engaged in sampling. There is a complicated argument behind that position. So let us cut corners and talk about our collection of cases. Of course, in gathering that collection we are selecting,[13] and I suppose our selection is rather close to what sociologists following Glaser and Strauss would recognize and call a 'theoretical sample' (cf. Glaser and Strauss, 1967). Basically the attempt is to get an extended range of different settings and different problems. We looked for three public boarding schools and got one boys', one girls' and one mixed. Our public day schools differed in size. Two were boys' schools, one girls'. We went for two sixth-form colleges, two tertiary colleges and two colleges of further education. The rest — apart from one local authority grammar school — were comprehensive schools of various kinds. We bore in mind the need to have some access to different social and environmental settings: for example, in rural areas we looked for plains villages as compared to linear valleys and the like. And of course we went for schools with different levels of library provision; indeed, our main reason for taking more than one school from a local authority was to balance a badly provided school with a well provided one in order to protect the Chief Education Officer who would be vulnerable if he allowed us to represent his authority only with a poorly provided school.

We also selected three Advanced level subjects for the centre of our attention: history, French and biology. The idea was to protect us from promising too much, but at the same time to draw into the penumbra of our vision the other subjects which A-level candidates in these subjects were also taking. We could then follow interesting trails that presented themselves. For example, in my state grammar turned comprehensive, it became clear that there were particularly interesting things going on in Russian and chemistry and I followed these up.

One particular case shows how far from experimental controls our selection of cases was. In one independent day school the head, with regret, rejected my first request to study the use of the library — he was dissatisfied with the condition of the library and the way it was being run. Some months later, he 'phoned me up and said that he had taken my first visit as a cue to approach his governors, and the library was now being reformed and revitalized. He was happy that we should study it. Although it was our approach that had changed the situation, we were very happy to get an example of what such an independent school regarded as the provision that should be aimed at, and how they went about their programme of renovation.

Interviewing on the Project

One is naturally sensitive to the effects of sponsorship on interviews. My judgement is that there were virtually no effects of this kind. No-one, I think, disbelieved me when I described the conditions of confidentiality before the interview. I think some felt that I was perhaps being overscrupulous. The most serious possibility was in the one case where I was entertained to coffee and tea daily by the head. However, I think this was scarcely seen by any of the staff. In that school I had an interviewing room off the library and never entered the staffroom until the day of my last visit.

The undesirable aspect of that study was that my fraternization with the head produced an intimacy that led to a taped interview in which the head exercised too little restraint. This led in turn to censorship of the transcript. I thought of the classic advice to fieldworkers: 'Never accept hospitality and always take your own marmalade.' In this case there was little or nothing crossed out which bore on my interests, but what I did was to go back and explain why I thought that the head had had to cross out so much and then I interviewed her again and now I have two interviews, one hacked and one complete.

I ought to say perhaps at this point something about my own interviewing style, though, of course, this is not something of significance across the project, since the view we took was that each was free to develop a style within the critical framework provided by project discussions. I am rather keen not to sit facing the interviewee, but rather side by side or angled towards each other. This allows me to seek or to avoid eye contact. I explain to interviewees that I prefer to sit beside them and look out at the world with them, sharing their view.

As an interviewer I try to be polite, attentive, sensitive, thought-ful, considerate, but not familiar — rather respectful. I feel it is part of my job to give people the feeling not merely that they have my ear, my mind and my thoughts concentrated on them but that they want to give an account of themselves because they see the interview as in some way an opportunity: an opportunity of telling someone how they see the world. I hope that the occasion is slightly flattering to the person being interviewed.[14] Interviewees should recognize that they are more important than they thought they were by reflecting about themselves and their work. I am told by readers of my transcripts that my questions encourage by naiveté, but I really only muse about what is being said and follow my curiosity:

Example 1

LS: If I knew a mathematician — well I'm only saying I'm not a mathematician myself, so don't feel you have to talk for me — but if I knew a mathematician is there any way in which I could describe to him the kind of maths that you are teaching in this school? It might not be comprehensible to me but might be comprehensible if I knew more.

Teacher: Well I suppose you mean whether it's modern or traditional? Is that the kind of crude terminology?

LS: I don't know enough about maths to know whether that's a question I should be asking or whether I should be asking, 'Is it pure or applied'? (Case Record No. 5 B (Teacher Interview) p. 51)[15]

[This exchange was followed by a long response from the teacher.]

Example 2

Teacher: ... the ... edition [of Shakespeare's plays] is now become the one bought in school because the footnotes are on the page that you're reading and not at the back....

LS: I suppose the annotations are the beginning of study skills.

Teacher: I'm sure they are ... all the staff here have had this broader study skills course you know with our felt tip pens and our diagrams, etc. so that creeping into lessons from time to time must be, as you say, study skills — how to plan an essay and all those other things but I don't know if I'm referring to quite what you mean by reference books and books of criticism.

LS: Well, I don't know. I'm trying to —

Teacher: You're just asking me.

LS: Yes. I'm trying to see what's in the word, and feeling that the phrases that I pick up from a conference about libraries and schools, I'm not sure what they mean either.

Teacher: Well study skills to me very often means that they have to rule off at the end of one piece of work and date each piece of work and head it properly so that they know where they're going and so do I. But I suppose that's extremely primitive and has nothing to do with the subject.

(Case Record No. 5 B (Teacher Interview) p. 68)

Example 3

LS: If one were to drive that to its furthest point and say,
'Well yes there are a lot of books that aren't used but it's a
kind of wall covering that reminds people about books and
if it were a bare study room people would perhaps study
less and...' Is there anything in that or is that just a sort of
romance...?
(Case Record No. 5 B (Teacher Interview) p. 88)

Example 4

LS: I've become interested without really being able to
come to any conclusion as to whether the solitary practice
of a musical instrument, training in physical education — I
mean training means trotting round on your own, working
on your own, that kind of thing — actually contribute to
the capacity for independent study, to habituate people to
the notion of something, some learning entered into
through an effort of concentrated application, conducted
on your own without supervision.
(Case Record No. 5 D (Senior Management Interview)
p. 13)

There is then a loose form to my interview. For example, in my
interviews with sixth-form pupils I asked them first for a job
description of being a pupil in the lower school:

Example 1

LS: Now what about your experience in the lower school.
Let me talk about the job of being a pupil. What was the
job of being a pupil like in the lower school?
(Case Record No. 5 A (Student Interview) p. 95)

Example 2

LS: And you studied those for five years, starting off at the
beginning. Did you.... I'm trying to get some notion of

what the job of being a pupil in the lower school is like. Did
you have to use the library in any of those subjects?
(Case Record No. 5 A (Student Interview) p. 2)

I then explored the difference in the sixth-form, then looked at the
differentiation of job between subjects ... and so on.

On the whole I feel that if you are not ethnographically inclined,
but closer, as I am, to oral history, and if you are not doing
evaluation, that is to say, if you are clearly concerned with an
educational problem that is of interest to teachers, then the business
of getting response is pretty robust. In the end, however, my
judgement can only be confirmed by looking at my interview
transcripts and making up your own mind about it. My contention is
that these matters are much more readily judged on the basis of
interview scripts than on the basis of described procedures. But then
my position close to historians naturally leads me to believe that
documents (including interview transcripts) can be criticized and that
well-grounded judgements can be made about them.

Another problem is that in all my case study settings I got at the
students through the teachers. I am still unsure how I feel about that.
A lot depends on the kind of study you are trying to do. I've got lazy
people among the students, academics and also highly utilitarian
people who have specific uses for A-levels and no great interest
beyond them. I don't think I've got many disruptors, but then it is
doubtful how many disruptors you would get in the academic sixth
form anyway. I'm just not sure about this factor; and my feeling is
that my own view will become clearer as I work through the materials
closely.

What I feel pretty sure about is that we were much more
concerned with people's perceptions and conceptions — their meanings — than with their behaviour or with events. That is not to say
that we never asked people about what they did or what they
observed, but rather that we should treat accounts of behaviour or
events with scepticism and with a greater interest in the meanings they
revealed than their direct evidential status. It is only when particularly stringent critical controls are exercised, and material survives them,
that one can use interview data as a source of information about
happenings. If a pupil says: 'I don't often go to my local library
because it's not much use to me for A-level work — it's really a
general library', I'd rather conclude that the library is perceived in
that way either because it is true or because of some factor that hides
its potential from that pupil than accept the statement as reliable

direct evidence. On the other hand, I would accept that he or she doesn't often go, because I can see in context no reason why he or she should be self deceived or intentionally deceiving in saying that.

Interview and Observation in Multi-Site Case Study

So much for the witness gathered from interview. But let's contextualize that. When you are working in multi-site case study, you are working lightly in each case and trying to get out of the comparison among cases something of the force that the classic ethnographer gets from depth in a single case. We bargained for twelve days of fieldwork in each school, and immediately that seems to me to mean that the case studies are predominantly interview-based. You are not getting enough time to do true participant observation, and therefore you are trying to collect, in interview, observation from participants.

Observation by fieldworkers is brief and, mainly non-participant (though not necessarily non-reactive). For my part, I spent some time in the library, sitting and working at taking notes, and I also visited the libraries in the catchment area of the schools, observing in the process something of the area itself. You must, however, beware of false impressions gathered from the observation of what just happens to come your way over a short period of time.

In both interviewing and observation it is important that one has some experience of schools and of libraries — a good second record, to use a phrase of Hexter (1972). I think I feel as an interviewer that I am trying to help the interviewee to give me a skilled interview. A lot of my work is in helping interviewees to structure their statements. Sometimes it will be as simple as reminding them when they have made three points, that they were going to make four; but it isn't easy to describe the pattern and function of one's interventions. It is as if one were helping the interviewee to master an unaccustomed art form. I did a paper on interviewing for the project (1979b), but it's a highly provisional piece which I hope to revise when I have been through all the records.

Styles of Data Recording

Our interviews are always tape-recorded unless the interviewee demurs, which we find rather rare. In that case, however, I take notes, always in two columns, the left column being a running record of the interview in catchword and brief note form, the right column being literal quotation. If the transcription is not possible because of resource constraints, I generally advise note-taking from tape in this form.[16]

I never try to hide or play down the tape recorder. On the whole I find that most subjects forget it or ignore it very quickly indeed. I think that is because I find it easy to ignore myself. If the interviewer is relaxed and natural, then that helps the interviewee. I would not under any circumstances choose to use notes to help me to conduct the interview. I think that really does destroy my rapport with the person I am interviewing. I also find it unacceptably intrusive when people are interviewing me.

The interviews come back from fieldwork and they are transcribed from tape by our secretaries, who are skilled and experienced in this kind of work. In fact they preserve more in the way of hesitation phenomena than I think is important for our purposes, but that is the way to have it, because that leaves the professional researchers rather than secretaries in control. When the transcriptions come back to me, I'll either go through them listening to the tape if I think there is any difficulty, or I'll read them carefully in the light of my memory of the interview and my 'second record';[17] and I'll make corrections, usually very few. For example, the typist may fail to pick up proper names, titles of textbooks, initials of examination boards and the like. After I've been through the transcripts, I post them back to the people who gave me the interviews, inviting them to correct any errors of fact that may have crept in and to strike out anything which must be off the record. Overall, we have had very few

---

CENTRE FOR APPLIED RESEARCH IN EDUCATION
University of East Anglia, Norwich, NR4 7TJ

I am prepared to give authority for the transcript of this interview of myself by (name of fieldworker) to be reproduced in an anonymised form for use in conferences, teaching and research and for lodgement in an archive in print or microfiche which shall be open to researchers.

Signed . . . .

Date . . . .

alterations or excisions in most interviews. About one in twenty or one in thirty people want to make fairly extensive alterations, most often to improve the grammar and syntax of the spoken word. I try to dissuade them if I can but accept their alterations if I have to.

Transcripts go back with a cover sheet which the interviewee is asked to sign: in this project this gives clearance for the use of material in anonymized form by researchers in conferences and in teaching. I would not anonymize again if I could avoid it, though I recognize that abandoning anonymization necessitates a gradual progress to greater honesty about schooling that cannot too much be hurried. I feel we should have taken that line in LASS. One of the things that attracts me to the project is that it seems to me relatively rich in research meaning without being very sensitive, and that favours openness.

We are only now (March 1982) beginning to tackle the problem of data analysis and reporting. Thus this account is necessarily truncated. We sit in a room with twenty-four box files along a shelf and various other bundles of documents, and discuss where we hope to get and how we are going to get there.[18]

One hope I have is that participants in the project will find the archive useful both in generating grounded theory and in testing theory, that the sponsors will find the report useful for their formulation of future policy and that teachers and students will find the report, the book and other materials produced useful in developing more emancipatory forms of sixth-form *and* lower school work. I certainly believe that such an emancipatory thrust is possible. Resistance is not the only escape from reproduction of the hegemony at cultural levels.

Notes

1 This paper was revised after the death of the author. The revisions, the notes and some examples have been provided by Robert Burgess, David Jenkins and Jean Rudduck who have, where possible, used the author's work and words. Some material has been taken from a tape recording of the session at which the first draft of this chapter was discussed by Lawrence Stenhouse at the Whitelands College workshop in March 1982.
2 Throughout this chapter the term 'case study methods' is used rather than 'ethnographic methods', for Stenhouse considered that ethnography is not devoted to the people it studies while, in contrast, he was devoted to the teachers and pupils with whom he worked. Stenhouse

saw ethnography as tainted with colonialism (cf. Asad, 1973). Furthermore, for him ethnographers were strangers to the situations they studied, while he was no stranger to educational settings as he maintained: 'There is one place where I feel that I understand the environment and that I am at home and that is in schools' (taped discussion).

3 For discussions of the Humanities Curriculum Project see, for example, Stenhouse (1973; 1975; 1980b; 1983), Rudduck (1976), Verma (1980), MacDonald (1979), Elliott (1983).

4 For discussions of Stenhouse's style of work in this area and his ideas on the approach involved see Stenhouse (1978; 1979a; 1979b; 1980a; 1982a).

5 For an account of this approach see Walker (1974), and for Stenhouse's interpretation of this style of work see Stenhouse (1982a).

6 See Stenhouse *et al.* (1982), pp. 119–84.

7 An account of this work is given by Jean Rudduck in chapter 8 of this book: 'A Study in the Dissemination of Action Research' (see also Rudduck and Stenhouse, 1979).

8 The project proposal, which was called 'Exemplary case studies: Towards a descriptive educational research tradition grounded in evidence', was submitted to the SSRC in December 1977. Exemplary records were produced but remain unpublished:
ECR 1 Hawthorn School: A Case Record
ECR 2 Furzedown Comprehensive: A Case Study
ECR 3 Senior Management at the Jepson School: A Case Record
ECR 4 Towards the History of Risby Church School 1914–1918.

9 See Stake and Easley (1978). The two studies by Rob Walker are collected in volume I of the project publication:
No. 6 Pine City: A Rural Community in Alabama.
No. 11 Greater Boston: An Urban Section in Metropolitan Boston.

10 When Lawrence Stenhouse died Jean Rudduck took responsibility for writing up the project report (Rudduck *et al.*, 1983). Rudduck had to work quickly and therefore did not pursue the idea of the 'open invitation' to fieldworkers to contribute to the final report. Indeed, Rudduck feels that she will be unable to operationalize this idea in the book that may follow, since it will reflect very closely the structure of the report.

11 This was the standard letter that was used in the project, modified according to the circumstances that have been discussed. The letter to independent schools included the following statement: 'We are keen to study three public schools where the sixth-form tradition has deep roots because we think this will place the situation in state schools in a properly broad perspective.'

12 In several settings the librarian acted as internal coordinator of the study and the fieldworker tended to spend more time with the librarian, developing a relationship that led to an easy flow of data, with the result that the librarian became an informant.

13 For discussions of selection in case study work see Stenhouse (1978; 1980a) also see the chapters by Martyn Hammersley and Stephen Ball in this book that discuss this issue.

14 For a discussion of interviewing see Stenhouse (1979b).

15 The twenty-four interview-based case records produced for this project are publicly accessible and are indexed and anonymized. They can be consulted at the Centre for Applied Research in Education, University of East Anglia, Norwich.

16 It was this style of note-taking that Lawrence Stenhouse used when reading through the case record to prepare for writing the report.

Interview with boy

CR4/A/85	Change to less directed work in VIth	
CR4/A/86	Use of library & use of common room	
CR4/A/87		'We're given textbooks, so I just use those. I find I don't need to use it. If we're told to look at something in the library, we do.'
CR4/A/88	Manner of writing essays. Subjects: maths, combined maths & physics and economics	
		'I study most upstairs' (common room) 'Well, physics and maths, it's generally having to consult with people.....'
CR4/A/89	Interested in physics, electronics	

Interview with two girls

CR4/A/90	Girl students (2) (1) A level Art, English & some O levels, more freedom, not treated as children in VI form	
CR4/A/91	Classes smaller	
CR4/A/92	Of essays —	'You've got to be more aware of how you write it and what you put into it — the way you set it out to get better marks....' 'Well, I study most at home — but I do a lot of my studying in free time upstairs in the common room, because I can't work when it's too quiet.'

| | Sometimes if it's too noisy comes to library, but lighting isn't good (fluorescent) |
| CR4/A/93 | Picks relevant chapter from contents |

KEY: CR4 = Case record 4
      A = Interview with students
     85 = Page reference within student interviews in CR4

17 The idea of the 'second record' comes from Hexter's book, *The History Primer* (1972) (Chapter 4, 'The sown and the waste or the second record'). Stenhouse introduced the idea in a paper written in 1981, 'The Verification of Descriptive Case Studies'. He begins by talking about fiction, suggesting that 'in realistic fictions verification depends upon the reader's judgments about the trustworthiness of a portrayal in terms of verisimilitude: a likeness to factual truth'. He goes on to suggest that the 'organized trace of the reader's experience' to which appeal is made in the verification of a realistic fiction might be called 'a general second record'. If the account offered is not confirmed by the general second record of the reader, 'either the portrayal will be dismissed or it must be upheld by a revision of the record of one's own experience'. Stenhouse then moves the argument across from fiction to history and thence to case study. A later paper (1982b) defines the second record as 'the accumulated experience of the reader'. Here Stenhouse argues that while verification may appeal to the second record of the reader, authentication requires a first record — the documents of the case.

18 Lawrence Stenhouse was working on the case records until ten days before he died in September 1982, trying to immerse himself in the data and making notes for the report. Jean Rudduck, who was one of the eighteen fieldworkers, agreed to take over responsibility for writing the report. She completed it in March 1983 (see Rudduck *et al.*, 1983). She invited two people who had not been involved in the fieldwork to make a contribution to the report: the two outsiders were thus able to test the potential of the archive of twenty-four case records as a source which people who had not taken part in the project could use; they also provided a check on the lineaments of her own interpretation of the situation. Jean Rudduck also took responsibility, but with very limited time and resources, for preparing the archive for use: this involved completing the indexing of the case records and their anonymization. The state of the case records in terms of uniformity of typeface and general presentation is poor: there was no money to have pages retyped after correction by interviewees and after anonymization.

In addition to the report to the British Library Research and Development Department, a number of articles and a book are planned.

References

ALTSCHULD, J. (1977) 'A retrospective analysis of the development of a project monitoring system', paper given at American Educational Research Association (AERA), New York City

ASAD, T. (Ed.) (1973) *Anthropology and the Colonial Encounter*, Ithaca, University of Ithaca Press.

BERK, L. (1977) 'Characteristics of good retrospective analysis', paper given at AERA, New York City.

ELLIOTT, J. (1983) 'A curriculum for the study of human affairs: The contribution of Lawrence Stenhouse', *Journal of Curriculum Studies*, 15, 2, pp. 105–23.

GLASER, B. and STRAUSS, A.L. (1967) *The Discovery of Grounded Theory*, Chicago, Aldine.

HEXTER, J.H. (1972) *The History Primer*, London, Allen Lane; first published New York, Basic Books, 1971.

LE ROY LADURIE, E. (1978) *Montaillou*, London, Scolar Press.

MacDONALD, B. (1979) *The Experience of Innovation*, Norwich, CARE, University of East Anglia.

PARLETT, M. and HAMILTON, D. (1977) 'Evaluation as illumination', in HAMILTON, D. *et al.* (Eds) *Beyond the Numbers Game*, London, Macmillan, originally published in 1972.

RUDDUCK, J. (1976)*The Dissemination of Innovation: The Humanities Curriculum Project*, Schools Council Working Paper 56, London, Evans/Methuen Educational.

RUDDUCK, J. and STENHOUSE, L. (1979) *A Study in the Dissemination of Action Research*, report to the SSRC, HR 3483/1.

RUDDUCK, J., HOPKINS, D., GROUNDWATER SMITH, S. and LABBETT, B. (1983) *Library Access and Sixth Form Study*, report to the British Library Research and Development Department.

SIEBER, S. (1973), 'The integration of fieldwork and survey methods', reprinted in BURGESS, R.G. (Ed.) *Field Research: A Sourcebook and Field Manual*, London, Allen and Unwin.

SINGER, N. (1977) 'A retrospective analysis of the development of program criteria', paper given at AERA, New York City.

STAKE, R.E. and EASLEY, J. (1978) *Case Studies in Science Education*, Centre for Instructional Research and Curriculum Evaluation and Committee on Culture and Cognition, University of Illinois School of Education.

STENHOUSE, L. (1973) 'The Humanities Curriculum Project', in BUTCHER, H.J. and PONT, H.B. (Eds) *Educational Research in Britain 3*, London, University of London Press.

STENHOUSE, L. (1975) *An Introduction to Curriculum Research and Development*, London, Heinemann.

STENHOUSE, L. (1978) 'Case study and case records: Towards a contemporary history of education', *British Educational Research Journal*, 4, 2, pp. 21–39.

STENHOUSE, L. (1979a), 'The problem of standards in illuminative research', *Scottish Educational Review*, 11, 1, pp. 5–10.

STENHOUSE, L. (1979b) 'Gathering evidence by interview', Norwich,

CARE, University of East Anglia, mimeo; later published in KEMMIS, S., BARTLETT, L. and GILLARD, G. (Eds) *Perspectives in Case study 2: The Quasi-Historical Approach — Case Study Methods*, Deakin University Press.

STENHOUSE, L. (1980a), 'The study of samples and the study of cases', *British Educational Research Journal*, 6, 1, pp. 1–6.

STENHOUSE, L. (Ed.) (1980b) *Curriculum Research and Development in Action*, London, Heinemann.

STENHOUSE, L. (1981) 'The verification of descriptive case studies', in KEMMIS, S., BARTLETT, L. and GILLARD, G. (Eds) *Perspectives in Case Study 2: The Quasi-Historical Approach — Case Study Methods*, Deakin University Press.

STENHOUSE, L. (1982a) 'The conduct, analysis and reporting of case study in educational research and evaluation', in MCCORMICK, K. (Ed.) *Calling Education to Account*, London, Heinemann.

STENHOUSE, L. (1982b) 'Case study in educational research and evaluation', in FISCHER, D. (Ed.) *Methodische Traditionem und Untersuchungsalltag in Fallstudienterrinder Padagogik: Aufgaben Methodein Wirlungen*, Konstanz, Fauder.

STENHOUSE, L. (1983) *Authority, Education and Emancipation*, London, Heinemann Educational.

STENHOUSE, L., VERMA, G.K., WILD, R.D., and NIXON, J. (1982) *Teaching about Race Relations*, London, Routledge and Kegan Paul.

VERMA, G.K. (Ed.) (1980) *The Impact of Innovation*, Norwich, CARE, University of East Anglia.

WALKER, R. (1974), 'The conduct of educational case study: Ethics, theory and procedures', in MACDONALD, B. and WALKER, R. (Eds) *Innovation, Evaluation, Research and the Problem of Control — Some Interim Papers*, Norwich, CARE, University of East Anglia, pp. 75–115; reprinted in DOCKERELL, W.B. and HAMILTON, D. (Eds) (1980) *Rethinking Educational Research*, London, Hodder and Stoughton.

WISE, R. (1977) 'A case for the value of retrospective accounts of curriculum development', paper given at AERA, New York City.

10 Chocolate Cream Soldiers: Sponsorship, Ethnography and Sectarianism

David Jenkins

Editor's Commentary. In recent years educational researchers have witnessed a change in the style of curriculum evaluation. No longer is there a preoccupation with evaluation studies based on quantitative measures, for many research workers have adopted an illuminative or naturalistic style of evaluation using ethnographic or case study methods of research. As David Jenkins shows, it was this research style that was adopted by the team who were engaged in evaluating the Schools Cultural Studies Project in Northern Ireland.

In this chapter David Jenkins highlights particular aspects of the research process involving an ethnographic evaluation that is reported in *Chocolate Cream Soldiers* and *Chocolate Drops*. In particular, he focuses upon the character of the sponsorship by the Department of Education in Northern Ireland and the Joseph Rowntree Charitable Trust, the evaluation contract, the value position of the investigators, and the process of writing up. A major theme throughout this chapter concerns ethical and political issues involved in this style of evaluation.

David Jenkins provides ethnographic material to discuss the setting in which the research project and the project evaluation were located together with a commentary on two meetings which chart the changing relationships with research sponsors. Among the questions that this chapter raises are: who owns data? What ethical and political issues are involved in report writing and in the reception of evaluation reports? In this first person account of an evaluation study David Jenkins demonstrates that ethnographic methods not only raise technical problems associated with data collection but also contribute to a number of complex issues associated with writing up and with the reception of a report. This chapter therefore deals with crucial aspects of the research process that have often been overlooked.

Northern Ireland is a very particular place. Not only do a number of terms at least relatively unproblematic in Britain (like 'policing' or 'political education') pose unique problems over here, but the whole society is shot through with a phenomenon of particular interest to the ethnographer, battles over crucial definitions. Social research in any aspect of life infiltrated by sectarianism is likely to place the researcher in an arena for conflict between antithetical accounts. When an armoured pig ran into Catholic youths in the Bogside it was immediately processed for public consumption by both sides: the RUC press statement spoke of a 'road accident'; *Republican News* hinted at psychopaths on the loose. The most familiar recent example, outside education, of conflicting definitions must surely be the H-Blocks hunger strikers, variously held to be suicidal criminals or murdered martyrs. The educational researcher is caught in a not dissimilar cross-fire.

Schools arguably respond to 'the Troubles' in one of three ways; some implicitly declare school to be 'time-out' and keep community issues off the curriculum; others teach from the local subculture, reflecting its values in a way that is implicitly sectarian; a third group sees the curriculum, particularly in social and cultural studies, as having a critical or reconstructionist potential.

This report concerns an evaluation study directed by the author and Father Sean O'Connor, a Jesuit priest who had strayed purposefully into the North, crossing the symbolic border at some unguarded point. The study was a broadly ethnographic account of the Schools Cultural Studies Project (SCSP), sponsored by DENI (the Department of Education, Northern Ireland) and the Joseph Rowntree Charitable Trust (JRCT). The study was commissioned in 1977 and was dramatized on public hordings as a high-risk exposure of a high-risk programme; independent, issues-based, methodologically eclectic with its commitment to 'illuminative portrayal', and likely to be close-up, possibly to an unnerving extent. Its enigmatic title, *Chocolate Cream Soldiers*, was borrowed from Shaw's *Arms and the Man*. The original 'chocolate cream soldier' was a pacifist who found himself inadvertently in a war zone; 'chocolate' is intended to suggest the quaker Rowntree Trust, 'cream' the curriculum task force, and 'soldiers' the Northern Ireland problem. Like the report itself, the title had a somewhat mixed reception.

It is probably useful to sketch something of the Schools Cultural Studies Project itself. The original funding proposal, by Professor Malcolm Skilbeck, sought to use schooling in a concerted attempt to blunt the edge of sectarianism in Northern Ireland schools by using the curriculum system of its secondary schools as an instrument of cultural change. Its novel features vis-à-vis current models of curriculum development were that it was *school-based* (thus valuing selective adaptivity rather than proposing a 'course of study' to be tested by teachers); premissed on a philosophy of *'cultural reconstructionism'* (and thus, ambiguously, believing that the Province's teachers, erstwhile 'naive bearers of the sectarian culture' could become, virtually overnight, 'cultural change agents'); and *open* (thus committed to painful self-analysis and seeking to promote a general unfreezing of attitudes).

Although Skilbeck's original funding proposal stressed analytical processes, and envisaged a community-wide cultural critique (with education an important part of, rather than monopolizing, the exercise), subsequent changes in the leadership of the project led to a redefined more restrictive brief, with the production of curriculum material and a common teaching strategy acquiring a central emphasis. Hooked into the Schools Cultural Studies Project pedagogy was a version of the 'values clarification process', by which the project hoped its teachers would avoid using the classroom as a platform for sectarian indoctrination. It thus echoed Lawrence Stenhouse's Humanities Curriculum Project which also put controversial issues on the secondary school curriculum, but espoused a different solution to the underlying problem in so-called 'neutral chairmanship'.

The Evaluation Contract

Much of the discussion leading up to the final version of *Chocolate Cream Soldiers* hinged on the initial contract. The main issue was whether groups other than the evaluators had proprietorial rights over the data rather than a point of view that we were committed to listen to. Yet the notion that there was an agreed initial contract itself became cloudy, even ambiguous; the surviving document is the proposal, said by some parties to have been modified in discussion. Even the proposal was not without some internal inconsistency and unfortunately might (viewed in retrospect) have disguised the extent to which non-recommendatory reports might nonetheless be implicitly judgemental. It was, however, quite clear on the independence of the evaluation. As presented to the Consultative Committee and Schools Cultural Studies Project teachers, the stance of the evaluators was characterized as follows:

1   *independent*, the project allowing reasonable access and accepting the final report, although negotiated for fairness

and accuracy, would be the responsibility of the evaluators, not the project team or the Consultative Committee;

2 *non-judgemental*, not making crude recommendations but seeking instead to write an issues-centred portrayal, collecting judgements rather than making them;

3 *methodologically eclectic*; although broadly working in an illuminative tradition, the evaluation team would gather survey data and perhaps employ measurement techniques in relation to some of the more crucial objectives;

4 *responsive*, trying to assess the audiences for its reports and what questions they want answered, rather than simply posing its own;

5 *short, sharp, intensive*, writing up quickly while hot.

At the meeting called so that project teachers might endorse or reject the proposal for an evaluation, the evaluators' 'sales pitch' was constructed around ten reasons why the teachers might legitimately *not* want the evaluation. The teachers, to their credit, agreed to cooperate. ('You've been honest with us; we'll be honest with you.') The evaluators were also open about secondary agendas. We wanted hands-on experience for a group of MA students studying programme evaluation. We also wanted to press the chosen model (the close-up issues-based portrayal) in circumstances that would test it to the limit.

The Evaluation in Retrospect

In the event it went ahead. Yet those who took part in it, sponsored it, and underwent its scrutiny, felt in general to have been a little bruised by the experience. The final report, *Chocolate Cream Soldiers*, has been lauded, denounced, suppressed, surreptitiously circulated, methodologically attacked, ethically condemned, cited as exemplary practice, and humanly criticized. What happened? What, if anything, went wrong? This chapter is an attempt to reflect on the discomforting experience of the exercise. In particular it takes the view that ethnographic research in educational settings, particularly in an 'evaluative' role, cannot treat its methodology as if it were abstractable and separable from more complex problems of role performance, and the need to generate 'understandings' in situ. Lying behind this issue is a more general snare, the evolution of a rhetoric of research methodology that claims spuriously to 'guarantee the findings'. Yet threats to the validity of an account at times feel more like the familiar problem of trying to 'tell the truth' in ordinary social life. The worries expressed about *Chocolate Cream Soldiers* barely touched upon technical matters like 'triangulation' or the basis upon which we had selected 'quotable quotes' from the mass of interview transcripts. It focused rather on the evaluators' 'value position', whether we had demonstrated 'bad faith', or whether we were politically bright enough to anticipate and appropriately forestall potential 'adverse' consequences. A crucial series of episodes surrounded our attempts to 'negotiate' with the sponsors and subjects of the report concerning its accuracy and fairness; the unambiguous emergence of an unacknowledged political agenda characterized these negotiations.

Politically, and in terms of its stylistic aspirations, the ethnographic style of evaluation (also called 'naturalistic', 'illuminative' or 'portrayal')[1] has been reasonably well documented recently. The aim of such evaluations, broadly, are to portray innovative programmes in action. Such portrayals tend to be intimate, analytic, emotive, concerned with processes and performances as well as effects, but tending to use issues as advance organizers. *Chocolate Cream Soldiers*, within this tradition, was not overtly theoretic and aspired to a balance of 'thick description' and analysis. But the evaluators were also attracted to Elliot Eisner's notion that the tools of literary criticism might make a legitimate contribution to alternative evaluation.[2] Concepts like 'tone', 'irony' and 'paradox' moved nearer the centre. The evaluators also accepted the appropriateness of 'portrayal of persons' in evaluation reports, and were prepared to experiment with wit and humour as heuristic devices for 'getting inside' situations characterized by conflicting definitions and inner tensions. Perhaps not surprisingly, this was often misunderstood, and parts of *Chocolate Cream Soldiers* were widely perceived as flippant.

The evaluators' reports (two *Interim Reports, Chocolate Cream Soldiers* and the digest, *Chocolate Drops*)[3] evidenced considerable sympathy for the Schools Cultural Studies Project, which has been facing bravely one of the most intractable social and cultural problems in Western Europe, recording that 'the great success of the Project can be simply stated; it introduced sharp issues into the curriculum of Northern Ireland schools, and has produced many many examples of courageous, high risk, and seemingly successful probing. In other words, there does seem to have been an unfreezing. . . .' Yet some slightly disturbing aspects were highlighted: the personality-dependence of the innovation, oscillating wildly

under its changes in directorship, unchallenged in the Rowntree pre-
dilection for trusting people rather than ideas; the regression back
towards a non-adaptive first-generation curriculum project ('centre-
peripheral' rather than 'school-based') increasingly 'technologizing'
its problems in a flight from direct confrontation with the sacrosanct
(even SCSP's 'value-clarification process' appeared in a curious
technical guise as a value-free heuristic); the overconcentration on the
five-year 'course of study' (which was neither envisaged nor financed
in the funding proposal) in a way that encouraged an assimilative
rather than a critical response.

Some problems, too, arose out of the ambiguous political image
of SCSP, perceived variously as a 'state sell', 'the educational wing of
the Alliance Party', 'the soft under-belly of English liberalism', or
even 'in a republican corner'. Certainly Malcolm Skilbeck's early
formulations (built into the funding proposal to Rowntree, but to
some extent subsequently reneged on) envisaged a community-wide
attack on the problems of cultural reconstruction in the Province,
spear-headed through the school curriculum. The teachers, it was
supposed, were to become 'change agents' through a kind of shoe-
strap self-enhancement with the self-lift coming through a commitment to analytical processes. But their 'diagnosed' starting point, in
the Skilbeck scheme, was as 'naive bearers of a sectarian culture'.
Their working situation was held to be substantially infiltrated by
unexamined social meetings; only by considerable reflexivity could
they avoid failing by default. The subcultures, *as represented in the
schools*, seemed to Skilbeck to be ideological, militant, aggressive, and
highly reproductive, although thin and translucent, lacking complexity and internal diversity.

The evaluators saw themselves as portraying the project wholis-
tically, disclosing its perceived meanings, inner tensions, natural
history, and educational issues, but also contributing to an analysis of
the 'logic of the problem', particularly the role that might be played
by schooling. In charting what turned out to be the rather deviant
natural history of the innovation, we felt able to generalize tentatively
concerning personality-dependent innovation. But our stance was
important for another reason; since the evaluation claimed to be non-
judgemental in any strong sense of that term, its own value position
(that is, the basis of its adjudication) did not have to be 'on the line'.
Indeed, when pressures grew we took the view that a project, and a
Department, and a Trust, so unequivocally committed to a liberal
intervention might adequately and legitimately be chastened, as
appropriate, *by confrontation with their own rhetoric*. Yet our

comment on DENI's geographical carve-up (that gave Skilbeck, at the New University of Ulster (NUU), Derry and the north of the Province, and Queens' John Malone and his project Belfast and the South) was not appreciated by those who held that the notion of 'liberal critique' did not properly extend to criticizing the sponsors ('statements should be deleted that in the view of the Management Committee might be detrimental to the Department, the Trust or the Project'). Yet, astonishingly, a project 'blunting the edge of sectarianism' in Northern Ireland had been established in a way that gave it no presence in Belfast, and only an equivocal toehold in Derry where it has been taught almost entirely by schools in the Catholic sector. The relative acceptability (after what might euphemistically be described as 'soundings by local community entrepreneurs') of the Derry materials in the Creggan rather than the Waterside is clearly of public interest; yet the evaluation team was all-but-instructed not to present its data.

Relationships with the Sponsors

Relationships with the sponsors became increasingly brittle over time. In December 1979 an international workshop was held at Girton College, Cambridge to review the use of naturalistic enquiry in educational evaluation.[4] Most of those at the workshop admitted to major problems with sponsors or clients at one time or another. The first source of discontinuity appeared to be the unexpected difficulty in 'targeting' evaluation data to the information needs of the decision-maker. Certainly DENI wanted from the evaluators recommendations and supporting evidence of a kind that would allow them to adjudicate whether the Schools Cultural Studies Project merited further funding. The second discontinuity was the perceived gap between programme evaluation, with its invitation to concentrate on a putative solution, and policy-related research, which allows independent access to the logic of the problem. *Chocolate Cream Soldiers*, from the sponsors' point of view, offered the worst of both worlds, claiming the right to comment upon policy and the underlying logic of the problem, but not offering the policy-makers much by way of 'indicators' against which they might 'measure' success. Ethnography, in other words, becomes what Paul Atkinson called a kind of 'surrogate theory', offering description rather than analysis or recommendation.[5] Even the concentration on issues is sometimes seen by the administrators as a kind of fence-sitting. We were consequently perceived as appealing over the heads of the sponsors to some 'hidden audience', perhaps academic peers, perhaps the population-at-large, perhaps the verdict of history.

The Tale of Two Meetings: (i) Coleraine

The edginess of the relationship between the evaluators, the project, and the sponsors can most readily be exemplified by two meetings. Both of these concerned the report, *Chocolate Cream Soldiers*, which appears to have taken the sponsors by surprise. It was regarded as overpersonal, even hurtful, lacking decorum, and naive about its own predictable consequences. An affronted Management Committee requested to meet the evaluators on 5 November 1979, two hours after high noon. Sean O'Connor and I had been excluded from the immediately prior morning session. The agenda indicated an afternoon session 'in the presence of Professor Jenkins'. It was a long time since things had looked this formal.

The first snippet of news came from the New University of Ulster's Professor Hugh Sockett over a lunchtime beer. According to Hugh, the morning had been inconsequential ('They haven't a clue how to handle an issues-centred portrayal. I keep telling them what kind of report they have got'). Hugh saw the morning meeting as 'nitpicking' and 'preoccupied with procedures'. At the Private Dining Room lunch, due to a symbolically apt oversight by the university catering department, the visitors had not been provided with knives.

Chairman Tom Cowan (ex-DENI) opened the afternoon session briskly, putting the meeting on a short fuse. The Management Committee had concluded a 'long complex discussion' in the morning. The 'major points of conclusion' were that *three copies only* of the report were to be circulated, to those committee were 'duty bound' to supply (the University, the JRCT and the DENI). Any wider circulation would have to be 'subject to two conditions', the 'deletion of references to individuals unless agreed', and the deletion of statements that in the view of the Management Committee might be 'detrimental to the Department, the Trust, or the Project'.

I felt unable to endorse this suggestion. It had been made clear from the start that the evaluation team, not the Trust, the Project or the Department would be responsible for the products. I reminded the meeting of the 'contract'; the evaluation was offering to negotiate, not the fact of a report, but its content, mainly for accuracy and fairness. But Tom Cowan held that the evaluation's known view of itself notwithstanding, there had been no 'agreement'. Besides, the Management Committee *per se* could not deliver on such a contract. He felt we were back to the legal position that sponsors 'buy' an evaluation. (Cowan: 'I have worked for the Department for more years than I care to remember. Every single word I have written has been their property.') He claimed that, as a·general principle, every report is 'the property of those that sponsor it'. Hugh Sockett, on the other hand, felt that copyright had not been surrendered. Professor Joe Nesbitt (NUU) said that he did not suppose the university, in any particular sense, to have been 'party to a contract'. NUU had however, joined in a decision to fund an avowedly *independent* evaluation ('I don't think we should have the intention of interfering'). The rest was a matter of 'occasional phraseology' which could safely be left to the writers.

I responded that the evaluation team did not need to be taught lessons on the sensitivity of the exercise. On the other hand, the principle that the sponsors can claim automatic protection from detrimental comment seemed a weak one. The evaluation saw the conduct of the sponsors as lying within its legitimate range of interests. Nicholas Gillett of JRCT agreed. The report's probing was useful ('I would be worried if the report were so bland that it worried nobody'). He himself had found it 'sharp and readable' (a letter saying just that was already on the table). Hugh Sockett capped the point: 'If *Chocolate Cream Soldiers* does not raise suspicions, then it ain't worth reading.' At this point Joe Nesbitt vigorously shook his head, but said nothing. But SCSP Director Alan Robinson was still unhappy. He did not 'want *Chocolate Cream Soldiers*, unrevised, landing on the desk of an uncommitted headteacher in Belfast'. He had also exhibited slight defensiveness with Hugh Sockett, sitting bolt upright, arms folded, as Hugh used his 20:20 hindsight to indicate what SCSP should have done. Sockett added that one problem that the evaluators had missed concerned the 'high risk funding'. It was 'amazing' that the university had touched SCSP in the first place. SCSP exhibited 'something unusual: a conservative Department of Education in partnership with an avowedly radical funding body'. That these unlikely bedfellows got together at all was 'a comment on the depth of the problem'. ('I don't know what Hugh was driving at there', confided Professor Nesbitt afterwards, 'the Department are far from conservative and some people might suppose that in one sense quakers are conservative.')

Suddenly Tom Cowan comes in line with the Trust. The evaluators have produced a 'worthwhile report', if somewhat 'jargon-ridden' and a bit of an 'insiders' document'. Circulation will be to the trial schools, the project and evaluation teams, professional developers/evaluators likely to find it of practical interest, and the sponsors. It can also be used as part of the NUU in-service award-bearing programme, but it should not, without further thought and negotiation, go into general circulation. The Rowntree representative, Nicholas Gillett, keeps up the Trust's recessiveness to the end, although putting his weight behind the eventual 'reconciliation'. Both sides fibbed that the original clash was a misunderstanding, a trick of the shifting light. It was a big step for the evaluation; although doubtless a tiny step for mankind.

The Tale of Two Meetings: (ii) Belfast

But the reconciliation didn't stick, and the low point in our relations with DENI came in December when Sean O'Connor and I were suddenly summoned to Belfast, instructed to attend a meeting convened to convey something of the Permanent Secretary's displeasure at the final draft of *Chocolate Cream Soldiers*. This meeting was in effect a re-run, with rhetorically more powerful backing, of the Management Committee meeting. The directors of the evaluation elected to attend, whilst reserving their position. Nevertheless, the chairman felt able to open matters firmly; we were all there 'to consider what action needs to be taken to make the Report one that the Department can associate itself with and endorse'.

They were genuinely puzzled that the evaluators appeared indifferent to Departmental endorsement. The argument used by DENI officials: ('if people realize how liberal SCSP is, Paisley and the DUP[6] will be down on our heads like a ton of bricks') was similar to that posed by Harry Wolcott at an AERA discussion: 'How should ethnographers feel if their data could be used to *terminate* cultures?' Again the bifurcation. Where does argument for responsible and prudent behaviour end and illicit pressurizing begin? Can an evaluator play God and construct a morality of consequences? Or is one on surer ground in emphasizing a truth-telling role?

The meeting ended with the conflicting definitions unresolved. DENI supposed itself to have blocked circulation of the report by dictat. The evaluators supposed the sensitivities of the situation to require delay, but saw the locus of the decision as resting with them. It was several years before *Chocolate Cream Soldiers* achieved reasonably wide circulation in Northern Ireland, mainly through the taught Masters and Diploma Programme at NUU. To the irritation of some, it was well regarded by some of the better-known portrayal evaluators in the United States, adding fuel to the argument that the exercise was 'really' aimed at its professional peer groups.

Reflections: *Chocolate Cream Soldiers* as Exemplum

Evaluation products may be created in circumstances of benign complicity or creative tension. A recent paper by Sean O'Connor,[7] 'The Social Role of Evaluation Products', explored the mismatch between overlapping subcultures, those of the sponsors, the research setting, the perceived audiences and the evaluation team itself. Ploys establishing or negating 'comfortablness' may be constructed around focal issues, the evaluator's alleged subject area competence, milieu-brightness, or ideological/political compatibility, as well as his or her prestige as a researcher and the 'constraints' imposed by contractual negotiation. O'Connor concluded that mismatched programme evaluations are typically conducted alongside problematic subtexts, involving possibilities of cooption, collusion, renegotiation of restricted contracts, deflection towards peripheral 'surrogate tasks', distancing, rejection, labelling as deviant, rhetorical acknowledgement divorced from political action, the management of counter-denunciations, the use of social sensitivities as instruments of social control, and the sponsorship of 'rival products'. Nevertheless, the evaluator had a recognized 'corner' from which to fight.

There is also an epistemological issue. The critics of *Chocolate Cream Soldiers* came armed with lists of passages they wanted deleted from the report. These were so extensive that a full analysis of the 'requests' has not yet been completed, but it went way beyond anything that might be termed 'negotiation for fairness and accuracy'. The wider question is whether any substantial process of negotiation (such as has been envisaged by the SAFARI researchers) is incompatible, ultimately, with the truth-telling role. The defences to the SAFARI[8] line, that social truths are relativistic, or that iterative discourse 'improves' an account, seem to me to be rather weak.

The study leading to *Chocolate Cream Soldiers*, viewed methodologically, owed some of its idiosyncrasies to an unusually composed research team. Also, as I have indicated, other agendas were involved. The evaluation was offered to SCSP in part because I was seeking a 'hands-on' exercise in which the bulk of the fieldwork could be conducted by an MA group at the New University of Ulster who were studying curriculum theory and programme evaluation. Although none of the group had any research experience as such, a certain amount of training was offered.[9] Many were experienced teachers, and were perceived by the trial schools as sympathetic but knowledgeable in a way that precluded them being 'fobbed-off'. Perhaps ill-advisedly, we allocated the students in teams to a small number of trial schools in a particular area. In the main, on a limited budget, this was to keep travelling expenses down. So the student-researchers gained extensive experience of SCSP in one or two well-defined geographical settings, but their view of the project was somewhat overfocused. This left a problem. Any confident cross-project generalizations[10] necessarily depend on some attempt at aggregation and interpretation of the ethnographic and survey data. Overall, the study relied heavily on participant observation, document analysis, observed episodes in classrooms, analyzed 'curriculum discourse', and semi-structured interviews concerning emerging pedagogical, curriculum, and community issues. But the unit of analysis (or 'bounded system') in *Chocolate Cream Soldiers* was necessarily the Schools Cultural Studies Project itself. Consequently the evaluation team faced problems equivalent to those faced in the kind of geographically-dispersed research that combines 'local' case study with a commitment to produce tentative cross-site generalizations. These problems of research in multi-site settings have been exemplified recently by the 'Executive Summary' included by Bob Stake and Jack Easley in their *Case Studies in Science Education* (1978), and by Lawrence Stenhouse's account of the LASS project in this volume.

The end-in-view of methodological practice is for the researcher to find himself or herself in a position to be able to say something with known levels of confidence or speculation. It is pertinent for us, as authors of *Chocolate Cream Soldiers*, to remind ourselves of the dichotomy between how it felt to be involved in the writing and the available justifying paradigms, positivistic or interpretive, for 'writing it up'. The task of putting the reports together in the centre fell to myself, as principal editor, Sean O'Connor, and the three outside consultants, who had been brought in partly to offset the embarrassment that the evaluation study had the same institutional base as SCSP, partly to 'front' certain aspects — Dr Stephen Kemmis from Deakin, Australia looking at the SCSP rationale; Chicago's Sister Anne Breslin measuring civil and moral reasoning; Dr Tom Anderson on sabbatical from the University of Illinois focusing on pedagogy. Altogether *Chocolate Cream Soldiers* has seventeen named authors!

The conditions under which it was written up, under pressure of deadlines, felt so culpably 'seat of the pants', so hair-raising, so magical, so unlike what any 'justifying' account might look like, that one simply has to say so. All I remember is the weariness, the emotional high, the savagery of the selection, the willingness to begin arguments with only a hazy idea of where they might lead, the hail of crumpled discarded notepaper, and the pure relief when the sacred slog eventually shuddered to a halt. It felt a bit like what I imagine to be the experience of writing a novel. Any judiciousness of comment must have come more out of a sensitivity to language than any explicit weighing of cross-tabulated evidence. At the risk of sounding complacent, I was truly surprised by how much of it sounded about right on my first 'read' of it a couple of days later.

There is no attempt to describe the research process behind *Chocolate Cream Soldiers* as exemplary; indeed, one strong assertion is that we need to learn from our mistakes. But the problems also relate to idiosyncrasies in the setting and it is an open question the extent to which even remotely similar circumstances might be replicated elsewhere. Yet overall it might be possible to identify a trend. Perhaps the climate of the times, stressing accountability, outcome measures, output budgeting, and so on is hostile to expansive non-recommendatory ethnographic reports. Decision-makers are declaring their information needs to lie elsewhere. Social relations in educational settings where ethnographic evaluation research has been conducted have not infrequently deteriorated in spite of protective rules designed to prevent this. Ploys designed to reduce the effectiveness of an evaluation, or deflect it, or manage a counter-denunciation, have become unremarkable and normal. There have been examples of tears, tantrums, ostracization, heavy-handed humour, dismissive silences, threats of litigation. Warmth is possible, but rare.

Research Processes in Cross-Site Settings

Chocolate Cream Soldiers was faced with a problem of distilling 'understandings' in a cross-site study that involved a largish team of experienced and inexperienced personnel. As Matthew Miles pointed out in his widely circulated *Memo to Dave Crandall*, the technical problems of data overload and conceptual focus are likely to be severe. Although 'grounded theory' suggests a careful attentiveness ('watchful of serendipity'), the conditions under which the evaluation of the Schools Cultural Studies Project was attempted (short time scales, limited but intensive school visits, a lot of thematic focusing at the Centre, relatively inexperienced fieldworkers) meant that the drive towards a clarity of framework was possibly too strong. At worst the fieldwork could be said to have been constructed around a framework of *'known'* issues rather than having the time and space to evolve its own. This problem was worsened by the *partial* view of SCSP available to any particular fieldworker, although weekly team meetings obviated the difficulty to some extent.

Each fieldworker had a research agenda that included observing and reporting classroom 'episodes' and the collection of testimony, wherever possible in the form of a taped interview, with subsequent protocol analysis and edited transcript. There was considerable variation, too, in the style of interviewing employed with the trial school teachers. The aspiration towards gentle probing proved a difficult one to realize in practice, and a certain passivity and blandness developed, particularly where the interviewers were over-recessive. Some of the paradoxes and ambiguities of SCSP came out rather surprisingly through the survey data. Because these were processed *after* the school visits, opportunities for methodological cross-fertilization were limited. In retrospect it would have been better to have armed the fieldworkers with basic data on the pattern of implementation before placing them in the setting.

As new researchers they weren't always able to 'read' the initial overview in a way that suggested the 'right' follow-up questions. My own view is that recessive interviewing is less a virtue than some educational ethnographers first supposed. But much of the final selection went on the 'newsroom' and was handled (at times brutally) by the subs. One equivocal possible advantage of this type of research is that it by-passes problems of data overload; ethnographic researchers immersed in day-to-day data are not always able to 'extract it out' around an analysis. Also skill at collecting data may not itself confer an ability to write it up, not least in a multi-author set-up where there are problems of an aggregate tone of voice.

Methodological Rhetoric and Retrospective Distortion

Finally, as the exercise itself became under seige, the authors of *Chocolate Cream Soldiers* have felt at times under pressure to give a retrospectively distorting account of how the study was actually conducted. What was essentially a modest proposal, a hand-to-mouth low-budget exercise somehow contrived to end up as a *cause célèbre*. The surprisingly dramatic impact of the exercise carried with it a concomitant temptation — to offer a methodological rhetoric as a professional defence. For example, we were a little bit slow to admit that there is something dishonest in castigating a project for abandoning its initial logic that sectarianism in education can only be combatted by engaging in a fine-grain cultural and ideological critique and then conducting an evaluation exercise curiously opaque in its squareness to the same challenge. For all its rich episodic detail, *Chocolate Cream Soldiers* splits on the analysis/portrayal dilemma. The analysis is an issues-based thematic overview of the whole exercise. The 'ethnography' was too often unthematic episodic elaboration for which the summarizing expression is the chapter tellingly called 'Glimpses'. There is something of a gap in the centre. Either as a piece of 'illuminative evaluation', or as a piece of ethnographic research, *Chocolate Cream Soldiers* stands rather awkwardly in relation to the approved animals in the research zoo. Historically it became instead something of a sacred monster, unswallowable like Harry Recher's unpunctured puffer-fish in *Man: A Course of Study*; perhaps what a moralistic pamphleteer might call 'a warning to all'.

Notes

1 See Shaw (1978) and Hamilton *et al.* (1977).
2 See Eisner (1972) and Eisner (1981).
3 See Jenkins, O'Connor *et al.* (1980a; 1980b).
4 See Jenkins *et al.* (1981) for some reflections on the Nuffield International Workshop held at Girton College, Cambridge, 17–20 December 1979.
5 At the workshop on the ethnography of educational settings at Whitelands College, London in March 1982 Paul Atkinson referred to ethnography being in some circumstances a kind of 'surrogate theory'.
6 The Democratic Unionist Party, led by the Rev. Ian Paisley. The DUP is in opposition to the Republican parties but in rivalry with the Official Unionists.
7 See O'Connor (1980).
8 SAFARI is an acronym for Success and Failure and Recent Innovation, a research project directed by Barry MacDonald at the Centre for Applied Research in Education, University of East Anglia to monitor the medium-range effects of curriculum projects. See Jenkins (1978).
9 In the main, the training that was offered was feedback to individual students on their fieldnotes and protocol analysis, together with seminars on interviewing and data analysis.
10 See Crooks (1982) and Stake and Easley (1978).

David Jenkins

References

CROOKS, T. (1982) 'Generalization in educational research; through a 'glass darkly'', mimeo, University of Otago, New Zealand.

EISNER, E.W. (1972) 'Emerging models of educational evaluation', *School Review*, 70.

EISNER, E.W. (1981) 'On the differences between scientific and artistic approaches to qualitative research', *Educational Researcher*, 10.

HAMILTON, D. *et al.*, (Eds) (1977) *Beyond the Numbers Game: A Reader in Educational Evaluation*, London, Macmillan.

JENKINS, D. (1978) 'An adversary's account of the ethics of case study', in RICHARDS, C. (Ed.) *Power and the Curriculum*, Driffield, Nafferton.

JENKINS, D. *et al.* (1981) 'Thou nature art my goddess: Naturalistic enquiry in educational evaluation', *Cambridge Journal of Education*, spring.

JENKINS, D., O'CONNOR, S. *et al.* (1980a) *Chocolate Cream Soldiers: Final Report on the Rowntree Schools Cultural Studies Project*, Coleraine, New University of Ulster (available from the Education Centre).

JENKINS, D., O'CONNOR, S. *et al.* (1980b) *Chocolate Drops* (a summary of the Rowntree Schools Cultural Studies Project), Coleraine, New University of Ulster (available from the Education Centre).

O'CONNOR, S. (1980) 'The social role of evaluation products', mimeo, New University of Ulster.

SHAW, K.E. (1978) 'Understanding the curriculum: The approach through case studies', *Journal of Curriculum Studies*, 10, 1.

STAKE, R. and EASLEY, J. (1978) *Case Studies in Science Education: Volume 2 Design Overview and General Findings*, Centre for Instructional Research and Curriculum Evaluation and Committee on Culture and Cognition, University of Illinois School of Education.

11 *Autobiographical Accounts and Research Experience*

Robert G. Burgess

Editor's Commentary. This chapter does not attempt to provide a summary of the accounts that have been provided by the contributors who are able to speak for themselves. Instead, the purpose of this closing chapter is to consider some of the characteristics of autobiographical accounts and the lessons that can be learned from them. It attempts to make comparisons between the work done by the researchers in a variety of educational settings. Among the issues that it highlights are the diverse attributes of the settings that have been described and some of the points that are of common concern in all the research projects. The chapter, therefore, examines some of the links between the different projects and discusses ways in which researchers might in future collect data that will be of direct relevance to autobiographical accounts of the research process while advancing our knowledge and understanding of research methodology.

In writing the preface to his autobiography, Clive James (1980) begins to identify some of the characteristics of autobiographical accounts. He maintains that autobiographies are little more than disguised novels where names and attributes of real people are changed and scrambled so as to make identification impossible and to spare other people's feelings. Furthermore, he indicates that many autobiographies are confessions, but selective confessions as it is rare for individuals to put themselves in a bad light or to write candidly about their activities (cf. Burgess, 1978; Burgess and Bulmer, 1981). In these terms it would appear that the task of the researcher who attempts an autobiography is not an easy one. Inevitably the accounts are retrospective and selective. They are reconstructions of a research programme. What then can be learned from autobiographical accounts of the research process?

The accounts that have been provided in this book focus upon personal and professional issues in the research process as well as technical matters. While each account highlights different aspects of the research process they all point towards several broadly similar lessons that can be learned. First, that research is a social process and as such is worthy of study in its own right. Secondly, that doing research is not merely about techniques of social investigation but about the ways in which studies begin and are funded, access is obtained, relationships formed, methods used, data recorded and analyses conducted. Finally, they also indicate the importance of examining the ways in which evidence is accepted, rejected and received. In these terms, the accounts would seem to have much to offer. However, individual autobiographies have been the subject of some criticism, as Dingwall (1980) has remarked:

> In general ... these accounts [autobiographies] are stronger on anecdotes than on drawing out more general implications in theoretical terms. This may reflect the limits of a reliance on single case studies rather than on explicit comparisons of experience in a number of settings ... (Dingwall, 1980, p. 872).

While Dingwall has raised an important issue, it is essential to appreciate that there are severe difficulties in making comparisons between different types of research experience. If we take the accounts that have been provided on educational settings we have to bear in mind that while all have the study of education in common they nevertheless display numerous differences. To begin with, the areas of investigation are different even when schools are being studied. King has examined three infant schools, while Hammersley has worked in two secondary modern schools.

Meanwhile, where individual schools are concerned Ball has looked at a mixed comprehensive school in the state system, while Delamont has examined classrooms in an elite girls' independent school. In turn, Stenhouse's LASS project covers schools in the independent and state sectors, a tertiary college and a college of further education. Furthermore, the LASS project (in common with David Jenkins' evaluation study) is a multi-site project, while the other studies focus upon one case or a series of cases. In some projects questions of gender, class and race are taken as given, while in Fuller's project they are rendered problematic. Meanwhile, in the projects by Atkinson, Stenhouse and Jenkins the 'curriculum' and 'knowledge' are rendered problematic by the researchers. A further difference is evident in the projects reported by Porter, Atkinson and Rudduck where the focus shifts away from the school towards higher education in the studies by Porter and Atkinson and beyond institutions to an educational event in the case of Rudduck.

Beyond these differences in terms of subject matter it is important to recall that these projects, although adopting a similar methodological approach, have been conducted using perspectives that have been derived from sociology, social anthropology and educational studies. Indeed, the researchers have been trained in different disciplines: Atkinson, Delamont and Porter in social anthropology, Hammersley and King in sociology, and Stenhouse in history. However, some of our researchers have provided no clues to their disciplinary allegiances nor to their initial training, or their training in research methodology.

As with any group of research projects, these studies have been conducted at different points in research careers. For Delamont, Hammersley, Ball, Fuller and Atkinson, the studies were initially presented as PhD theses. In all cases, apart from Fuller's, they were the first major pieces of work that had been conducted by the individuals concerned. In this respect, we might consider the extent to which the age and experience of the investigator influence the conduct of the study and the final research report. Indeed, Fuller and King had come to their studies after being involved in large-scale survey research; Fuller as a research assistant and King as the director of several projects. Fuller explains how her approach to research design was influenced by her earlier experience involving quantitative research. Meanwhile, Porter was a member of a research team and was employed by John Wakeford to do research on 'his' project. Here, her work has some links with Rudduck's project which was initially designed by Stenhouse and was part of the broader programme of work at the Centre for Applied Research in Education at the University of East Anglia. However, here there is a further contrast in terms of experience. For Rudduck this was one of several projects on which she had worked, while Stenhouse indicates how his multi-site study is part of a cumulative research experience that he is able to trace from an initial (although unsuccessful) research proposal written in 1957, through the now famous and influential Humanities Curriculum Project to the project on the teaching of race relations. In these terms, we have to remember that our investigators had different degrees of research experience, were of different ages and had different types of training. Furthermore, they worked in different research settings within the broad field of 'education'. Given that the projects were all located in university departments or research centres, we hear relatively little about the ways in which the locations and other staff and students within them have informally influenced the projects. Yet if we turn to the prefaces of many studies, including texts and monographs produced by our investigators, we are provided with data on the ways in which ideas have been shared, developed, modified and changed on the basis of discussions and comments from colleagues (cf. Delamont, 1976; 1980; Ball, 1981; Atkinson, 1981). Yet in these accounts we hear little about the academic location of the projects or of those individuals who worked alongside our investigators apart from Delamont and Atkinson who indicate that their work was conducted alongside several other ethnographic studies in education that have subsequently become influential.

In Porter's account of the postgraduate education project she discusses relationships between the project and the project's location in the Lancaster University Department of Sociology. First, we are told that some members of the department favoured other candidates for appointment to the project staff and there were rumours about why John Wakeford had appointed two women. Secondly, that there was ill-feeling in the department because John Wakeford had set up the project. Finally, she goes on to discuss the marginality of the project within the department. Certainly, physical marginality was involved as the project room was located some distance from the department because no need was seen for the researchers to be near the rest of the department. This brief case study indicates that academic politics and academic gossip surrounded this project in the Lancaster Sociology Department. But, we might ask, how did this effect the conduct of the project and the discussions that could be held between project staff and members of the tenured staff? Indeed, it is important to consider the relationships between research and teaching. Certainly, research is a key element of academic life which the Robbins Committee (1963) argued should feed into teaching, for they remarked:

> There is no borderline between teaching and research; they are complementary and overlapping activities. A teacher who is advancing his general knowledge of his subject is both improving himself as a teacher and laying foundations for his research. The researcher often finds that his personal work provides him with fresh and apt illustration which helps him to set a subject in a new light when he turns to prepare a lecture. (Robbins, 1963, p. 182)

However, in the accounts in this book we appear to hear little about the relationship between research and teaching, apart from Hammersley's comments in the latter part of his paper about the overlap between his research and his teaching at the Open University. Here we appear to have located a gap in our knowledge about the relationships that surround social research. However, we might speculate about this omission along the lines suggested by Platt (1976), who indicates the difficulties that researchers have in reporting their relationships with one another when they know that the report will be most likely read by the people about whom they are writing. Secondly, as Bell and Newby (1977) have indicated, the British libel laws prevent the publication of candid accounts. Yet this is to suggest that we only have negative remarks to make about our colleagues — really we need to be given access to accounts of the assistance provided by departments and by colleagues; that is, we need analytic accounts about the support we briefly read about in the prefaces of studies. Here, we have much to learn from natural scientists. For example, Watson (1968) reports conversations between scientists in coffee breaks and the ways in which these discussions influenced the direction of his project on DNA.

Among our accounts it is David Jenkins' presentation that takes us into conversations between sponsors and researchers. He gives us the flavour of the academic committee meeting with its debate, conversation and gossip; all of which can help contribute to our understanding of the research process. Clearly, researchers need to provide more detail of the contributions that colleagues make to discussions of research projects if we are to advance our understanding of the informal processes that surround the conduct of social research.

The Pre-Fieldwork Phase of Social Research

We are all aware that research does not start with a visit to the field of investigation but more often begins as a project proposal submitted to a department for a PhD place or to a funding body. Yet as Eggleston (1980) has remarked, given the importance of this phase of research, we know little about the way in which project proposals are written and the way in which they are subsequently modified. A brief glance at research application forms provides data on the origins of a research project that are rarely reported in the final study, apart from the standard quasi-bibliographical literature review that is provided in the early chapters of many studies. Yet, as Wright Mills (1959) has indicated, it is when requests are made for funds that most 'planning' is done or at least carefully written about. However, Mills indicates that writing research proposals:

> is bound in some degree to be salesmanship, and given prevailing expectations, very likely to result in painstaking pretensions; the project is likely to be 'presented', rounded out in some arbitrary manner long before it ought to be; it is often a contrived thing aimed at getting money for ulterior purposes, however valuable, as well as for the research presented. (Mills, 1959, p. 197)

This statement alone raises questions about the politics of research funding and the writing of research proposals. Among the clearest statements about writing proposals and about funding are those from individuals involved in project teams. Stenhouse indicates that within the Centre for Applied Research in Education, research funds are essential if individuals are to be kept in post, with the consequence that writing research proposals becomes a 'normal' activity. Indeed, he argues that the funding process involves a partnership with the funding agency where researchers attempt to find scope for their own aims alongside the aims of the sponsor. However, the experience that is recounted by David Jenkins indicates that there are problems associated with the kind of relationship which Stenhouse identifies. For Jenkins draws on field data to discuss the reception that his sponsors gave to the project report. Clearly, questions can be raised about the ethics and politics of the relationship between researchers and sponsors, and the degree to which sponsors might attempt to exercise control over project findings and patterns of dissemination.

Another dimension to the start of social research concerns the relationship between the sponsors, the project director and the members of the project team who have to interpret the aims and objectives that have been identified by the proposal writer. However, even this is not as straightforward as it may seem; especially where project staff are involved. Rudduck indicates that in her work she found some difficulty in interpreting Stenhouse's intentions in the race relations evaluation project. Meanwhile, this is taken further by Porter who discusses the remoteness of the project director who writes the initial proposal. Here she indicates how she and Sue Scott were responsible for 'translating' Wakeford's proposal into fieldwork terms with the consequence, she concludes, that while the project was John Wakeford's, the fieldwork was their own as inevitably Wakeford became distanced from the project. Here a point of comparison can be noted in Stenhouse's LASS project where Stenhouse sees the project coordinator being closer to the fieldwork experience despite the fact that he was personally involved in the collection and interpretation of data.

One further area which our studies have in common is that among the funded research projects it is the project directors (males) who write the research proposals, and the research staff (predominantly females) who conduct the fieldwork. Here, it might be argued that this reflects the pattern of staffing in higher education and the process of academic gatekeeping (cf. Spender, 1981). In addition, we might consider the extent to which gender influences the origins of research projects together with the concepts and questions that are used.

When the origins of projects are discussed it is interesting to note that they are firmly contextualized within previous academic work. In the case of PhD theses, the studies are frequently located within the context of a previous line of inquiry. Indeed, both Ball and Delamont indicate how their own studies were seen to be extensions of the work of Hargreaves (1967) and Lacey (1970). Both King and Fuller also indicate how their work grew out of particular substantive concerns and gaps in the literature. In King's case, he indicates how his work was in response to a 'new' theoretical perspective and to a gap in the study of classrooms in general and infant school classrooms in particular. Meanwhile, Fuller indicates that her project was created in response to the psychological literature on sex differences and cross-cultural studies of gender. Indeed, Fuller, unlike many other researchers, indicates that she came to the study of an educational setting from a different perspective with the result that she was unaware of some of the studies that already had been done in schools and some of the literature on education (cf. Freilich, 1977, p. 17). Meanwhile, some writers locate their studies within their own intellectual biographies as Ball indicates how his study was originally intended to take up themes that had been developed in his MA thesis, while Stenhouse begins to locate the LASS project in his long-standing interest in the problem of emancipation through schooling in the face of the social control problem in school — a theme which he traces through earlier projects on which he worked. This situates the project within the biography of the individual researcher. Indeed, we might take this further by considering the ways in which the experience of a particular project resulted in a number of published materials. For example, Fuller explains how her research has given rise to a series of papers and articles that focus on one aspect of her original enquiry. However, we still need to consider what elements of our researchers' experience have resulted in them engaging in ethnographic studies and case studies of educational settings rather than in other social and cultural situations — perhaps Stenhouse gives part of the 'answer' when he indicates that schools and classrooms provide familiar territory. Yet such a situation is not without difficulty as researchers who work in familiar social settings need to make the familiar setting strange by asking questions about the activities that occur in them rather than taking them as given (cf. Spindler and Spindler, 1982; Burgess, 1984a). Such an approach demands that researchers handle this problem through their fieldwork experience (cf. Atkinson, this volume).

Fieldwork Experiences

An early fieldwork problem for all researchers is how to gain entry to social situations that are to be studied. In a recent account of educational case studies, Walker (1980) indicates that the researcher engaged in studying a school needs to consider how to gain access to the head, staff and pupils without being captured by any one group. To avoid this dilemma he offers the following advice:

> To gain access to the school you need to first approach the Local Education Authority; to gain access to the staff, you need to approach the Head; to gain access to the pupils you need to approach the staff. Each fieldwork contact is thus sponsored by someone in authority over those you wish to study. (Walker, 1980, p. 49)

This relates to what Dingwall (1980) has referred to as a hierarchy of consent; a situation in which sponsorship is provided by individuals who stand in positions hierarchically above those who are to be studied. Several of the accounts indicate that this is a common feature in the studies. Porter explains how access to her graduate students was 'instantly' gained through John Wakeford's links with a professor or head of sociology department who gave permission for her to include the department in the study after consulting with a departmental committee or a staff meeting. However, she indicates that later she and her co-researcher had to introduce themselves to graduate convenors and students in order to explain who they were and what they were doing. In this sense, they were passed down the hierarchy.

A similar experience is reported in our school studies by King, Fuller and Delamont, who negotiated with headteachers, and by Stenhouse who negotiated with headteachers in independent schools and chief education officers in the state system.

A clear case of the way in which this operates in revealed by Hammersley in his discussion of his two approaches to Downtown Secondary Modern School. Initially, on approaching the English teacher in the school, he was passed up the hierarchy to the headteacher and on to the chief education officer. Meanwhile, on his second fieldwork trip he approached the chief education officer only to find that he was passed back down the same hierarchy to the English teacher. Schatzman and Strauss (1973) indicate that researchers have to be able to explain their research requirements clearly and concisely to those individuals who control entry to an organization. While textbooks often indicate that a letter written to the head of an institution is a preliminary step in gaining access, it is rare to find examples of the letters used. Here, Hammersley and Stenhouse provide examples of letters which they actually used in the initial stages of gaining entry to a school.

However, we might consider in this context the rights of those at the bottom of the educational hierarchy. What right, if any, do pupils and students have to withdraw from studies? It would appear that pupils are seen to be docile and available, as we hear virtually nothing about how access was gained to the pupils other than through the teachers. However, Fuller indicates how she not only negotiated research access with the head but also with teachers and with pupils. Indeed, she explains how these negotiations took place in the term before her main fieldwork began. Here pupils were not considered to be compliant 'subjects' but were told they were free to decide for themselves whether they wished to participate in interviews or complete questionnaires (cf. Burgess, 1983). While this appears to be a move towards democracy it is still evident that it is the teachers rather than the pupils who take decisions concerning the researcher's observational activities. We might, therefore, consider whether a set of democratic principles can be established where observation and participant observation are used in the study of schools and classrooms. Meanwhile, other studies highlight the problem involved in negotiating with a large number of participants. For example, Rudduck had to gain access to conference members. This raises the question as to how a researcher successfully negotiates access to a large number of potential informants.

Turning to Fuller's study, we find that in the beginning she was casting about for a specific focus to her study with the result that her initial research problem was transformed on the basis of wide reading and further study of gender, ethnicity and the problems of interviewing. However, the project still had to be explained to the potential informants, who in turn influenced the overall design of the project. In this respect, access and project definition are not one-off situations but are part of the constant negotiation and renegotiation that takes place between researcher and informant throughout a project (cf. Geer, 1970; Burgess, 1980; 1982a; 1984a), with the result that research projects are subject to almost constant change.

We might consider how these changes influence the methods of investigation that are adopted and the roles that are used by the researcher. Our project reports indicate that no single method is identified with the case study or ethnographic style of research. In many of the studies, observation is used (by Delamont, Fuller, King and Atkinson) and participant observation (by Ball and Jenkins). In many of these studies, observation is complemented by interviews (by Porter and Stenhouse), by documentary materials (Stenhouse, Rudduck and Ball) and questionnaires (Fuller and Delamont). The key question that we need to address in this context is how methods of social investigation are *actually* used to study educational settings. If we consider the observational approaches that have been used, we find that they are all very different. In several instances it might appear that the observers were passive. Yet Rudduck tells us that she intervened in the conferences she studied at points where she thought her knowledge of conference organization would be of use to the participants. Furthermore, she indicates how her relationships with individuals influenced the ways in which she wrote up her report.

Similarly Porter tells us that when postgraduate students in her study asked for advice this was freely given. In these ways the researchers were not detached from the surroundings in which they conducted their investigations. They were involved observers; participants in the situations under study. In a similar situation, Hammersley discusses observation from the rear of a school classroom. Here again we find that it is not simply a question of passivity on the part of the researcher who is sat at the back of the room, as he soon finds that teachers begin to direct comments to him and one teacher actually 'fills in time' during the lesson by going to the back of the class to engage him in conversation. In these terms, observation is not simple and straightforward. Again, in King's work, we are told that he decided to actively avoid any participation with such ploys as avoiding eye contact with pupils, hiding behind furniture and hiding in the Wendy House within his infants' classrooms. In these circumstances, we might question the extent to which some of his work becomes covert or semi-covert, as we are told that individuals who entered the classroom were unaware of his presence. Furthermore, King indicates that he had to avoid friendship and involvement in the schools in which he worked by actually leaving the premises during the lunch hour. We need to explore how these field tactics influenced the kind of data that were collected. Finally, at the other extreme we have the participant observer role taken by Ball who goes into Beachside Comprehensive School and teaches a class. Here we might consider the ways in which friendship and participation influence the data collected. Certainly, these different roles that are adopted by our researchers indicate that simple typologies of observer, observer-as-participant, participant-as-observer and participant as suggested by Gold (1958) and Junker (1960) cannot be easily deployed within a research situation. In some situations, researchers have played all these roles within the research setting (cf. Burgess, 1983; 1984a). However, in other settings, roles are not 'played' or 'taken' but are products of the situations in which researchers find themselves. Nevertheless, we need to enquire how the roles that are used influence the data that are gathered and ultimately the research report that is provided.

Many of our researchers indicate that interviews were used within their studies. However, as several commentators have explained, there is no such thing as the 'standard interview' as reported in the methodology textbooks; for researchers, especially researchers engaged in ethnographic work, enter into relationships with their informants (cf. Oakley, 1981; Finch, 1984; Burgess, 1984a). Oakley (1981) discusses the way in which this operates when women interview women. However, questions may be raised about interview style: especially when adults interview pupils (cf. Burgess, 1984a) and where researchers interview individuals who are higher or lower in the status hierarchy than themselves. Stenhouse provides examples of his interview style with teachers and with pupils, while Porter highlights the problems involved in interviewing postgraduate students who are drawn from different disciplines: chemistry and sociology. Indeed, she indicates how when interviewing sociology students she was confronted with informants who were not only fellow researchers but also knowledgeable about the discipline and the associated research process (cf. Platt, 1981). In these terms, this influenced the course which the interviews took, and the shared meanings that were established between the researcher and the researched. Furthermore, we find that the interviews which many of our researchers discuss are more like conversations having no prede-termined form as they are based on a series of topics or an agenda which arises out of situations in which both researcher and researched have been involved (cf. Porter and Stenhouse). In these circums-tances, researchers are involved not only with flexibility in terms of research design but also with research practice.

The flexibility that is involved in qualitative projects becomes evident when researchers discuss sampling strategies. Here sampling is not viewed in a rigorous statistical sense, as discussed by Moser and Kalton (1971), but involves the researcher in considering principles of selection which may be modified on the basis of research experience. This is clearly revealed in Stenhouse's account in which he indicates how sampling strategies were used on the LASS project for institu-tions and for subjects. However, he considers the importance of flexibility in the research process when he discusses the way in which he started out working on history, French and biology but subse-quently found it desirable to follow up themes that arose in his study with reference to Russian and chemistry. In another study, Ball indicates how sampling strategies adopted within the research in-fluence those parts of schools on which researchers focus and those elements which remain unseen and are not written about. In many traditional ethnographic studies conducted by social anthropologists, those aspects of life that were studied and unstudied were, in part, the result of the aspects of social life to which informants directed the researchers. Yet as Ball remarks, informants are scarcely discussed in educational studies. However, they do have an important role as they can open up situations for study. Indeed, informants can guide the researcher and teach the researcher about relevant customs, traditions and practices within a social setting. For example, in an educational setting teacher and pupil informants may teach the individual about attributes associated with their positions in the school (cf. Burgess, 1982b; 1983; 1984a). Indeed, in our accounts we find that informants are used in some of the studies. Ball discusses how five young teachers who distanced themselves from the school became his informants and provided some feedback and validation for his observations. Meanwhile, Stenhouse indicates that on the LASS project a deputy headteacher in one of the schools, who had previously been known by the project coordinator, became an informant. However, it was much more common for the librarians to be the key informants. In these projects we are told about the informants, but we are not told about the specific ways in which they influenced the research in terms of topics studied and perspectives adopted. However, in all these cases it is essential for researchers to consider how the assistance which they obtain from informants will influence what is seen, how it is seen, what is recorded, and how this contributes to the analysis and subsequent dissemination of data.

Recording and Analyzing Data

In many basic textbooks devoted to research methodology much space is devoted to the effort that is required on data collection but little is said about how to record data or strategies involved in analysis. Yet data recording and data analysis are essential components of the research process (cf. Lofland, 1971; Burgess, 1982a); they are the basic building blocks involved in doing research and in report writing. Fuller shows how data recording needs to be programmed into the research timetable as she stresses the importance of writing up observations on a regular basis within the classes that are observed. She indicates how note-taking is dependent on the social setting in which the researcher is located and how some field settings, such as school classrooms, permit the researcher to make jottings (on a prepared sheet) which can later be augmented and amplified into full field notes. Field notes are seen by many of our researchers to be the key element involved in data recording, alongside tape recordings which are subsequently transcribed. We might consider *how* notes are made, what format is used, what types of field notes are produced. Rudduck indicates the different types of notes that she used in her study: documentary notes, personal comments and reflections (cf. Geer, 1964; Burgess, 1981). She indicates that notes could be kept on the basis of taking the role of 'clerk' to the groups she was studying. Indeed, she indicates that her notes were open to inspection, in contrast to Hammersley who attempted to disguise his handwriting and so prevent open access to his notes.

However, producing field notes and transcriptions from interviews is but one part of the research process. We need to consider how field notes and transcriptions are produced and their relationship with data analysis. Several researchers indicate that their field notes were confidential and that informants were allowed to check, correct, and delete sections of transcribed material; an essential component where 'raw data' are to be stored in a data archive (Rudduck and Stenhouse). Indeed, Rudduck and Stenhouse discuss the way in which field notes may be used to produce not only case studies but also case records that may be publicly accessible in the form of an archive. Such a collection of material Stenhouse (1978; 1979) has argued could be used in the course of cross-checking data and in turn for comparative analysis. As Rudduck indicates, such a collection of material has been established at the Centre for Applied Research in Education at the University of East Anglia; it has yet to be developed by other researchers. Meanwhile, we need to consider how researchers have used their data.

Several researchers indicate the ways in which field notes and transcriptions need to be annotated and categorized (where possible throughout the research process, although it is evident from the remarks made that this is difficult to attain). As many researchers report, note-taking is a personal activity but researchers can establish a format within which to work. Indeed, Stenhouse demonstrates the way in which he engaged in systematic note-taking while doing research. Such sets of notes are analytic (Burgess, 1982a; 1984a) in that they help the researcher to highlight major themes that can be used in the process of analysis. In these terms, analysis is not something which occurs at the end of the research but is a continuous process (cf. Becker and Geer, 1960; Macintyre, 1979). Indeed, King lets us in on this process when he indicates that field notes were the first step in establishing the social structure of the classrooms he studied. As a consequence, analysis was a continuous process in which preliminary interpretations were recorded in the field notes.

However, we might ask: how do themes emerge from the notes that are taken? How are links made between the data that are recorded and subsequent theoretical writings? In this situation we find that formal and informal research activities become intertwined and emerge during the research process. Ball argues that the researcher needs to have a clear idea about what constitutes data, while other researchers have indicated how the themes and categories emerge during the research process and after the fieldwork has been completed. Porter indicates that some of the categories emerged from the data during the course of the transcription of tapes. However, she also points to the importance of discussion with her co-researcher during the research, as she indicates that while they were away from Lancaster they discussed the interviews they had conducted and their observations with a view to considering further implications for the research process. This approach is also mentioned by Stenhouse in terms of the discussions that are held between workers on the multi-site case study. However, in both instances we need to know more about how these informal activities link up with the process of theorizing. This process of themes emerging during the course of the fieldwork is also discussed by Hammersley in relation to the selection of material from staffroom conversation. He points to the difficulties involved in deciding which indicators were conceptually relevant for his research. However, his work does illustrate how data analysis takes place alongside data collection. Meanwhile, Delamont points to a different way of working whereby the researcher looks for incidents that can be used after the data have been collected. This style of working highlights the importance of considering the extent to which researchers are involved in taking critical incidents and situations to illustrate a particular theoretical point or the extent to which cases are fully developed so that theoretical propositions can be refuted or sustained.

Another dimension to this issue concerns what constitutes theorizing in the projects that have been discussed. Several of the projects (Porter, King and Stenhouse) point to the use of Glaser and Strauss' (1967) work and their notion of grounded theory. However, we might ask what operations are involved in using Glaser and Strauss' approach within a project. Meanwhile, some of the sociological contributions point to the use of particular perspectives that informed their observations. Delamont discusses the relevance of symbolic interactionism. King points towards a theoretical approach that draws on action theory utilizing the work of Weber and W.I. Thomas. Indeed, he demonstrates how his study was also used to examine theoretical propositions in the work of Basil Bernstein and Sharp and Green.

In common with many feminists working from a sociological perspective (Roberts, 1981; Stacey, 1981), Fuller (like Delamont) discusses how there was relatively little work that questioned sex and gender and took a critical stance towards these areas of investigation, when she began her study in the early 1970s. However, she indicates that towards the end of her research period there was a growing literature on sexual divisions which highlighted the way in which questions of gender should be the subject of serious consideration. Such a position indicates that new concepts are required if data are to be analyzed from a feminist perspective. Furthermore, it suggests that the generation of theory is an integral part of the research process and that 'discovery' is an essential component in that process. However, we still need to consider *how* this theoretical discovery takes place and for what purpose. In these terms, reflections on the research process need to be concerned with some evaluation of the processes involved in analyzing data and writing the research report; processes that are only briefly touched upon in our accounts.

The Dissemination of Data

Data dissemination is an aspect of the research process that is often overlooked as if the researcher had no responsibility for the reception, interpretation and use of data. Here, researchers need to consider questions that relate to writing up and to the ethics and politics of the research process. Ball indicates how the dissemination process within the school constituted data that could be used to illuminate themes on which he had already written. One area on which he dwells is the reception that his data received from teachers. We might consider the extent to which teachers see case studies and ethnographies pointing to contradictions in their activities. Often these presentations are seen as misrepresenting teachers, and involving implicit criticism of their activities. Here the researcher is presented with an ethical dilemma about what material should be included or excluded from the final report as data that might advance a research career might be subject to reinterpretation by teachers and headteachers resulting in non-advancement for the practising teacher. Furthermore, much data that we collect on schools and schooling can often be deployed on initial teacher education and in-service courses. Here pupil strategies are subjected to some scrutiny. But we might ask what are the repercussions for pupils? For teachers to have an understanding of these strategies is an essential component of their education, but if this results in pupil mechanisms for coping with schooling being curtailed, might we not consider whether we have rendered a disservice to pupils who have 'cooperated' with our research activities? (Cf. Burgess, 1984a; 1984b; Davies, 1984.)

In writing up his experiences of using ethnography to engage in the evaluation of a curriculum project, David Jenkins indicates how the writing and reception of a research report are integral features of the research process and take us back to issues that were involved in sponsorship when the project was initially established. Similarly, King highlights another aspect of the reception of evidence by focusing on the reviewing process. Such procedures indicate the way in which evidence is evaluated, cited, quoted and used. Indeed, Atkinson indicates how this can result in some data being pigeonholed into categories that were not originally intended by the researcher, while Delamont discusses problems surrounding misrepresentation and misunderstanding by reviewers (cf. Shipman, 1976, p. x).

Conclusion: A Future for Autobiographical Accounts?

This chapter has attempted to synthesize some of the main themes and issues which have been discussed in the autobiographical accounts in this volume. In turn, an attempt has been made to raise questions which need to be addressed about the processes involved in the conduct of research in educational settings. In these terms, some encouragement has been given to researchers to be more reflexive about their research activities. But how is this to be achieved? Platt (1976) gave researchers an opportunity to discuss their research activities with her, but this, like autobiographical accounts, is retrospective.

In these terms, I would argue that researchers need to keep not only detailed diaries on the substantive materials that they investigate but also detailed diaries of their own research practices (Burgess, 1981). On this basis, researchers would then have the materials to conduct research on themselves and to provide a confessional account about doing research. Secondly, such accounts might include reactions from those who have been researched as well as some commentary from them as this will help to promote wider debate and discussion on the research process. Finally, triangulation of accounts from different participants could be invoked as a way in which researchers could provide more detailed studies of the research process. The result would, hopefully, make discussions of research practice more public and we might get closer to understanding the mistakes, problems and satisfactions involved in doing research in educational settings. However, here we might go back to the point at which we started by looking at Clive James' work. For James (1980) remarks that 'the mainspring of a confessional urge is guilt; and somewhere underneath the guilt there must be a crime' (p. 9). But what constitutes our 'crime'? Some researchers might argue that research itself (especially if it is covert) constitutes a crime. Yet is it more than this? Is it a crime if as researchers we do not address the social, ethical and political problems that surround the research process in the study of educational settings?

Robert G. Burgess

Acknowledgements

I would like to thank all the participants at the ethnography of educational settings workshop held at Whitelands College, London in March 1982 for their helpful comments on this chapter. I am especially grateful to David Jenkins, Mary Porter, Marten Shipman and Helen Simons who gave me detailed comments. However, any errors are my own.

References

ATKINSON, P. (1981) *The Clinical Experience*, Aldershot, Gower.

BALL, S. (1981) *Beachside Comprehensive: A Case Study of Secondary Schooling*, Cambridge, Cambridge University Press.

BECKER, H.S. and GEER, B. (1960) 'Participant observation: The analysis of qualitative data', in ADAMS, R.N. and PREISS, J.J. (Eds) *Human Organisation Research: Field Relations and Techniques*, Homewood, Ill., Dorsey Press, pp. 267–89; reprinted in BURGESS, R.G. (Ed.) *Field Research: A Sourcebook and Field Manual*, London, Allen and Unwin.

BELL, C. and NEWBY, H. (Eds) (1977) *Doing Sociological Research*, London, Allen and Unwin.

BURGESS, R.G. (1978) 'Researchers come clean' (review of BELL, C. and NEWBY, H. (Eds) *Doing Sociological Research*), *The Times Higher Education Supplement*, no. 325, 27 January.

BURGESS, R.G. (1980) 'Some fieldwork problems in teacher-based research', *British Educational Research Journal*, 6, 2, pp. 165–73.

BURGESS, R.G. (1981) 'Keeping a research diary', *Cambridge Journal of Education*, 11, 1, pp. 75–83.

BURGESS, R.G. (Ed.) (1982a) *Field Research: A Sourcebook and Field Manual*, London, Allen and Unwin.

BURGESS, R.G. (1982b) 'The practice of sociological research: Some issues in school ethnography', in BURGESS, R.G. (Ed.) *Exploring Society*, London, British Sociological Association.

BURGESS, R.G. (1983) *Experiencing Comprehensive Education: A Study of Bishop McGregor School*, London, Methuen.

BURGESS, R.G. (1984a) *In the Field: An Introduction to Field Research*, London, Allen and Unwin.

BURGESS, R.G. (1984b) 'The whole truth? Some ethical problems in the study of a comprehensive school', in BURGESS, R.G. (Ed.) *Field Methods in the Study of Education*, Lewes, Falmer Press.

BURGESS, R.G. and BULMER, M. (1981) 'Research methodology teaching: Trends and developments', *Sociology*, 15, 4, pp. 477–89.

DAVIES, L. (1984) 'Ethnography and status: focussing on gender in educational research', in BURGESS, R.G. (Ed.) *Field Methods in the Study of Education*, Lewes, Falmer Press.

DELAMONT, S. (1976) *Interaction in the Classroom*, London, Methuen.

DELAMONT, S. (1980) *Sex Roles and the School*, London, Methuen.
DINGWALL, R. (1980) 'Ethics and ethnography', *Sociological Review*, 28, 4, pp. 871–91.
EGGLESTON, J. (1980) 'The perspectives of the educational research project', *British Educational Research Journal*, 6, 1, pp. 85–9.
FINCH, J. (1984) '"It's great to have someone to talk to": The ethics and politics of interviewing women', in BELL, C. and ROBERTS, H. (Eds) *Social Researching: Policies, Problems and Practice*, London, Routledge and Kegan Paul.
FREILICH, M. (Ed) (1977) *Marginal Natives at Work*, New York, Wiley.
GEER, B. (1964) 'First days in the field', in HAMMOND, P. (Ed.) *Sociologists at Work*, London, Basic Books.
GEER, B. (1970) 'Studying a college', in HABENSTEIN, R.W. (Ed.) *Pathways to Data*, Chicago, Aldine.
GLASER, B. and STRAUSS, A.L. (1967) *The Discovery of Grounded Theory*, Chicago, Aldine.
GOLD, R. (1958) 'Roles in sociological field observations', *Social Forces*, 36, 3, pp. 217–33.
HARGREAVES, D.H. (1967) *Social Relations in a Secondary School*, London, Routledge and Kegan Paul.
JAMES, C. (1980) *Unreliable Memoirs*, London, Picador.
JUNKER, B. (1960) *Fieldwork: An Introduction to the Social Sciences*, Chicago, University of Chicago Press.
LACEY, C. (1970) *Hightown Grammar: The School as a Social System*, Manchester, Manchester University Press.
LOFLAND, J. (1971) *Analysing Social Settings*, Belmont, Calif., Wadsworth.
MACINTYRE, S. (1979) 'Some issues in the study of pregnancy careers', *Sociological Review*, 27, 4, pp. 755–71.
MILLS, C.W. (1959) *The Sociological Imagination*, Oxford, Oxford University Press.
MOSER, C.A. and KALTON, G. (1971) *Survey Methods in Social Investigation*, 2nd ed., London, Heinemann.
OAKLEY, A. (1981) 'Interviewing women: A contradiction in terms', in ROBERTS, H. (Ed.) *Doing Feminist Research*, London, Routledge and Kegan Paul.
PLATT, J. (1976) *Realities of Social Research*, London, Chatto and Windus for Sussex University Press.
PLATT, J. (1981) 'On interviewing one's peers', *British Journal of Sociology*, 32, 1, pp. 75–91.
ROBBINS, (1963) *Higher Education*, Cmnd. 2154, London, HMSO.
ROBERTS, H. (Ed.) (1981) *Doing Feminist Research*, London, Routledge and Kegan Paul.
SCHATZMAN, L. and STRAUSS, A.L. (1973) *Field Research: Strategies for a Natural Sociology*, Englewood Cliffs, N.J., Prentice Hall.
SHIPMAN, M. (Ed.) (1976) *The Organization and Impact of Social Research*, London, Routledge and Kegan Paul.
SPENDER, D. (Ed.) (1981) *Mens Studies Modified*, Oxford, Pergamon.
SPINDLER, G. and SPINDLER, L. (1982) 'Roger Harker and Schönhausen: From the familiar to the strange and back again', in SPINDLER, G. (Ed.)

Robert G. Burgess

Doing the Ethnography of Schooling, New York, Holt, Rinehart and Winston.
STACEY, M. (1981) 'The division of labour revisited or overcoming the two adams', in ABRAMS, P., DEEM, R., FINCH, J. and ROCK, P. (Eds) *Practice and Progress: British Sociology 1950–1980*, London, Allen and Unwin.
STENHOUSE, L. (1978) 'Case study and case records: Towards a contemporary history of education', *British Educational Research Journal*, 4, 2, pp. 21–39.
STENHOUSE, L. (1979) 'The problem of standards in illuminative research', *Scottish Educational Review*, 11, 1, pp. 5–10.
WALKER, R. (1980) 'The conduct of educational case studies: Ethics, theory and procedure', in DOCKRELL, W.B. and HAMILTON, D. (Eds) *Rethinking Educational Research*, London, Hodder and Stoughton.
WATSON, J.D. (1968) *The Double Helix*, Harmondsworth, Penguin.

Notes on Contributors

Sara Delamont graduated in Social Anthropology from Girton College, Cambridge in 1968, and went to Edinburgh to do a PhD on an SSRC award. Between 1971 and 1973 she was a research associate for J.A.M. Howe in the Bionics Research Laboratory at Edinburgh. In 1973, after getting her PhD, she went to lecture in the School of Education at Leicester University, working with Gerry Bernbaum and Tom Whiteside. Since 1976 she has been in the Sociology Department at University College, Cardiff. She has written numerous articles and edited several collections of papers on the sociology of education. She is the author of *Interaction in the Classroom* (1976), *Sex Roles and the School* (1980), and *The Sociology of Women* (1980). She was the first woman President of BERA in 1983–84.

Martyn Hammersley was previously a research fellow in the Department of Sociology, University of Manchester. Currently, he is a lecturer in the Sociology of Education in the Faculty of Educational Studies at the Open University. His main research interests are the study of classroom interaction and the methodology of social research. He has written articles in both fields as well as a book on *Ethnography* (1983) with Paul Atkinson. He is also the editor of *The Process of Schooling* (1976) and *School Experience* (1977) with Peter Woods. His current research project (working with John Scarth and Sue Webb) concerns the effects of different types of external assessment on teaching and learning in secondary schools.

Stephen J. Ball has been a lecturer in Education at the University of Sussex for eight years, and for five years has been the Director of Studies of the MA in Education (Curriculum Development in Schools); previously he had worked in a bank, in a library and taught sociology in further education colleges. He is author of *Beachside Comprehensive: A Case Study of Secondary Schooling* (1981) and co-editor of *Defining the Curriculum* (1984); he was written a number of articles on classroom interaction, participant observation methods and education in developing societies and also teaching materials for the Open University course, *Conflict and Change in Education.*

Mary Fuller attended a girls' grammar school in Kent. She obtained a BSc (Sociology) from Bath University and worked as a researcher at Bath University, at the SSRC Research Unit on Ethnic Relations and at the Department of Mental Health (both at Bristol University). She was awarded a PhD from Bristol University in 1978. Since 1979 she has been Senior Lecturer (Sociology) at Bulmershe College of Higher Education, Reading. She has published articles on ethnic minorities and education, sex-role stereotyping in the social sciences and several papers arising from the research discussed in her chapter. She has edited *Sex Role Stereotyping* (with O. Hartnett and G. Boden) (1979) and is currently working on a unit entitled 'Inequality: Race, Gender and Class' for the Open University course, *Conflict and Change in Education.*

Ronald King is Reader in Education at the University of Exeter where he has taught the sociology of education since 1966. His PhD is reported in *Values and Involvement in a Grammar School* (1969). *School Organization and Pupil Involvement* (1973) and *School and College: Studies of Post-Sixteen Education* (1976) are the main reports of research funded by the Schools Council and the Social Science Research Council respectively. *All Things Bright and Beautiful?* (1978) is the principal account of his study of infants' schools. He has recently completed a study of changes in school organization funded by the SSRC, and his most recent book is *The Sociology of School Organization* (1983).

Mary Porter graduated from the University of Manchester in 1978 having read social anthropology. She worked as a research assistant for Oldham Metropolitan Borough until February 1979 when she moved to the University of Lancaster Department of Sociology where she was a research associate on the postgraduate education project until February 1982. She has been the convenor of the BSA ethnography study group and has written several articles with Sue Scott on women postgraduates. In the USA she has worked on the oral history of Washington women with the University of Washington Archive. She is now registered for graduate study in cultural anthropology at the University of Washington at Seattle.

Paul Atkinson graduated in Social Anthropology from King's College, Cambridge, in 1969. Between 1969 and 1973 he was a research student and research associate in the Centre for Research in the Educational Sciences at the University of Edinburgh. After a year as a temporary lecturer in Sociology at Stirling University he went to University College, Cardiff, where he is currently a senior lecturer. He was editor of *Sociology of Health and Illness: A Journal of Medical Sociology* between 1980 and 1983. His publications include: *The Clinical Experi-*

ence: The Construction and Reconstruction of Medical Reality (1981); *Medical Work: Realities and Routines* (ed. with Christian Heath) (1981); *Ethnography: Principles in Practice* (with Martyn Hammersley) (1983).

Jean Rudduck is a senior lecturer at the Centre for Applied Research in Education at the University of East Anglia. Before joining the Centre in 1970, she was a member of the Schools Council/Nuffield Humanities Curriculum Project team. She has directed various projects, including the Small Group Teaching Project, Pupils and Innovation, Making the Most of the Short In-Service Course, Teachers in Partnership, Sex-Stereotyping in the Early Years of Schooling. Her main publications include: *Dissemination of Innovation: The Humanities Curriculum Project* (1976), *The Dissemination of Curriculum Development* (with P. Kelly) (1976), *Teaching through Small Group Discussion* (1978), *Learning to Teach through Discussion* (ed., 1979), *Making the Most of the Short In-Service Course* (1981) *and Teachers in Partnership: Four Studies of In-Service Collaboration* (1982). She has recently been appointed Professor of Education at the University of Sheffield.

Lawrence Stenhouse was director of the Centre for Applied Research in Education (CARE) at the University of East Anglia from its inception in 1970 until he died in 1982. He was given a personal chair, in applied research in education, in 1979. In 1967 he was appointed director of the Schools Council/Nuffield Foundation Humanities Curriculum Project. He came to the Humanities Curriculum Project from Jordanhill College where he was head of the education department. At CARE he directed two projects on teaching about race relations, undertook pioneering work in case study methods which influenced the design of his last project, a multi-site case programme looking at library access and sixth form study. His publications include *Culture and Education* (1967); *Discipline in Schools (1967); An Introduction to Curriculum Research and Development (1975); Curriculum Research and Development in Action* (1980); *Teaching about Race Relations: Problems and Effects* (1982) and *Authority, Education, and Emancipation* (1983).

David Jenkins taught for eight years in Duffryn High School, a comprehensive school in Newport, Monmouthshire, before becoming Deputy Director of the Schools Council/University of Keele Integrated Studies Project, which was exploring new maps of knowledge and pedagogies for humanities teaching in secondary school. He then moved to the Open University, first as Staff Tutor for the South-West Region, later as a central academic working in the curriculum studies area. He was seconded for four years to the Centre for Applied Research in Education at the University of East Anglia to work with Barry MacDonald on the UNCAL evaluation of the National Development

Programme in Computer Assisted Learning. This was followed by a spell of seven years as Professor of Education at the New University of Ulster. It was in Ireland that he conducted the research, reported in his chapter, into the Rowntree Schools Cultural Studies Project, which was an attempt to use the curriculum of its secondary schools to blunt the edge of sectarianism in the province. His publications include *Chocolate Cream Soldiers* (1980) and *Chocolate Drops* (1980), both with Sean O'Connor, and a collection of edited papers entitled *Beyond the Numbers Game, A Reader in Educational Evaluation* (1977), with David Hamilton and others. He has recently been appointed Professor of Arts Education at Warwick University.

Robert Burgess   is a Lecturer in Sociology at the University of Warwick. His teaching and research interests include the sociology of education and social research methodology; especially field research. He is particularly interested in ethnography and its use in educational settings. He is the author of *Experiencing Comprehensive Education: A Study of Bishop McGregor School* (1983), *In the Field: An Introduction to Field Research* (1984) and the editor of *Teaching Research Methodology to Postgraduates: A Survey of Courses in the U.K.* (1979), *Field Research: A Sourcebook and Field Manual* (1982), and *Exploring Society* (1982). He is Honorary General Secretary of the British Sociological Association, 1982–4.

Author Index

Subject Index